BARRON'S

ACT®

ENGLISH, READING, AND WRITING WORKBOOK

3RD EDITION

Linda Carnevale, M.A.

BARRON'S

DEDICATION

To my husband Sandro, whom I treasure, and my precious son-shines, Phillip, Andrew, and Luca, who inspire me daily; to my supportive family, friends, former colleagues at Cold Spring Harbor Schools, current colleagues at Sage Test Prep, and my superlative students; and much gratitude to my cherished parents Anne and Ernest and supportive in-laws Nicoletta and Filippo.

ABOUT THE AUTHOR

Linda Carnevale holds a Master of Arts from Columbia University's Teachers College. Formerly an English teacher at Cold Spring Harbor High School, Long Island, New York, she currently prepares students for the ACT and SAT and is the author of Barron's *Hot Words for the ACT*, *Hot Words for the SAT*, and *SAT 1600*, and has published in a variety of local and national publications. Her poem "Daisies Grow on My Windowsill" was recently selected for publication in an anthology of poems about Long Island.

© Copyright 2019, 2013, 2008 by Kaplan, Inc., d/b/a Barron's Educational Series

Published by Kaplan, Inc., d/b/a Barron's Educational Series
750 Third Avenue
New York, NY 10017
www.barronseduc.com

ISBN: 978-1-4380-1112-7

9 8 7 6 5 4 3 2

Kaplan, Inc., d/b/a Barron's Educational Series print books are available at special quantity discounts
to use for sales promotions, employee premiums, or educational purposes. For more information or
to purchase books, please call the Simon & Schuster special sales department at 866-506-1949.

Contents

Introduction

Good for you! You got your hands on this information-packed workbook, and you are ready to roll up your sleeves, learn all that you need to know, and achieve your personal best score on the ACT.

The main intentions of this prep book are to inform you about the specifics of the test, to let you know what to expect, to strengthen particular skills that are important in order to perform well, and to allow you to try your hand at some practice test questions.

Here is a summary of all that this workbook contains.

THE SELF-ASSESSMENT TEST

Where are you at? This is your chance to find out how you perform on the English Language Arts portions of the ACT: English Test, Reading Test, and Writing Test. This section provides a diagnostic test with timing goals clearly indicated. To make your practice test as accurate and as real as possible, be sure to time yourself precisely on each of the sections.

Do not give yourself extra time; if you fudge even by a few minutes and stretch your testing time, you'll only end up cheating yourself in the long run. If you give yourself a couple of extra minutes here and there, you might end up with an "inflated" or unrealistic score. An inflated score will not give you a clear sense of your strengths and weaknesses pertaining to each of the three English Language Arts sections. This is your chance to give it your all, to be real, and to get a sense of your performance in terms of reading comprehension, English grammar and usage, and essay writing.

When you are done with the entire Self-Assessment Test, definitely peruse the Answer Explanations that appear at the end. Many students find the answer explanations within such workbooks to be the most valuable sections of all. The explanations are thorough, user-friendly, and provide valuable test-taking instruction. Be sure to read through all answer explanations, even for the questions that you answered correctly. Reading through the explanations will help you to shed light on any "doozies," the tricky questions that you happened to get wrong. The explanations will also reinforce topics and grammatical conventions that can help you not only maintain but surpass your current score.

> **TIP**
>
> Keep this win-win situation in mind as you work your way through the Self-Assessment Test: On the ACT, you are not penalized for incorrect answers!

Keep this win-win situation in mind as you work your way through the Self-Assessment Test: On the ACT, you are not penalized for incorrect answers! These words sound like a test-taker's dream. But, guess what? It's true! Test takers are not penalized for incorrect answers, so educated guessing is always advisable. Do not omit any questions. That would not make any sense. Consider this hypothetical, worst-case scenario: you have five questions left and forty seconds on the clock! What do you do? Just fill in those bubbles on your answer sheet. You have nothing to lose, literally, and the potential to gain a few last-minute points.

OVERVIEW AND TEST-TAKING TIPS

CHAPTER 1 gives you an Overview and the Format of the ACT

For each of the three English Language Arts sections—English Test, Reading Test, and Writing Test (optional)—you will learn about the format, types of questions, and percentage breakdown of those questions. You will also be given a suggested timing plan and will learn about the various verbal skills that will be assessed.

CHAPTER 2 shows you how to Be a Class ACT on Test Day

Nuts 'n' bolts, the basics, and a bevy of handy reminders in the form of checklists make up this chapter. Here you will find valuable test-taking tips. You will also be told what to bring to the test center and what *not* to bring to the test center so that you are organized and prepared to do your very best. You will also get a practical heads-up regarding test day: you'll know what to expect at the test center and what to expect during the testing circumstance itself!

SPECIFIC TEST REVIEW

CHAPTER 3 focuses on the English Test of the ACT

You deserve to be a class ACT on test day. Using an original acronym for ACT, this chapter meticulously presents key English conventions.

ACT ENGLISH PRINCIPLES

A covers **A**uthor's Style and **A**ccuracy in Grammar, Usage, and Sentence Formation.

C covers these important aspects of sound and competent English:

Conciseness, **C**oherence, **C**ommas, **C**olons, Semi**C**olons, and other Punctuation.

T covers **T**echnique used by the Author, in particular, Strategy and Organization. **T** also refers to the **T**one used by the Author.

Making Sense of the Double-Column Format

Have you seen the strange-looking, double-column format that is used on the ACT English Test? It's probably quite unlike anything you have seen in English class before! An entire section of this chapter is devoted to helping you make sense of these quirky columns and their unusual features such as: numbers within boxes, numbers within brackets, small numbers beneath underlined parts, uneven white space between lines of text, various types of questions, and so on. After reading through and digesting this section of the chapter, you will be well-equipped to navigate the, *before now*, enigmatic (mysterious) double columns of the English Test.

Workbook Advantages

Since this is a workbook (and not pleasure reading), you are given many opportunities to sharpen your pencils and practice your ACT grammar and usage principles with Quick-Drills. You are also given opportunities to practice your skills with various Practice Mini-Passages, each featuring a different genre and containing about five to nine questions. (Recall that reading passages on the ACT feature a set of ten questions.)

If you crave more opportunities to test your skills, rest assured that at the end of the book you can work through a full-length practice test. As always, thorough answer explanations are provided so that you can make sense of and learn from the ones that you got wrong.

As you work through this book, keep your eyes peeled for the dude in the hammock:

No Sweat Points

The good stuff: This chapter also lists the things that you will *not* be tested on, happily referred to as "No Sweat Points." Believe it or not, there are many aspects of standard, written English grammar and usage that you do *not* need to worry about! As if that weren't enough of a win, this chapter also gives you test-taking tips that apply particularly to the English sections.

CHAPTER 4 focuses on the Reading Test of the ACT

To keep you in the driver's seat, a four-stage strategy plan is laid out and elaborated on for you: *Preview, Focus, Read, Answer.* Here you will dive into reading skills in closer focus. These diverse reading skills include finding the main idea, interpreting details, understanding sequence of events, drawing comparisons, understanding cause and effect, understanding meanings in context, making generalizations, and examining author's voice and method.

Good news: The passages won't all be the same flavor and they won't all sound the same. On the English Test, passages come in four varieties. If you are not a natural science type, don't worry because there's a prose fiction piece. If you are not a fiction buff, don't worry because there's a social studies piece coming up. If neither prose nor social science holds your interest, don't worry because there's a humanities piece to follow.

In this chapter, you will focus on reading skills that relate to comprehending and interpreting a variety of passages that fall into four main categories: natural science, humanities, social science (sometimes referred to as social studies), and prose fiction.

Workbook Advantages

Once again, since this is a workbook, you will have many opportunities to practice on abridged passages with corresponding questions. Practice reading selections are provided for those same four genre types: Prose Fiction, Social Science, Natural Science, and Humanities. No outside knowledge is required to answer the questions. All of the information you will need is contained within the passages themselves; the correct answers are unconditionally based on what is directly stated or implied (suggested, hinted at) in the passages.

CHAPTER 5 focuses on the Writing Test of the ACT

As you work through this chapter, you will focus on a repertoire (a list or supply) of skills that are particular to this section of the ACT. For example, a workable, three-step, no-sweat plan is provided for writing the essay: *Prewriting, Freewriting, and Revising/Editing.* These three classic stages are tried-and-true, so be confident that they will work for you as you embark on composing your thirty-minute essay.

Many test takers, like you, are talented and very capable writers. However, timing is often an issue with these same test takers. In this chapter, you are provided with a flexible timing plan. Saving time is something everyone likes. You will even get some ideas and suggestions about how you can actually prepare (to some extent) for the ACT Writing Test during your everyday life. No kidding!

This is a workbook, so you are encouraged to write essays for the sample writing prompts that are provided, and you are encouraged to create brainstorming notes on the corresponding planning pages.

FULL-LENGTH PRACTICE TEST

A complete Practice Test along with thorough answer explanations and a scoring guide is provided at the end of this book. Here's the bottom line: Try your hand at a couple of *timed* practice tests. Time yourself using an egg timer, a kitchen timer, or your watch. You should take these tests under "testing conditions"—no radio, no iPod headphones, no television humming in the background, no snack food. Your cell phone should be off. You get the idea. Take these practice tests as if it were "independence day": the day on which you take the test on your very own.

Do not make your testing conditions at home too perfect, though. As we'll discuss in Chapter 2, actual testing conditions at a variety of official testing centers are far from perfect.

ACT FAQs

The purpose of this FAQs section is to provide responses to questions that are often asked by students and parents about the ACT college entrance exam.

Q: What is Test Information Release?

A: After the test administration, a student's test answers can be ordered up to three months after he or she has sat for the exam. This service can greatly help to identify strengths and weaknesses and refine a student's course of test preparation.

Q: Is the ACT accepted by most colleges and universities?

A: Yes, all four-year colleges and universities in the United States accept the ACT for college admissions purposes.

Q: Is the ACT the easier or harder of the two college entrance exams?

A: This depends on your academic strengths. Stronger math and science students tend to perform slightly better on the ACT. For some test takers, their SAT and ACT scores are the same. For still others, their SAT scores show off more strongly. Try both exams, under timed test-taking conditions to discover which exam is the better fit for you.

Q: Does taking the ACT satisfy a student's college application requirement for an SAT II Subject Test?

A: For some schools, the ACT with Writing (the 30-minute essay) satisfies a Subject Test requirement. Check with each individual college's specific application requirements and guidelines. College websites typically have the most up-to-date information.

Q: Compared to the SAT, is the ACT a faster-paced test?

A: Yes. On average, a student has less time per question. On the essay, however, the ACT test taker has 5 minutes more than he or she has on the SAT.

Q: ACT Math versus SAT Math—which is harder?

A: The answer depends on the individual strengths of the test taker as a math student. However, most agree that ACT Math is somewhat harder because it contains some trigonometry questions. You may also have a handful of questions on conic sections or scatter plots.

Q: How much time do I have to work on each Reading and English passage and its questions?

A: On the English Test, you have 9 minutes per passage and its corresponding set of 15 questions. On the Reading Test, you have 8.5 minutes per passage and its corresponding set of 10 questions. It is helpful to bring a watch with you on test day. Make sure audible alarms are not programmed.

Q: Do all colleges and universities superscore the ACT?

A: For the most part, the answer is yes. However, check the websites of the individual schools to be sure. Score choice policies may change among schools from one academic year to the next.

Q: Does vocabulary matter on the ACT?

A: Yes. The most recent ACT reveals that a rich, upper-level vocabulary appears in the Reading Test passages and their corresponding questions. The English Test also contains potentially challenging words. Vocabulary is often an obstacle for students, costing them a number of questions. Many ACT students will stop mid-passage and ask, "What does *prose* mean?" or "What does *soundly* mean?" or "What does *attributed* mean?. . . *scarcity*? . . . *prevalence*?" Learning more words will improve your ability to make your way through the passages with greater ease and clarity of understanding.

The Reading Test passages come in four genres: Prose Fiction, Humanities, Natural Science, and Social Science. To thoroughly absorb the information in these passages, it is beneficial for you to enrich and expand your vocabulary.

Summer offers an ideal time to read widely across a variety of topics and genres that you find interesting. Seek out books and articles that hold your interest. You can read from your school's recommended summer reading list, which may include classics, such as *The Hobbit* or *Jane Eyre*. Or you can read *It* or another science fiction or adventure-suspense book that you will find enjoyable. Check out Amazon's recommendations or the *New York Times* best-seller lists for suggestions. If you read on a Kindle, consider its suggestions, too, based on the type of books you tend to read.

In addition, you can read scientific articles—from *Scientific American* or *Wired*, or from a reputable scientific journal, for example—about nanotechnology, earthquakes, or solar energy. Push yourself to read articles from *National Geographic* from beginning to end, annotating the passages along the way. Moreover, you can read social science and economics articles—in print form or online—in the *Wall Street Journal* or *New York Times*.

While in school, try your best to select Honors, AP, and IB courses that will challenge and hone your reading skills across a variety of academic disciplines. Push yourself to read material that is harder, denser, and contains more intricate patterns of reasoning as well as college-level and beyond vocabulary.

Certainly, both memorizing the meanings of words and gleaning meanings from context are valuable to test takers. Refer to "Grasping Meanings in Context" on page 139.

ACKNOWLEDGMENTS

With love and gratitude to my husband and sons, Phillip, Andrew, and Luca. Thank you, Sandro, for your steady encouragement and voice of positivity.

Special thanks to my dedicated editor, Linda Turner, and to acquisitions manager Wayne Barr, for bringing me on board to Barron's once again. Thank you for your confidence. I greatly appreciate the contributions of my copyeditor, Nina Hnatov, and the efforts of the production manager, Debby Becak.

With much gratitude to those authors, many of whom are experts in their respective fields, who generously allowed me to feature their work as practice reading or English passages in this book. Your contributions will help hundreds of students who are working hard to prepare for this challenging college entrance exam.

Pages 9–12: "Lake View," by Phillip Ernest Carnevale.

Pages 19–22: Introduction to *Good Eats:* Long Island Edition, 1993, by Chet Halperin, editor and publisher. Used by permission of Laura Halperin.

Pages 25–26: "Augmentative and Alternative Communication," by Lauren Beth Benzoni, MA, CCC-SUP.

Pages 28–29: "Addicted to Fame: From the Greeks to Lady Gaga," *National Endowment for the Humanities.*

Pages 30–31: "Urbanization and Malaria: The Most Important Environmental Health Effect," by Jason Halperin.

Pages 124–125: "My Locker," by Phillip Ernest Carnevale.

Pages 150–152: "The Magician," from *The Cloud King,* by Michael Jan Friedman.

Page 154–155: "Mobilization for Youth," by Edythe K. Scro, LCSW, CASAC.

Page 156: "The Yamas and Niyamas," by Donna Rovegno.

Pages 157–159: "Loving the Questions" by Brooke Huminski, from *We Are the Ones We've Been Waiting for: Reflections on Life and Service from the Public and Community Service*, a publication by the Capstone Class of 2007, Providence College, Rhode Island.

Pages 161–162: "The Dynamic Cross Cylinder," by Mark Rosenfield, PhD, MCOptom, FAAO, and Jaclyn Anne Benzoni, BS, OD, MS.

Pages 164–165: "Cheetah's Inner Ear Is One-of-a-Kind, Vital to High-Speed Hunting," *National Science Foundation.*

Pages 165–166: "Older Is Better for Hunting Dogs," *National Science Foundation.*

Pages 219–222: "The Hero's Journey," by Andrea Benz Goetz.

Pages 223–226: "Miguel Hidalgo," by Andrea Benz Goetz.

Page 237: "Single Breath Meditation," by Rebbie Straubing.

Page 239: "Hurricanes," by Greg Goebel, from *www.vectorsite.net.*

SELF-ASSESSMENT TESTS

- English Test (Test of Grammar, Usage, and Rhetorical Skills)

- Reading Test (Test of Reading Comprehension Across Four Genres)

- Answer Key and Explanations

- Diagnostic Charts

ANSWER SHEET
Self-Assessment Tests

English Test

1. Ⓐ Ⓑ Ⓒ Ⓓ
2. Ⓕ Ⓖ Ⓗ Ⓙ
3. Ⓐ Ⓑ Ⓒ Ⓓ
4. Ⓕ Ⓖ Ⓗ Ⓙ
5. Ⓐ Ⓑ Ⓒ Ⓓ
6. Ⓕ Ⓖ Ⓗ Ⓙ
7. Ⓐ Ⓑ Ⓒ Ⓓ
8. Ⓕ Ⓖ Ⓗ Ⓙ
9. Ⓐ Ⓑ Ⓒ Ⓓ
10. Ⓕ Ⓖ Ⓗ Ⓙ
11. Ⓐ Ⓑ Ⓒ Ⓓ
12. Ⓕ Ⓖ Ⓗ Ⓙ
13. Ⓐ Ⓑ Ⓒ Ⓓ
14. Ⓕ Ⓖ Ⓗ Ⓙ
15. Ⓐ Ⓑ Ⓒ Ⓓ
16. Ⓕ Ⓖ Ⓗ Ⓙ
17. Ⓐ Ⓑ Ⓒ Ⓓ
18. Ⓕ Ⓖ Ⓗ Ⓙ
19. Ⓐ Ⓑ Ⓒ Ⓓ

20. Ⓕ Ⓖ Ⓗ Ⓙ
21. Ⓐ Ⓑ Ⓒ Ⓓ
22. Ⓕ Ⓖ Ⓗ Ⓙ
23. Ⓐ Ⓑ Ⓒ Ⓓ
24. Ⓕ Ⓖ Ⓗ Ⓙ
25. Ⓐ Ⓑ Ⓒ Ⓓ
26. Ⓕ Ⓖ Ⓗ Ⓙ
27. Ⓐ Ⓑ Ⓒ Ⓓ
28. Ⓕ Ⓖ Ⓗ Ⓙ
29. Ⓐ Ⓑ Ⓒ Ⓓ
30. Ⓕ Ⓖ Ⓗ Ⓙ
31. Ⓐ Ⓑ Ⓒ Ⓓ
32. Ⓕ Ⓖ Ⓗ Ⓙ
33. Ⓐ Ⓑ Ⓒ Ⓓ
34. Ⓕ Ⓖ Ⓗ Ⓙ
35. Ⓐ Ⓑ Ⓒ Ⓓ
36. Ⓕ Ⓖ Ⓗ Ⓙ
37. Ⓐ Ⓑ Ⓒ Ⓓ
38. Ⓕ Ⓖ Ⓗ Ⓙ

39. Ⓐ Ⓑ Ⓒ Ⓓ
40. Ⓕ Ⓖ Ⓗ Ⓙ
41. Ⓐ Ⓑ Ⓒ Ⓓ
42. Ⓕ Ⓖ Ⓗ Ⓙ
43. Ⓐ Ⓑ Ⓒ Ⓓ
44. Ⓕ Ⓖ Ⓗ Ⓙ
45. Ⓐ Ⓑ Ⓒ Ⓓ
46. Ⓕ Ⓖ Ⓗ Ⓙ
47. Ⓐ Ⓑ Ⓒ Ⓓ
48. Ⓕ Ⓖ Ⓗ Ⓙ
49. Ⓐ Ⓑ Ⓒ Ⓓ
50. Ⓕ Ⓖ Ⓗ Ⓙ
51. Ⓐ Ⓑ Ⓒ Ⓓ
52. Ⓕ Ⓖ Ⓗ Ⓙ
53. Ⓐ Ⓑ Ⓒ Ⓓ
54. Ⓕ Ⓖ Ⓗ Ⓙ
55. Ⓐ Ⓑ Ⓒ Ⓓ
56. Ⓕ Ⓖ Ⓗ Ⓙ
57. Ⓐ Ⓑ Ⓒ Ⓓ

58. Ⓕ Ⓖ Ⓗ Ⓙ
59. Ⓐ Ⓑ Ⓒ Ⓓ
60. Ⓕ Ⓖ Ⓗ Ⓙ
61. Ⓐ Ⓑ Ⓒ Ⓓ
62. Ⓕ Ⓖ Ⓗ Ⓙ
63. Ⓐ Ⓑ Ⓒ Ⓓ
64. Ⓕ Ⓖ Ⓗ Ⓙ
65. Ⓐ Ⓑ Ⓒ Ⓓ
66. Ⓕ Ⓖ Ⓗ Ⓙ
67. Ⓐ Ⓑ Ⓒ Ⓓ
68. Ⓕ Ⓖ Ⓗ Ⓙ
69. Ⓐ Ⓑ Ⓒ Ⓓ
70. Ⓕ Ⓖ Ⓗ Ⓙ
71. Ⓐ Ⓑ Ⓒ Ⓓ
72. Ⓕ Ⓖ Ⓗ Ⓙ
73. Ⓐ Ⓑ Ⓒ Ⓓ
74. Ⓕ Ⓖ Ⓗ Ⓙ
75. Ⓐ Ⓑ Ⓒ Ⓓ

Reading Test

1. Ⓐ Ⓑ Ⓒ Ⓓ
2. Ⓕ Ⓖ Ⓗ Ⓙ
3. Ⓐ Ⓑ Ⓒ Ⓓ
4. Ⓕ Ⓖ Ⓗ Ⓙ
5. Ⓐ Ⓑ Ⓒ Ⓓ
6. Ⓕ Ⓖ Ⓗ Ⓙ
7. Ⓐ Ⓑ Ⓒ Ⓓ
8. Ⓕ Ⓖ Ⓗ Ⓙ
9. Ⓐ Ⓑ Ⓒ Ⓓ
10. Ⓕ Ⓖ Ⓗ Ⓙ

11. Ⓐ Ⓑ Ⓒ Ⓓ
12. Ⓕ Ⓖ Ⓗ Ⓙ
13. Ⓐ Ⓑ Ⓒ Ⓓ
14. Ⓕ Ⓖ Ⓗ Ⓙ
15. Ⓐ Ⓑ Ⓒ Ⓓ
16. Ⓕ Ⓖ Ⓗ Ⓙ
17. Ⓐ Ⓑ Ⓒ Ⓓ
18. Ⓕ Ⓖ Ⓗ Ⓙ
19. Ⓐ Ⓑ Ⓒ Ⓓ
20. Ⓕ Ⓖ Ⓗ Ⓙ

21. Ⓐ Ⓑ Ⓒ Ⓓ
22. Ⓕ Ⓖ Ⓗ Ⓙ
23. Ⓐ Ⓑ Ⓒ Ⓓ
24. Ⓕ Ⓖ Ⓗ Ⓙ
25. Ⓐ Ⓑ Ⓒ Ⓓ
26. Ⓕ Ⓖ Ⓗ Ⓙ
27. Ⓐ Ⓑ Ⓒ Ⓓ
28. Ⓕ Ⓖ Ⓗ Ⓙ
29. Ⓐ Ⓑ Ⓒ Ⓓ
30. Ⓕ Ⓖ Ⓗ Ⓙ

31. Ⓐ Ⓑ Ⓒ Ⓓ
32. Ⓕ Ⓖ Ⓗ Ⓙ
33. Ⓐ Ⓑ Ⓒ Ⓓ
34. Ⓕ Ⓖ Ⓗ Ⓙ
35. Ⓐ Ⓑ Ⓒ Ⓓ
36. Ⓕ Ⓖ Ⓗ Ⓙ
37. Ⓐ Ⓑ Ⓒ Ⓓ
38. Ⓕ Ⓖ Ⓗ Ⓙ
39. Ⓐ Ⓑ Ⓒ Ⓓ
40. Ⓕ Ⓖ Ⓗ Ⓙ

Self-Assessment Tests

GENERAL DIRECTIONS

Tests in English and reading are part of this self-assessment. These tests assess your proficiency in skills that are closely tied to those in high school courses and college success. Because this assessment test does not contain a math section, calculators may *not* be used.

Questions are numbered; answer choices are indicated by letters. Rows of ovals, which are lettered to correspond with the answer choices, appear on the answer sheet. Select what you believe is the *best* answer to each question; on the answer sheet, find in that row the oval that has the same letter as the answer you have selected. Using a soft, lead #2 pencil, fill in the oval completely. Make your marks clear, dark, and heavy. Do not use a mechanical pencil or a ballpoint pen.

For each question, indicate only one answer by marking your selected oval. If you want to change your answer, completely erase your original answer before you fill in your final answer. For each question on the test, be sure that you mark in the row of ovals whose number matches that of the question on which you are working.

You will not receive credit for any answers marked or written in your test booklet. Only answers that you indicate on your answer sheet will be electronically scored. You will earn points for only the questions you answer correctly; no half-credit or partial-credit is given. You will not lose points for guessing. It is in your best interest to answer *every* question, even if your answer is based on an educated guess.

Work on only one test at a time when the proctor tells you to begin working. If you finish a test before time is up, use the remainder of the time allotted to that particular test for checking your work and thinking over questions about which you were hesitant. Do not look back on the previous test, and do not begin working on the next test. You will be disqualified from the test if you work on any test other than the one indicated by the test proctor.

When time is called at the end of each test, put down your pencil right away. After time is called, you may not erase or darken in ovals on your answer sheet. If you do so, you will be disqualified from the test.

ENGLISH TEST

45 MINUTES—75 QUESTIONS

Passage I

Caring for Peaches

[1]

A yellow Lutino Cockatiel, Peaches 'n' Cream was born on August 11, 2017, in East Northport Long Island, New York. A male bird, Peaches (as we call him for short) was named for the perfectly round, peach-colored circles on the sides of his cheeks and his soft, crème-colored feathers.

1. (A) NO CHANGE
   (B) East Northport; Long Island, New York
   (C) East Northport, which is the name of a town found on Long Island, New York
   (D) East Northport, Long Island, New York

2. (F) NO CHANGE
   (G) as a shorthand name
   (H) for a short nickname
   (J) at his nickname

[2]

Taking care of Peaches is ratherly basic. Every day, give him clean water and a scoop of mixed seed. You can open

3. (A) NO CHANGE
   (B) is basic.
   (C) is basic, rather so.
   (D) rather than difficult, is basic.

GO ON TO THE NEXT PAGE

the front door of his cage to dispense the seed and water or—if a toddler or a hyper dog is around—simply lift the clear plastic sides of the cage to pull out and fill his seed and water cups.

[3]

For the most part, Peaches is—by and large—a low-maintenance pet. He can sleep during the day in the blazing sunlight, or he can sleep in the darkness of night. There's no need to drape a towel or blanket over his cage at night because he outgrew episodes of "night fright" when he turned one. Our dog still likes a blanket draped over his crate when he goes to sleep. He doesn't often whistle, except for occasionally in the mornings. He's usually quiet.

[4]

Just for fun, if you'd like, you can secure pieces of lettuce, small slices of bread, or pieces of cooked pasta to the sides of Peach's cage, using the plastic yellow treat clips. For a special treat, give Peaches scrambled eggs, which he loves! You can just spoon the eggs, with or without melted cheese, into one of his two feeding cups. Anytime you'd like to see him spread his wings, sing, and preen for a very long time, just sprinkle him with the water spritzer, filled with

4. As a topic sentence for Paragraph 3, which of the following choices would most clearly communicate how easy it is to care for Peaches?
   (F) NO CHANGE
   (G) Peaches, in most estimations, is a pet that is not high maintenance.
   (H) Most would agree that Peaches doesn't take a whole lot to care for.
   (J) Peaches is a low-maintenance pet.

5. During the revising and editing stages of writing this essay, the author considers the underlined sentence. Which move would you recommend?
   (A) NO CHANGE
   (B) Move it to the last paragraph of the essay.
   (C) Delete it entirely.
   (D) Leave it where it is, but reword it to fit the overall style and tone of the essay.

6. (F) NO CHANGE
   (G) one
   (H) he or she
   (J) bird breeders

7. (A) NO CHANGE
   (B) Peaches's
   (C) Peaches'
   (D) Peaches' and Cream's

GO ON TO THE NEXT PAGE

lukewarm water. Don't worry about getting his feathers too

wet, he loves bath time!
    8

[5]

When the bottom of his cage gets messy, one should
                                                    9
throw out the used paper towels and lay down new

ones. A thorough cage cleaning should happen about

once a week to keep him healthy and happy,
                          10

using soap and warm water.
        11

[6]

Peaches loves to play pick-up-sticks and is remarkably
                   12
dexterous when it comes to toting around those six-inch-

long plastic sticks. Spread the sticks out on a table, put

Peaches down, and watch him go to work! He invariably

picks up the yellow sticks first—his favorite color. 13

[7]

If you think Peaches is feeling under the weather, don't

delay. You can tell if he's feeling sick if he hangs out at the

bottom of the cage too much, if he fails to eat or drink, or

if he starts plucking out his own feathers! Call the Station

Plaza Veterinarian Clinic or his caring and knowledgeable

8. (F) NO CHANGE
   (G) wet because he loves
   (H) much wet, being he loves
   (J) wet; He loves

9. (A) NO CHANGE
   (B) then, the pet owner should
   (C) simply
   (D) now it's time for you to

10. (F) NO CHANGE
    (G) it
    (H) them
    (J) these species of birds

11. The writer is trying to determine whether to keep
    this gerund phrase where it is or move it. Which, if
    any, is the best revision?
    (A) NO CHANGE
    (B) Move the phrase after the word "happen"
    (C) Move the phrase after the word "cleaning"
    (D) Move the phrase after the word "him"

12. (F) NO CHANGE
    (G) the playing of
    (H) when one plays with him
    (J) playing

13. Upon rereading this paragraph, the author considers
    deleting the prior sentence. If the writer were to
    omit this sentence, the paragraph would primarily
    lose:
    (A) a superfluous detail that weakens rather than
        strengthens the passage.
    (B) an illustration of the unpredictable behavior of
        most pets, especially birds.
    (C) a vivid detail that, to an extent, offers a glimpse
        into Peaches' personality.
    (D) a comment in defense of the case for animal
        intelligence that this author so strongly
        advocates.

GO ON TO THE NEXT PAGE

breeder, Norma, at Norma's Nest. She not only offers a

wealth of advice, <u>as well she</u> knows a great deal about
₁₄

emergency care.

14. (F) NO CHANGE
    (G) in addition breeders
    (H) but also a wealth she
    (J) but she also

> Question 15 asks about the preceding passage as a whole.

15. Suppose the writer wanted to write an essay that summarizes proper pet care. Would this essay accomplish his goal?
    (A) Yes, because several important steps pertaining to pet care are discussed.
    (B) Yes, because the reader readily gets a sense of how this author adores animals.
    (C) No, because some of the bird care advice is inadequate or faulty.
    (D) No, because this essay discusses some aspects pertaining to the care of a specific bird type and not of pets in general.

Passage II

"Lake View"

"Let me go see what's <u>outside." I looked</u> outside and
₁₆

my eyes popped; my chin dropped; and I stared. It was

definitely worth being out in the frigid weather. I probably

looked like I was staring at a huge dinosaur! 17

16. (F) NO CHANGE
    (G) outside," I looked
    (H) outside;" I was looking
    (J) outside," then, when I looked

17. The function of the simile in the preceding sentences is to depict:
    (A) childlike fantasy mingled with delusion.
    (B) humor to introduce the essay's overall comical tone.
    (C) ironic understatement in order to distort the actual scene.
    (D) exaggeration that emphasizes how awestruck the narrator was about what he saw.

GO ON TO THE NEXT PAGE

I could see the lake water softly skimming the shore

so serene like a vulture gliding in the smooth air. I could
_____
18

also see the tree branches clinching, slapping, and hitting as
                                      _____
                                                19

a gust of wind blew by. The rough wood of the

rickety porch railing rubbed against my stinging cold

hands. 20

The lake's thick blue color seemed unrealistic-like to me

as I peeked through the trees. 21 Being out in this

weather, I could hear the melodic sound of the birds chirp-

ing and the chattering of other bunks of classmates playing

outside. The birds didn't even know they were making

music.

18. (F) NO CHANGE
    (G) so serene as a vulture
    (H) as serenely as a vulture
    (J) so serenely like vultures

19. (A) NO CHANGE
    (B) slapping, and hitting like
    (C) to slap and hit while
    (D) with a slap and hitting as

20. If the writer were to delete the preceding sentence,
    which of the following would result?
    (F) The essay would lose a sense of the author's
         inner sensitivity.
    (G) The essay would lose emphasis pertaining to
         the setting's rustic nature and coldness.
    (H) The essay would gain a straightforward
         meaning.
    (J) The paragraph would end with more relevant
         detail.

21. Is this description of the lake an appropriate way to
    begin this paragraph?
    (A) Yes, because the ominous lake description
         predicts the unfortunate events that follow.
    (B) Yes, because the paragraph is about what the
         author experiences while in this lake setting.
    (C) No, because the topic of the lake is better
         addressed elsewhere in the passage.
    (D) No, because the paragraph is more about the
         birds and wildlife, and less about the lake.

GO ON TO THE NEXT PAGE

With the frosty wind at my back, I took two more steps
                                    22

closer to the lake, and I just couldn't believe what I saw. If

you really inspected the lake, like a detective, you could feel

how rural all of Greenkill was.

So in back of the lake was a rustic pure brown color like
23

a thick, deep brushstroke of paint. I discovered that the

brown color was towering trees without leaves. It looked as

if there were a million earthy-colored trees! Now every time
                                                24

I go into the center room, I look outside.

"Phillip, come on, we're having candy", James exclaimed,
                                          25

"It's your favorite!" I turned toward the cabin and
         25

am sprinting toward the center room, imagining Snickers
        26

bars and Reese's. I could taste the creamy, crunchy, crafted

candy melting in my mouth. Everyone is enjoying their
                                      27

candy—"cricket, cricket" meant total silence while everyone

munched.

22. If the author eliminates this underlined portion, the
    effect will most likely be that:
    (F) the reader gains a sense of comfort from the
        deletion of this prepositional phrase.
    (G) the essay moves more sluggishly.
    (H) the reader feels more a part of this descriptive
        scene.
    (J) the reader loses a reminder of how cold it is
        out by the lake.

23. (A) NO CHANGE
    (B) Being
    (C) And so,
    (D) Delete underlined word.

24. (F) NO CHANGE
    (G) Now and then,
    (H) Once in a while,
    (J) Occasionally, with

25. Which of the following sentences is punctuated
    correctly?
    (A) NO CHANGE
    (B) "Phillip come on! We're having candy!" James
        exclaimed, "It's your favorite!"
    (C) "Phillip, come on, we're having candy, James
        exclaimed." "It's your favorite!"
    (D) "Phillip, come on! We're having candy!" James
        exclaimed. "It's your favorite!"

26. (F) NO CHANGE
    (G) was sprinting
    (H) sprinting
    (J) sprinted

27. (A) NO CHANGE
    (B) is enjoying his and hers
    (C) enjoying their
    (D) is enjoying his

GO ON TO THE NEXT PAGE

Finally, I was back in the groove and I was joining
                                            _____
                                                 28

everybody in the huddle being around the steaming, red
                          _____
                               29

fire. [30]

28. (F) NO CHANGE
    (G) join
    (H) will join
    (J) joined

29. (A) NO CHANGE
    (B) that surrounded
    (C) which found itself surrounding
    (D) Delete underlined portion.

30. If the author wanted to add a closing line, which
    of the following sentences would most effectively
    conclude this essay?
    (F) James and I have been good friends since the
        second grade.
    (G) Eating candy and toasting marshmallows by a
        blazing fire was a great way to end a fun-filled
        day.
    (H) I wanted to head back outdoors.
    (J) I wished we could have tried skiing that
        weekend.

Passage III

Every Bride Needs a Printer

The bride anticipates appointments with her caterer,

clergyman, and meetings with her bandleader. She meets
              _____
                         31

ahead of time, with the hairdresser to preview her
_____
              32

"up-style." And the well-groomed bride conferring with her
                                       _____
                                           33
manicurist on whether to color her nails Pink Parfait, or

31. (A) NO CHANGE
    (B) their bandleader.
    (C) the person in charge of the band.
    (D) bandleader.

32. (F) NO CHANGE
    (G) ahead of time with the hairdresser
    (H) ahead of time, with the hairdresser
    (J) ahead of time with the hairdresser,

33. (A) NO CHANGE
    (B) is found to confer
    (C) might of conferred
    (D) confers

GO ON TO THE NEXT PAGE

in whispering elegance in a French manicure. Less often,
however, does the bride think about talking with her
printer; yet, for most brides the professionally printed
wedding invitation is an absolute necessity.

Beyond the invitation, there are many aspects of printing
that can enhance both the pre- as well as post-wedding

experience. So we asked Chet and Laura Halperin, who are
North Shore residents and owners of Len Rho Paperie gift
shop and printing shop in Roslyn Village, to share their
expertise on matters of print, from engagement announcements to place cards to thank-you notes.

Not all brides send announcements declaring their
engagement. However, as Chet Halperin notes, the
engagement announcement is "a festive preview to your
marriage." Engagement announcements are a practical
way to share the good news with your out-of-state family

34. (F) NO CHANGE
    (G) whether or not to whisper
    (H) to whisper
    (J) for the whisper of

35. (A) NO CHANGE
    (B) Omit the underlined portion.
    (C) both the two,
    (D) even the both:

36. (F) NO CHANGE
    (G) they are
    (H) Omit the underlined portion.
    (J) being

37. (A) NO CHANGE
    (B) his as well as her
    (C) both of there
    (D) his or her

38. (F) NO CHANGE
    (G) is, "a festive
    (H) is: "a festive
    (J) are "a festivity and

GO ON TO THE NEXT PAGE

members and friends. You'll be able to tell all the significant
_____
39

people in your life about your future plans.
_____
39

Invitations are sent for the following events: the engagement party, the bridal shower, the rehearsal dinner, and the
wedding. "We create invitations as various as the people who
send them out," says Halperin. "Invitations can be simple,
understated and elegant—or bold, trimmed in a red border,
wearing a long, red feather!"

The repertoire of printing brims with choices:
the embossing process, engraving, raised lettering,
_____
40

monogramming. Your selections can also be personalized
using type styles and ink color. Paper choices are
vast, they include handcrafted vellum, parchment, and
_____
41

heavy bond.

Printing can also add memorable touches to your
wedding day. Traditionally, leaflets are given out at the
ceremony as programs, featuring the music played or sung,
persons delivering readings, candle lighting ceremony and
any other rituals.

Scrolls are the printed words, rolled up and tied with
pretty ribbon. Poetry scrolls can celebrate a couple's favorite
poem or song or they can be created to thank the important
people in your lives. Personalized wedding vows can also be

39. Given that all of the following choices are reasonable,
which one provides the most logical extension of
the concept of "practical" that is described in the
preceding sentence?
(A) NO CHANGE
(B) Your future guests will get a sense of the theme
and/or style that you have in mind for your
wedding.
(C) You will also trim your long distance telephone
bill.
(D) Your guests will have ample time to make
travel plans in order to attend your upcoming
wedding.

40. (F) NO CHANGE
(G) that are including embossment
(H) which include embossed
(J) embossing

41. (A) NO CHANGE
(B) vast, including
(C) vast; they including
(D) vast; which including

GO ON TO THE NEXT PAGE

immortalized on colored parchment and wrapped and tied as a scroll.

Place cards are usually handwritten in calligraphy. However, they can be professionally printed instead to match the style of your invitations.

Etiquette decrees that every bride needs thank-you notes. Ones printed with your names are particularly nice, for example, "Mr. and Mrs. John Jones." Traditional monogrammed notes are another classic choice. Or, you might prefer a more casual approach, "Mary and John." Think carefully about how you would like your wording to be printed. You don't want to pick up your print order and find yourself saying, I <u>should of used</u> our first names, or our
                                    42
nicknames would have been warmer.

[1] Laura Halperin advises using simple stationery so that <u>your handwriting</u> sentiments stand out. [2] Traditional
        43

paper in ivory, ecru, or white <u>is a timeless elegant choice.</u> [3]
                                                    44

42. (F) NO CHANGE
    (G) should've have used
    (H) should been using
    (J) should have used

43. (A) NO CHANGE
    (B) they're handwriting
    (C) their handwritten
    (D) your handwritten

44. (F) NO CHANGE
    (G) make a timeless and create a choice of elegance.
    (H) provide choices—timeless and elegant.
    (J) is a timeless, elegant choice.

GO ON TO THE NEXT PAGE

Use navy or black ink to maintain a classic style. [4] A simple satin ribbon may be all that is needed to add an elegant, finishing touch. [45]

45. The writer is considering adding the following sentence to the final paragraph of this article:

> You wouldn't want your heartfelt words of appreciation to be overshadowed by a too-heavy border or an all-over design that obscures your message.

Should the sentence be added to this paragraph, and, if so, where should it be placed?
(A) Yes, after Sentence 1.
(B) Yes, after Sentence 2.
(C) Yes, after Sentence 3.
(D) The sentence should NOT be added.

Passage IV

A Hearty Brew

If you're feeling sluggish and run-down, or if someone
      46
you love is under the weather, cook up this "hearty brew," which guarantees that you or your loved one will be feeling better soon.

First, dice the following vegetables: several carrots, one large sweet Vidalia onion, two cloves of fresh garlic, one green bell pepper, and one large yam. Sauté these vegetables in a few tablespoons of extra virgin olive oil until it is
                                                          47
somewhat tender; as for the onions, they should be
                 48
translucent. If a fork can easily pierce the peppers and

46. (F) NO CHANGE
    (G) you have been
    (H) your
    (J) someone is

47. (A) NO CHANGE
    (B) being
    (C) becoming
    (D) they become

48. (F) NO CHANGE
    (G) the onions
    (H) and regarding the onions, they
    (J) for onions, these

GO ON TO THE NEXT PAGE

carrots, <u>this way</u> they are soft enough. Pour in two large
₄₉

cans of organic chicken broth and one large can of crushed

tomatoes. If you have it on hand, <u>they</u> can even add one
₅₀

small bouillon cube for extra rich flavor and color.

Let simmer for a solid hour. While the soup simmers,

the flavors will blend and the vegetables <u>would get</u>
₅₁

<u>tenderized</u>. Prepare your favorite small-sized pasta or
₅₁

<u>grain;</u> brown rice, whole grain couscous, star-shaped
₅₂

"pastina." Once done, spoon grain or pasta into a bowl and

use a ladle to pour a good portion of vegetables and broth

on top. If you'd like, top with a sprinkle of grated cheese or

<u>black pepper that is coarsely ground.</u>
₅₃

    This hearty brew has many benefits. It will warm you,

serve as a tasty meal, <u>and fill you up</u> with a good dose of
₅₄

nutrition. It works as either a first course or as a satisfying

main course, particularly when served with a hefty slice of

flaky bread. Make a big pot of this soup; the <u>remainders</u>
₅₅

49. (A) NO CHANGE
(B) carrots; so
(C) carrots, as such,
(D) Delete "this way"

50. (F) NO CHANGE
(G) he or she
(H) you
(J) the chef or gourmet

51. (A) NO CHANGE
(B) they tenderizing
(C) will become tender
(D) meanwhile would become tender

52. (F) NO CHANGE
(G) grain-
(H) grain,
(J) grain:

53. (A) NO CHANGE
(B) pepper, black and ground coarsely.
(C) coarse grinding of pepper, which is black.
(D) coarsely ground black pepper.

54. (F) NO CHANGE
(G) and also filling
(H) and fill you
(J) the brew will be filling

55. (A) NO CHANGE
(B) leftovers
(C) leftover remains
(D) leftover portions

GO ON TO THE NEXT PAGE

can be frozen in portion-sized freezer containers. [56]

Next time the weather forecast says "chilly," simply defrost a portion of this soup and you will enjoy a meal that gratifies your body, soul, and palate. [57]

Though this soup is homemade, so you control the
58   59

ingredients, the portions of each, and the flavorings. [60]

56. Consider the structure and format of this paragraph as it has unfolded up to this point. With which of the following critical assessments do you agree?
(F) It is soundly organized, with a topic sentence that opens the paragraph and is supported by the sentences that follow.
(G) It is organized fairly well, but the focus of the paragraph breaks down at the midway point.
(H) It is organized poorly. It begins with a sentence about the soup's benefits and appeal but does not follow with supporting ideas.
(J) It is a very poorly organized paragraph. The ideas lack focus and read like a staccato listing of thoughts.

57. This passage can be most accurately described as:
(A) dramatic.
(B) biographical.
(C) informative.
(D) academic.

58. (F) NO CHANGE
(G) Thus,
(H) Best of all,
(J) Even though

59. (A) NO CHANGE
(B) homemade;
(C) homemade—
(D) homemade:

60. This paragraph would be strengthened by:
(F) discussing the type of cookware that is most effective for making this soup.
(G) specifying the particular types of breads that best accompany this soup.
(H) including the names of well-known chefs that regularly make soups of this type.
(J) mentioning some specific nutritional benefits of the soup.

GO ON TO THE NEXT PAGE

Passage V

Introduction to *Good Eats*

Long Island Edition

[1]

Our inaugural issue of *Good Eats* <u>let</u>'s you in on where
₆₁
to eat good, inspired meals inexpensively on Long Island.

Unlike other <u>restaurants</u>, we've selected only those choice
₆₂
breakfast, luncheon, and dinner spots we believe are real

finds, <u>whereabouts</u> dinner for two can be purchased for
₆₃
under fifty dollars.

Some listings are hole-in-the-walls, some are landmarks,

some are <u>new and trendy</u>, some are old and established
₆₄
places, some are well-known diners, some are unknown

luncheonettes, some are tucked away treasures, and some are

places that <u>can be found</u> right on Main Street.
₆₅
I have always found it easy to find the expensive Long

Island restaurants for eating out, like Peter Luger's, The

Palm, and La Marmite, to name a few. However, until now,

<u>it's being</u> very difficult to locate new, exciting places to
₆₆
enjoy *Good Eats* at reasonable prices, some even dirt cheap!

---

61. (A) NO CHANGE
    (B) is letting
    (C) lets
    (D) let is

62. (F) NO CHANGE
    (G) types of restaurants
    (H) guides geared toward selecting restaurants
    (J) restaurant guides

63. (A) NO CHANGE
    (B) in where
    (C) regarding that
    (D) in which

64. (F) NO CHANGE
    (G) new as well as being trendy
    (H) new and trendy spots
    (J) new, trendy types

65. (A) NO CHANGE
    (B) while they are found
    (C) being found
    (D) they have been found

66. (F) NO CHANGE
    (G) it has been
    (H) being
    (J) it would have been

GO ON TO THE NEXT PAGE

In our *Good Eats* guide, you will find those special restaurants serving Long Island's *best* waffles, *best* Buffalo wings, *best* burgers, *best* knishes, *best* cole slaw, and the *best* BBQ for the best prices around.

I really have to thank my Mom, Rhoda, and Dad, Leo, for this dining guide. Mom never cooked—not breakfast, lunch, or dinner. Not even coffee. Growing up on Long Island, most of my home-cooked meals were eaten at my friend's houses. Even today, Mom still buys
67
large cups of take-out coffee at the famous Laurel

luncheonette and heats it up, one at a time, at home.
68

So, by necessity, I've come to know the Long Island
69
restaurant scene very well.

67. (A) NO CHANGE
    (B) houses belonging to my friends
    (C) friends, their houses
    (D) friends' houses

68. (F) NO CHANGE
    (G) them
    (H) the take-out cups
    (J) the coffee

69. (A) NO CHANGE
    (B) contradictorily
    (C) unexpectedly
    (D) unnaturally

GO ON TO THE NEXT PAGE

In closing, *Good Eats* was written from a compilation of reviews from family, friends, and acquaintances throughout Long Island's many communities. Some of them are former New York City residents, now living in the suburbs, who miss the neighborhood restaurant scene. Some are just plain folks who eat out often and know their particular area very well.

A special thanks to my fiancée, Laura, her who has been an invaluable source of information and inspiration in

producing the *Good Eats* guide. 72

70. (F) NO CHANGE
    (G) of them contributors
    (H) contributors
    (J) contributing

71. (A) NO CHANGE
    (B) who
    (C) being those who
    (D) will

72. At this point, the author has composed the following sentence:

> She has offered me insights into her own favorite dining spots and has encouraged and supported me every step of the way throughout the process of compiling this guide.

Should the author insert this new sentence here? Why or why not?

(F) Yes, because it dramatically juxtaposes Laura as a supporter with those who tried to dampen the author's efforts to produce this dining guide.
(G) Yes, because it elaborates on how Laura has been an "invaluable source of information and inspiration."
(H) No, because it ironically detracts from the prior sentence.
(J) No, because the sentence offers irrelevant details that slow the pace of the dining guide's introduction.

GO ON TO THE NEXT PAGE

Agents, please let us know if you have a favorite place
—————
73
you would like to share with our audience. We are in the

process of putting together separate guides for suburban

dining in your area. We would love to hear comments from

all of our friends in the tri-state area. [75]
          ————————————————
                    74

73. (A) NO CHANGE
    (B) Men and women,
    (C) People,
    (D) Readers,

74. (F) NO CHANGE
    (G) friends living in the tri-state area.
    (H) friends who live in the tri-states.
    (J) friends that are living within the tri-state region.

75. Which of the sentences below, if added here, would provide the most effective conclusion to this paragraph and is most consistent with the main point of this passage?
    (A) This dining guide should inspire reluctant restaurant-diners to eat out more often.
    (B) Please eat at local restaurants more often than at the "big chains" in order to support family-owned businesses.
    (C) With your input, hundreds of first-hand dining experiences and observations can be pooled, making the next edition of *Good Eats* even better!
    (D) Turns out, ambiance and service rank over how the food tastes and what the bill states as the bottom line.

STOP

READING TEST

35 MINUTES—40 QUESTIONS

Directions: The reading test consists of four passages. Ten questions follow each reading selection. After reading each passage, choose the best answer for each question and fill in the answer bubble on your answer sheet. You may refer to the reading selections as often as you like.

Passage I

PROSE FICTION: Written during a summer writing institute at Columbia University's Teachers College, this reading selection is adapted from Linda Carnevale's fictionalized memoir, *Excavating a Place*. The narrative is structured around building an outdoor patio.

I remember dreading that home improvement project. *Impossible.* Couldn't build a 550-square-foot patio ourselves, one of pavers in blue-gray. "Wedgwood," I'd say; the photo brochure called the pavers
5 "Camelot."

Impossible, turns out, were the estimates. So early one Saturday morning in April we began digging, digging deep—not as profound as the eight- by ten-foot mote that cradled our red ranch four years
10 earlier—digging a place for family roots so that more memories could grow. We dug with my dad's shovels, the ones he used twenty-five years ago when he excavated a place for the red brick patio of my childhood home. The patio he graced with cement
15 pots brimming with red and fuchsia geraniums. The same shovels my dad had used, deceased seventeen years ago, to turn over his backyard garden so asparagus, eggplant, and tomatoes could grow. There I was, digging up red clay in April, remembering when
20 I—five or six—would gather chunks of red clay from our garden and sculpt.

Digging and shoveling like kids at the beach, my father-in-law, husband, and me. Leveling and measuring the ground repeatedly to get the precise pitch,
25 flowing away from the house. Staying within the borders of the form that my husband constructed of knotted twine and wooden posts (remnants from our dining room's oak floor). Shoveling the earth deep, deep enough to hold four inches of gravel and three
30 inches of sand.

With a formidable claw and iron clad in industrial orange, it arrived. In a moment, my husband became the cougar behind the bobcat, shredding our newly seeded lawn like cabbage. Wheels like teeth.
35 Seven-foot high piles of black gravel and beige sand stood on our lawn like full-bellied soldiers, stalwart and waiting. To me, the piles were pyramids to dismantle. I felt the pressure of creating the Eighth Wonder of the World—in our backyard. One patio,
40 one bobcat, my husband, the pharaoh, and me.

"Slices stone like bread," Frank, the nine-fingered mason, had said about his tile cutter as he trimmed rose garland tiles for our new master bath the summer before. Now a wet stonecutter, rented
45 from Frank, became our main artillery. Armed with earplugs, waterproof gloves, and goggles, we began. "*Zzz . . . Chip! Chip! Zzzz . . . Chip!*"—Chips of paver leaped off the stonecutter, just as charred crumbs jump off burned toast when you scrape it!

50 In less than ten minutes, our hair was covered in powder as fine as flour. Like salt, it burned our eyes and singed our pores as we sweat and got wet by the Almighty Stonecutter! I saw an eighty-three-year-old countenance of my husband: white eyebrows, chalky
55 eyelashes, gray moustache. Gray forearms, too. A head of tight, raven-black curls turned to wet, sandy gray. The paver dust was unlike other dust we'd known over our four-year-long home renovation. There was the dust of sheetrock, as fine as powdered
60 sugar, finding its way into sock drawers and toilet paper. I sneezed from that dust and the dust from sanding wood molding. I cried over endless cleanups and tireless efforts to stay ahead of the mess.

White and wet, our pruned hands continued to
65 manipulate the cobblestones. The skin of our fingertips seemed to melt in the brew of the stonecutter's

GO ON TO THE NEXT PAGE

murky water, the humidity, and the paste of paver
dust mixed with water. A paste-like ground, like
the chalky stuff we used to grout our fifty-year-old
70 powder room. Paste, like the white caulking my
husband set around the kitchen sink and along the
narrow water canals where the Formica counter met
the backsplash tile.

So, following the warfare of masonry and settling
75 of the dust, we have our Camelot, a peaceful outdoor
place, a mini American Riviera. A peaceful place to
celebrate May birthdays with barbecues. A place for
weekend lounging, reading, evening daydreaming,
container gardening. A place to eat sweet-smelling
80 honeydew and tamari almonds. A place to gaze at
terracotta votives and the blazes of tiki torches that
burn oil with a tropical fragrance. A place for our
two-year-old son to leave a trail of his "na-nilla" ice-
cream cone, the dessert he chose over the American
85 classic, homemade apple pie. Like King Arthur and
Lady Guinevere, we triumphed as we will always
strive to do.

To this day, I love the solidity of our patio, the
color of seawater. The feel of stone beneath my bare
90 feet is strengthening, enduring like the antiquity of
old English cobble. With a girth of three inches,
the blocks promise the longevity of ages. We had
thought of building a half wall of brick around the
patio. I'm glad we didn't. Like Humpty Dumpty,
95 walls eventually fall down.

1. The author's narrative technique in the second and
   third paragraphs uses:
   (A) shifting back and forth between present day
       and reflection.
   (B) writing in second-person point of view.
   (C) juxtaposing images of strength with those of
       feebleness.
   (D) varying her tone from nostalgic to critical.

2. The descriptive sentence "With a formidable claw
   and iron clad in industrial orange, it arrived"
   (lines 31–32) primarily produces which of the
   following rhetorical effects?
   (F) It exaggerates the strength of the cougar.
   (G) It personifies the bobcat.
   (H) It is a euphemistic expression for destructive
       power.
   (J) It compares the patio project to the work of
       soldiers.

3. In writing this memoir, the author uses ALL of the
   following creative writing devices EXCEPT:
   (A) rhetorical questions.
   (B) stylistic fragments.
   (C) repetition of words and phrases.
   (D) allusions to historical legends.

4. The description of the bobcat's effect, "shredding
   our newly seeded lawn like cabbage" (lines 33–34)
   most closely illustrates which of the following
   literary devices?
   (F) Analogy
   (G) Alliteration
   (H) Simile
   (J) Hyperbole

5. The sentences "Now a wet stonecutter, rented from
   Frank, became our main artillery. Armed with
   earplugs, waterproof gloves, and goggles, we began"
   (lines 44–46) create which of the following effects?
   (A) The stonecutter is old and unreliable, therefore
       requiring its users to protect themselves to an
       excessive degree.
   (B) The homeowners and mason feel overwhelmed
       by not only the project but also the financial
       burden they have taken on.
   (C) Frank has enlisted the homeowners' help
       in alleviating some of the heavy burden of
       building a patio of stone.
   (D) The patio builders are home-improvement
       warriors who appear to face a military
       expedition as they embark on cutting the
       stones to fashion their patio.

6. The description "*Zzz . . . Chip! Chip! Zzzz . . .
   Chip!*"—Chips of paver leaped off the stonecutter,
   just as charred crumbs jump off burned toast when
   you scrape it!" (lines 47–49) illustrates ALL of the
   following literary devices EXCEPT:
   (F) simile.
   (G) imagery.
   (H) irony.
   (J) onomatopoeia.

GO ON TO THE NEXT PAGE

7. In the eighth paragraph (lines 74–87), the author most likely uses repetition of the phrase "a place" to:
   (A) baffle the reader about why she repeats herself.
   (B) attempt to induce a hypnotic effect in the reader.
   (C) emphasize how much pleasure the patio offers.
   (D) lull the reader by imitating the repetitive lyrics of a chorus.

8. The details that the author uses in describing the patio "A place to eat sweet-smelling honeydew and tamari almonds. A place to gaze at terracotta votives … son to leave a trail of his 'na-nilla' ice cream" (lines 79–84) are:
   (F) allusions to the carefree pastimes of most children.
   (G) an appeal to the senses.
   (H) a sense of detached interest when it comes to spending time outdoors.
   (J) a commentary on the cultural values of many Americans today.

9. The main contrast the narrator delineates between the "patio" (line 88) and the "half wall" (line 93) in the final paragraph is between:
   (A) transience and belligerence.
   (B) longevity and evanescence.
   (C) beauty and fancy.
   (D) durability and stability.

10. A reasonable conclusion you can draw about the author is that she:
    (F) will not tackle additional home-improvement projects in the near future.
    (G) prefers the outdoors to the indoors.
    (H) prefers things that are durable to those that do not endure for long.
    (J) favors working alone to working as part of a team.

Passage II

SOCIAL SCIENCE: This passage on alternative communication methods was written by Ms. Lauren Beth Benzoni, MS, a speech-language pathologist who is currently at North Shore Schools, New York. Ms. Benzoni's training and background include a Master of Science degree from the State University of New York at Geneseo and employment at the prestigious Long Island-based Mill Neck Manor for the Deaf.

Augmentative and Alternative Communication (AAC) refers to communication modalities, other than speech. Augmentative communication techniques range from simple to complex, and include
5 gestures, facial expressions, and writing. AAC is a system created for individuals who need to increase their expressive skills for functional communication. It involves enhancing or substituting speech with unaided or aided symbols.

10 Unaided symbols include manual signs, finger spelling, and gestures; aided symbols include picture communication symbols, line drawings, and tangible objects.

The American Speech and Hearing Association's
15 (ASHA) special division twelve, which is designed specifically for AAC, has four main components: symbols, aids, strategies, and techniques.

ASHA realizes that AAC providers must look beyond the individual client and examine the people
20 with whom they interact. The type of AAC must be specific to its user. This objective is imperative so that clients have as much access to the device as possible and recognize it as their mode of communication. Many are qualified to use AAC, including
25 those with Down syndrome or autism and people whose functional communication is not enhanced with standard speech-language therapy. People with medical issues preventing them from communicating entirely by speech, such as a cleft palate or a
30 tracheotomy, also fall into this category.

AAC focuses on people with severe and expressive communicative disorders, and attempts to compensate for the speech they lack temporarily or permanently. "Approximately two million Americans are

GO ON TO THE NEXT PAGE

35 unable to use speech and/or handwriting to meet their daily communication needs. This represents between 0.8% and 1.2% of the U.S. population" (ASHA 2004 1). ASHA has declared that any indi-vidual can use AAC; one does not have to meet

40 qualifying criteria. ASHA maintains a "zero exclu-sion criterion": rather than determining if a client is eligible for AAC, a speech-language pathologist determines where a client falls on a continuum of communication, explicitly identifying that client's

45 strengths. The speech-language pathologist then determines what type of AAC to use with the client.

A team of specialists should serve an individual who requires AAC. This team may include (but is not limited to) speech-language pathologists, occu-

50 pational therapists, physical therapists, physicians, rehabilitation engineers, educators, social workers, psychologists, computer programmers, vocational counselors, audiologists, orthodontists, and manu-facturers of communication devices. These practi-

55 tioners ensure that the client's fine and gross motor skills match the demands of the device. Usually, clients requiring AAC have global delays and need evaluations and therapies to address these deficits. The child who requires AAC is instructed on how to

60 use the device at school. The adult client is instructed by a local professional.

AAC is vital because it allows people with com-munication impairments to express their needs and emotions. AAC facilitates expressive communica-

65 tion, enhancing a person's speech. Although verbal communication may not be physically possible for certain clients, AAC provides options. Clinicians often use AAC devices in conjunction with literacy.

Although sign language uses no technology, other

70 intricate output communication systems are fully computerized. At a minimum, sign language helps individuals convey their ideas: Signed Exact English and American Sign Language are used. Sign language

is similar to speaking, allowing the individual to

75 comprehend and tell stories. Another form of AAC is communication boards, which have sets of photos, drawings, symbols, or words that help the individual communicate. The student points to a picture as an answer or request. A speech-language pathologist can

80 adapt a storybook to incorporate the board, using symbols to represent words. Another step up is the voice output communication device, which allows one to record his or her voice to correspond with a picture or symbol on the board. When a button is

85 pressed, a corresponding word or phrase comes from the device. The Macaw is a voice output communi-cation device that has multiple levels for recording one's voice. Its numerous settings enable pictures to be incorporated, thus providing for a longer, more

90 versatile lesson. This device can be used with differ-ent age groups, from preschoolers to adults.

Although the Macaw uses technology, more advanced devices allow for expressive communica-tion. For example, with the Dynavox, individuals

95 navigate from screen to screen, increasing the length of utterances and vocabulary. With one program, the individual types a word on the screen and that word is repeated. This device enables users to type words to form sentences. Individuals with severe commu-

100 nication impairments take longer to receive, process, and respond to literacy information. Alternative strategies are implemented to hone comprehension skills.

Clinicians can adapt activities to facilitate print

105 awareness and heighten vocabulary. Students with severe impairments are taught the same types of activities as other students, in differentiated ways. The therapist draws attention to print using aided systems, such as a communication board, a voice

110 output system, or the Dynavox. Each method teaches important concepts: phonemic awareness, word and syllable awareness, print awareness, the use of pictures, and reading.

GO ON TO THE NEXT PAGE

11. As it is used in line 80, the word "adapt" most nearly means:
    (A) acclimate.
    (B) modify.
    (C) camouflage.
    (D) familiarize.

12. Based on the information presented in lines 10–13, if unaided symbols include non-tangible methods, which of the following is the best example of an aided symbol?
    (F) Shapes made with the hands
    (G) Gesturing combined with lip movement
    (H) Colorful flash cards with drawings on them
    (J) Full and dramatic body movements

13. In lines 32–33, the word "compensate" most nearly means:
    (A) compound.
    (B) befriend.
    (C) make up.
    (D) pay back.

14. The Macaw (line 86) and the Dynavox (line 94) invoke the client's ability to:
    (F) manipulate objects.
    (G) sketch pictures.
    (H) navigate through pictures and choose the corresponding picture to communicate.
    (J) use the sense of sight to recognize pictures and/or objects.

15. Which of the following best explains a legitimate aspect of the "zero exclusion criterion," as described in lines 40–41?
    (A) The speech-language pathologist "measures" the client's communication abilities, then determines which AAC methods are best suited for that client.
    (B) The speech-language pathologist avoids the use of AAC unless the client displays a dire need for this type of intervention.
    (C) The speech-language pathologist uses AAC as a last resort, regardless of where the client falls on the communication continuum.
    (D) The speech-language pathologist administers AAC services to the client only if a doctor recommends it.

16. As used in line 88, the word "settings" could most reasonably incorporate ALL of the following aspects EXCEPT:
    (F) volume.
    (G) body temperature.
    (H) images.
    (J) a mixture of sounds and pictures.

17. As it is used in line 102, "hone" most nearly means:
    (A) memorize.
    (B) sharpen.
    (C) tone.
    (D) harness.

18. Based on the information presented in the passage, it can be inferred that related service providers should be included in the selection of an appropriate device because:
    (F) obtaining a large group of professionals and opinions is essential for a client to succeed.
    (G) the client can learn to remember names.
    (H) all areas of a client's functioning are evaluated and improved to ensure the selection of a device that is appropriate.
    (J) these providers can make it easier to address pragmatic concerns like availability of times and scheduling.

19. It can be reasonably inferred from the last paragraph (lines 104–113) that a student can develop "print awareness" by:
    (A) working with the therapist, using a device with aided symbols.
    (B) reading books that incorporate a challenging level of vocabulary.
    (C) accentuating syllable breaks while speaking with the therapist.
    (D) cutting and pasting sections of text from newspaper headlines.

20. For students who cannot speak and have limited use of their arms and hands, the *least* appropriate AAC device would be:
    (F) the Macaw.
    (G) sign language.
    (H) a communication board.
    (J) the Dynavox.

GO ON TO THE NEXT PAGE

Passage III

HUMANITIES: This passage was excerpted from the article "Addicted to Fame: From the Greeks to Lady Gaga," featured in Fall 2017 *Humanities* magazine published by National Endowment for the Humanities at *www.nea.gov.*

"Fame is a bee," Emily Dickinson wrote in one of her last poems. "It has a song— / It has a sting—." "Ah, too," she added, "it has a wing." The poem captures Dickinson resigning herself to how ephem-
5 eral fame can be, how effortlessly it moves from one person to the next, pleasing, wounding, and deserting them as it travels across the earth.

Dickinson's comparison came to mind as I pre-pared a course at The College of New Jersey on the
10 history of fame. On campuses across the country, one can find fascinating classes dedicated to the study of stars like Beyoncé, Madonna, and Bruce Springsteen. My course took a different approach. It focused not on individual personalities, but on the long line of
15 thinkers who have grappled with the meaning of fame.

Fame itself may be fleeting, but for centuries writers and artists have praised and lamented its grip on their lives. Dickinson is a case in point: Though she largely rejected publication and was virtually unknown in her
20 time, she wrote about fame as a fundamental part of her humanity.

Today's college students are part of a fame culture that is far more absorbing than the one in which their parents grew up. Waves of publicity crash over
25 them daily, with Twitter, Instagram, and BuzzFeed now added to the mix of dorm-room posters and fan magazines. But young people no longer see themselves as just spectators. Listen to the most savvy among them, and they'll offer detailed strategies for creating a
30 personal brand and curating a digital identity. As the phrase goes, they aim to *optimize their presence* in an attention-based economy.

My aim was to build a course that could defamil-iarize fame by exploring its roots in the ancient world.
35 I wanted students to see that fame was not always associated with glamor and excess. I wanted them to appreciate how previous cultures had integrated fame into treasured stories about virtue, character, mortality, and public life. But like Dickinson's bee,
40 our discussions took flight and frequently landed us in fields far removed from antiquity. In the end, my students discovered the remoteness of the past; what they taught me is its unmistakable presence today.

The Eternal Achilles
Our course began with Achilles, the great hero of
45 Homer's Iliad, who for centuries has epitomized the idea that fame is a kind of immortality. Disgusted by the waste of the Trojan War and suffering from injured pride, Achilles must choose between abandoning and rejoining the Greeks' siege of Troy in the war's ninth
50 year. "Two fates bear me on to the day of death," he laments:

If I hold out here and I lay siege to Troy,
my journey home is gone, but my glory never dies.
If I voyage back to the fatherland I love,
55 my pride, my glory dies . . .
true, but the life that's left me will be long,
the stroke of death will not come on me quickly.

A mortal by birth, Achilles can either die fighting—and be celebrated—or return to his peaceful fatherland,
60 where he will suffer in anonymity. Glory will give him new life and the godlike immortality that only artists and storytellers can confer.

Because heroics alone cannot preserve Achilles, he aspires to what the Greeks called *kleos*, which is the
65 immortality that comes from being part of the poet's song. Without a developed sense of an afterlife, the Greeks believed in the consecrating, imperishable power of art. Achilles has to die in Troy in order to claim his role in Homer's narrative. His eternal fame
70 remains inseparable from the artistic re-creation of his feats.

The Greeks had significant reservations about fame, which, for many students, resonated with their own. In the Odyssey, Odysseus is punished for brag-
75 ging after blinding the Cyclops, and when he visits

GO ON TO THE NEXT PAGE

the Underworld, Achilles tells him that life as a slave would have been better than ruling over "the breathless dead." But amid this ambivalence, we also saw how significant kleos continued to be. Hundreds of
80 years after the Iliad, Alexander the Great recognized the importance of art in keeping his conquests alive. As designed by his favored sculptor, statues of Alexander relied on certain trademark features (the curl of his hair, the cast of his eyes) that identified him for
85 posterity. Like a contemporary politician complaining about his press coverage, Alexander grumbled that, without a poet of Homer's skill, his fame would be more transitory than that of his hero Achilles.

21. The passage is best described as being told from the point of view of someone who is:
    (A) depicting the most desirable type of fame that all of modern humankind seeks.
    (B) examining various concepts of fame from across times and cultures.
    (C) surveying his students' notions about what types of fame are most desirable.
    (D) touting his ability to create fame for himself in various ways.

22. The passage as a whole best supports which of the following conclusions?
    (F) Fame is defined primarily by money and social status.
    (G) Fame that lasts indefinitely is more prized than that which is ephemeral.
    (H) Fame is among mankind's most deleterious enemies.
    (J) Fame is an undesirable state of being.

23. Lines 52–57 ("If I hold . . . quickly") primarily serve to suggest that:
    (A) only a fool would sacrifice a long life for honor.
    (B) in battling for one's country, one can only attain a fleeting sense of fame.
    (C) an individual's sense of immortality is tested only when he or she goes to war.
    (D) dying in battle can yield a type of eternal fame.

24. As it is used in line 15, the word "grappled" most nearly means:
    (F) faced.
    (G) collided.
    (H) wrestled.
    (J) handled.

25. Which of the following questions is most directly answered by the passage?
    (A) What inspired Emily Dickinson to write her poem about fame, "Fame is a bee … it has a wing"?
    (B) Who designed the form and content of the course taught at The College of New Jersey?
    (C) For how long did this course run at the college?
    (D) What type of fame do most college age students seek today?

26. According to the passage, which of the following pairs represents sources of fame that are most likely to endure the passage of time?
    (F) Battle victories and bravery
    (G) Slavery and humility
    (H) Public service and political writing
    (J) Art and poetry

27. As it used in line 72, the word "reservations" most nearly means:
    (A) qualms.
    (B) plans.
    (C) hindrances.
    (D) territories.

28. The passage suggests that the "discussions" referenced in line 40 were:
    (F) predictable and mundane.
    (G) unfounded and myopic.
    (H) expansive and reflective.
    (J) unprecedented and arbitrary.

29. The effect of the simile in lines 85–88 "Like a contemporary . . . hero Achilles" is best described as:
    (A) emphasizing Alexander's desire for everlasting fame through the pen of a skilled author.
    (B) deprecating Homer's skill as an author and poet.
    (C) exaggerating the effect that art can have on one's posterity.
    (D) contradicting Dickinson's notions about fame as expressed in her poem.

30. According to the author, all of the following are characteristics of the meaning of fame EXCEPT:
    (F) fleeting nature.
    (G) enduring pleasure.
    (H) eternal anonymity.
    (J) individual stardom.

GO ON TO THE NEXT PAGE

Passage IV

NATURAL SCIENCE: Entitled "Urbanization and Malaria: The Most Important Environmental Health Effect," this article was chosen as a finalist for submission to an environmental health journal. The author, Jason Halperin, graduated from New York University in 2001, then traveled with and worked for the international humanitarian organization, Doctors Without Borders in the United States, South Africa, and Sudan. He holds a Master's Degree in Public Health from Columbia University's Program on Forced Migration and Health. His research focuses on infectious disease epidemiology, with an emphasis on tropical medicine.

Malaria, one of the world's most common and serious tropical diseases, is a protozoal infection transmitted to humans by mosquitoes. Each year, malaria causes close to two million deaths and an
5 additional 300 to 500 million clinical cases, the majority of which occur in the world's poorest countries. Over ninety percent of mortality due to malarial infection occurs in pregnant women and children under five. Pregnant women, due to normal immune
10 suppression, have a much greater risk of contraction than nonpregnant women and men. Besides the typical flu-like symptoms, malaria often leads to the loss of pregnancy, low birth weight complications, and maternal anemia. Throughout the developing
15 world, malaria is the leading killer of children under five, with an African child dying every thirty seconds from malaria. The greatest burden from this infection falls squarely on the shoulders of women of reproductive age and women as the primary child
20 caretakers. Furthermore, the Washington-based Global Health Council has recognized that many cases are not documented saying, "reporting is particularly fragmentary and irregular in areas known to be highly endemic," leading to an unimaginable toll
25 of global mortality and morbidity.

Currently, developing countries, especially in sub-Saharan Africa, are experiencing the highest rates of urbanization in the world. These same locations comprise the greatest burden of malaria infec-
30 tions. This increase in urbanization is nested within our current framework of globalization. The World Health Organization (WHO) defines globalization as "the increased interconnectedness and inter-dependence of peoples and countries." But the WHO's
35 simple definition does not accurately capture the economic forces that are leading to the decline of

agriculture, green spaces and therefore rapid urbanization. For example, Nobel Prize-winning economist Joseph Stiglitz criticizes our current form
40 of globalization by noting "it completely neglects systems of democracy, sustainable development and traditional forms of farming." As families have become displaced economically from their customary forms of livelihood, they are invading the out-
45 skirts of cities desperately looking for employment, where they often find themselves in "black holes of social exclusion." Castell terms this shared reality of political, economic and social exclusion that connect the world's "ghettos" as the fourth world. These
50 "outposts of powerlessness" are inhabited, predominantly, by women and children who fall outside the opportunities of these new "globalized" cities.

Current estimates predict that half of the African population will live in urban settings by the year
55 2025. Proper city planning has not preceded this massive influx, and already poor countries are struggling to cope with the pace and extent of urbanization. Millions of people, throughout the world, are now residing in barrios, shantytowns, slums and
60 other informal settlements on the margins of urban areas. Keiser reports, "poor housing and lack of sanitation and drainage of surface water can increase vector breeding and human vector contact" and have been clearly demonstrated to "increase malaria trans-
65 mission." Furthermore, economic migrants, who have never been exposed to malaria, are moving from non-endemic rural areas to endemic urbanized areas, which will greatly increase global malaria incidence. For these reasons, malaria poses a very serious envi-
70 ronmental health effect, but prevention and control are possible in these settings.

The most important steps to decrease malaria prevalence in these settings include increased surveillance, access to artimisinin-based combination
75 therapy (ACT, which is the cheapest and most effective malaria treatment), use of insecticide-treated bed nets, good sanitation and access to clean water as well as the elimination of breeding sites. Proper sanitation and access to clean water have been shown
80 by Staedke to significantly decrease the prevalence of malaria when comparing wealthier areas of Kampala to Kawempe (the largest shantytown in Kampala, the capital of Uganda). Though the poor areas

GO ON TO THE NEXT PAGE

of cities, especially in the developing world, have
85 many mosquito breeding sites, cities such as Rio de
Janeiro have dramatically cut transmission in these
high-density communities by implementing environmental health strategies.

Malaria control in Rio de Janeiro, Brazil, utilizes
90 a visionary multi-pronged strategy: field sanitation
technicians visit outlying communities, spraying
insecticides in breeding areas, removing standing
water, increasing easy access to clean water as well as
taking blood samples to treat persons suffering from
95 malaria. Each community has a health office where
people who suspect they are infected can come for
an examination and treatment with ACT. Treatment
with highly effective anti-malarials is an important
component of malaria control, especially in urban
100 areas, as infected humans are the prime reservoir of
future infections.

Globalization is leading to increased urbanization worldwide, especially throughout the developing world. The prevalence of malaria continues to
105 steadily increase in these urbanized areas, primarily
in the low-income areas of these cities where women
and children are at most risk. Effective control
measures are urgently needed to protect against this
public health calamity, the most important environ-
110 mental health threat fueled by globalization.

31. The effect of the author's diction (word choice)
when he uses the word "squarely" in line 18 is to:
(A) reflect on the hardships women endure as
they care for themselves as well as their ailing
children.
(B) undermine how men, for the most part, flatly
disregard the destructive potential of this sickness.
(C) underscore the unfairness of health policies
that do not adequately protect victims of
malaria.
(D) emphasize the extent to which the burden of
this particular disease rests with women.

32. According to the author, the fact that some cases of
malaria are NOT being reported has what effect?
(F) It limits the resources and manpower that
are available both to research and to treat the
sickness.
(G) It saves funds on behalf of organizations like
the Global Health Council, who insist that
these funds are more urgently needed
elsewhere.
(H) It makes the potential for the scale of misery
and fatalities caused by malaria loom even
larger in people's minds and imaginations.
(J) It increases skepticism among doctors and
researchers who already doubt the widespread
negative effects of this infectious disease.

33. The passage indicates that an accurate depiction
of the future of "sub-Saharan Africa" (line 27) will
most likely portray it as:
(A) a region immune to the particular effects of the
diminution of the farming industry.
(B) an industrious area experiencing rapid economic growth and prosperity that will posi-
tively affect the poorest of regions.
(C) a location marked by the convergence of cultures that illuminates the various value systems
held by peoples worldwide.
(D) regions with higher occurrences of displaced
families, a decline of untouched greenery, and
increasing rates of malaria.

34. Based on the passage, it can be reasonably concluded
that which of the following physical locations has
the most promising future in terms of health and
human welfare?
(F) Sub-Saharan Africa
(G) Kawempe
(H) The outskirts of cities
(J) Rio de Janeiro

35. It can reasonably be inferred that, given the future
prospects pertaining to malaria, the author:
(A) is despairing and pessimistic.
(B) has resigned himself to a reality-based outlook of
steady, worsening doom.
(C) regrettably intermingles fact and fantasy.
(D) envisions the possibilities for human efforts to
result in significant positive outcomes.

GO ON TO THE NEXT PAGE

36. It can be reasonably inferred from the passage that given "current estimates" (lines 53–71):
    (F) women will likely pursue higher levels of formal education.
    (G) future migrants, children and adults alike, will learn to better protect themselves against infection.
    (H) more and more people will live in urban areas characterized by unsanitary, cramped living conditions that will, in turn, breed more cases of malaria.
    (J) the estimators will eventually be proven wrong, for urban populations will thrive, as a result of comprehensive prevention efforts.

37. As it is used in line 69, the word "poses" most nearly means:
    (A) portrays.
    (B) stands for.
    (C) causes.
    (D) impersonates.

38. In the fifth paragraph (lines 89–101), the author uses ALL of the following devices EXCEPT:
    (F) an abbreviation that has been previously defined.
    (G) a metaphor.
    (H) a vivid flashback.
    (J) a specific example followed by supporting details.

39. As used in line 96, the word "suspect" most nearly means:
    (A) scrutinize.
    (B) believe.
    (C) doubt.
    (D) conclude.

40. The overall effect of the final paragraph (lines 102–110) of this passage is to:
    (F) summarize the author's key point and put forth a plea to restrict the spread of malaria.
    (G) contradict several points that the author made earlier.
    (H) excessively exaggerate the current and potential harms of malaria worldwide.
    (J) cast doubt upon the main points the author has expressed throughout the article.

STOP

ANSWER KEY
Self-Assessment Tests

English Test

PASSAGE I: CARING FOR PEACHES

1. D	4. J	7. C	10. F	13. C
2. F	5. C	8. G	11. C	14. J
3. B	6. F	9. C	12. F	15. D

PASSAGE II: LAKE VIEW

16. F	19. A	22. J	25. D	28. J
17. D	20. G	23. D	26. J	29. B
18. H	21. B	24. F	27. D	30. G

PASSAGE III: EVERY BRIDE NEEDS A PRINTER

31. D	34. H	37. A	40. J	43. D
32. G	35. B	38. F	41. B	44. J
33. D	36. H	39. C	42. J	45. A

PASSAGE IV: A HEARTY BREW

46. F	49. D	52. J	55. B	58. H
47. D	50. H	53. D	56. F	59. A
48. G	51. C	54. H	57. C	60. J

PASSAGE V: *GOOD EATS*

61. C	64. H	67. D	70. H	73. D
62. J	65. A	68. G	71. B	74. F
63. D	66. G	69. A	72. G	75. C

Reading Test

PASSAGE I: PROSE FICTION

1. A	3. A	5. D	7. C	9. B
2. G	4. H	6. H	8. G	10. H

PASSAGE II: SOCIAL SCIENCE

11. B	13. C	15. A	17. B	19. A
12. H	14. J	16. G	18. H	20. G

PASSAGE III: HUMANITIES

21. C	23. D	25. B	27. A	29. A
22. G	24. H	26. J	28. H	30. H

PASSAGE IV: NATURAL SCIENCE

31. D	33. D	35. D	37. C	39. B
32. H	34. J	36. H	38. H	40. F

ANSWERS EXPLAINED

English Test

PASSAGE I: CARING FOR PEACHES

1. **(D) Choice D** uses a comma to separate the name of a town and the name of a region; it also uses a comma to separate the name of the region from the name of the state.
   Choice A is incorrect because it lacks a comma between the name of a town and the name of a region.
   Choice B is incorrect because it incorrectly sets off a town name with a semicolon.
   Choice C is undesirable because it is too wordy: *East Northport, which is the name of a town found on Long Island, New York.*

2. **(F) Choice F** is most economically worded.
   Choice G, *as a shorthand name*, is unnecessarily wordy.
   Choice H, *for a short nickname*, is slightly redundant since nicknames, by definition and purpose, are short.
   Choice J, *at his nickname*, is faultily worded; the preposition *at* is unidiomatic.

3. **(B) Choice B** (*is basic*) is clear and to the point.
   The original version, *ratherly basic* (Choice A) is incorrect because "ratherly" is not a word.
   Choice C contains the unneeded verbal fluff phrase, *rather so.*
   Choice D is unnecessarily drawn out and wordy.

4. **(J) Choice J** is clear and to the point.
   Choice F is incorrect because *for the most part* and *by and large* are redundant expressions.
   Choice G is undesirable because it contains the phrase *in most estimations*, which is awkward and does not add any significant information to the sentence.
   Choice H is out because it has a more casual tone than the rest of the essay.

5. **(C) The best answer is C.** This sentence strays from the main topic of the essay and therefore should be deleted.
   Choice A is incorrect because this sentence strays from the main topic of the essay and therefore should be deleted.
   Choice B would not work because the sentence is still unneeded and ineffective even in a different location.
   Choice D is out because the information is unnecessary even if it is rephrased.

6. **(F)** **Choice F** works to keep the second-person pronoun *you* since this pronoun is used throughout the essay.

   Choice G is incorrect because use of the singular-universal pronoun *one* is not consistent with the rest of the essay.

   Choice H is out; using the third-person pronoun *he or she* construction would be awkward and inconsistent with the rest of the essay.

   Choice J is also incorrect; even though *bird breeders* is a vivid and specific plural noun, the rest of the essay does not address bird breeders specifically.

7. **(C)** **The best answer is C.** If a noun ends with an *s*, you should simply add an apostrophe to make it possessive.

   Choice A is incorrect because the bird's name is not *Peach* but *Peaches*.

   Choice B is incorrectly punctuated: *Peaches's*.

   Choice D is out. *Peaches' and Cream's* implies that there are two birds with two separate names. The opening paragraph tells us that the essay is about only bird, whose full name is Peaches and Cream.

8. **(G)** **In Choice G**, the conjunction *because* correctly links the two clauses that make up this sentence.

   Choice F is incorrect because a semicolon is needed to separate two independent clauses.

   Choice H is incorrect because it is awkwardly worded.

   Choice J is incorrect. When semicolons are used to separate independent clauses, the second clause should start with a lowercase letter.

9. **(C)** **The best answer is Choice C** because it is the most concise, or economically worded.

   Choice A is incorrect because the use of the pronoun *one* is inconsistent with the rest of the essay, which uses the second-person pronoun *you*.

   Choice B is incorrect because the word *then* is not needed, and addressing *the pet owner* is inconsistent with the rest of the essay.

   Choice D is undesirable because it is diffusely worded.

10. **(F)** **The best answer is Choice F** because the pronoun *him* correctly stands for the male bird.

    Choice G is incorrect because now that we know the bird by name, it is best to refer to Peaches as *he*, and not as an inanimate *it*. Also, the rest of the essay refers to Peaches as *he*.

    Choice H is the wrong pronoun form; *them* is plural and so incorrectly refers back to the singular antecedent, Peaches.

    Choice J, *these species of birds*, is unnecessarily wordy. The sentence is specifically referring to Peaches—not to one or more species.

11. **(C) The best answer is Choice C.** The best placement for this phrase is after "cleaning," which is the word it modifies.
Choice A is incorrect because this modifying gerund phrase, *using soap and warm water,* is misplaced.
Choices B and D are both incorrect because positioning the phrase in these spots is awkward and does not correctly indicate how the "cleaning" of the bird cage should be carried out.

12. **(F) The best answer is Choice F** because it has a verbal infinitive, *to play,* correctly following a conjugated verb, *loves.* If you haven't learned this grammar rule in English class, you more than likely learned it in foreign language class.
Choices G and H are both unnecessarily wordy and therefore ineffective.
Choice J is not bad, but refer to the rule given to support Choice F as best.

13. **(C) The best answer is Choice C.** After all, vivid details make up part of "the stuff" of good, descriptive writing.
Choice A is incorrect because a lively detail does not necessarily weaken a piece of writing.
Choice B is incorrect because the fact that Peaches likes to play pick-up-sticks does not indicate the *unpredictable behavior of most pets.* This is a sweeping and unsubstantiated stereotype.
Choice D is incorrect because even though Peaches' playing this game might present a case for *his* intelligence, it does not testify to the intelligence of all animal life.

14. **(J) The best answer is Choice J.** *Not only...but also* are correlative conjunctions. *But also* correctly follows *not only.* In addition, Choice J makes the sentence contain parallel form.
Choice F is not correct because *as well* incorrectly follows *not only.*
Choice G is out because *in addition* incorrectly follows *not only.*
Choice H is incorrect because the resulting sentence is not parallel in form and structure. Language must be expressed in a balanced (parallel) fashion.

15. **(D) The best answer is Choice D.** This essay does not fulfill that particular writing goal because although it discusses some aspects pertaining to the care of Lutino Cockatiels, it does not address pets or proper pet care in general.
Choice A is incorrect because general pet care is a broad topic that is not addressed within the scope of this essay.
Choice B is reasonable, since the author apparently likes animals and finds them to be playful. Still, this idea does not support pet care specifically.
Choice C is incorrect. Unless the readers are experts on birds and their habits, it would be difficult to determine whether the information provided is *inadequate or faulty.*

PASSAGE II: LAKE VIEW

16. **(F) Choice F** correctly uses a period to divide the two independent clauses.
Choice G is incorrect because placing a comma between two independent clauses creates a comma splice.
Choice H uses the verbal phrase *was looking*, which is not parallel to the other verbs used in the sentence: *popped*, *dropped*, and *stared*.
Like Choice G, Choice J creates a comma splice with the use of a comma between the two independent clauses; it is also wordy.

17. **(D) The best answer is D** because the simile (comparison using *like* or *as*) stresses how amazed the narrator is by what he saw.
Choice A is incorrect because the sentence offers no evidence of something as severe as *delusion* (a false, psychotic belief).
Choice B is out because the essay's over-arching tone is arguably NOT comical.
Choice C is not correct because no textual evidence indicates that the narrator was intentionally trying to *distort* (warp) the scene he was viewing and describing.

18. **(H) The best answer is H**, *as serenely as a vulture*. This comparison is expressed in a grammatically sound manner. It uses *as…as* to compare two similar things, and it appropriately uses *serenely* as an adverb modifying the verb *skimming*.
Choice F is incorrect because the adjective *serene* should be changed to an adverb (*serenely*) to modify the verb *skimming*.
Choice G is incorrect because the adjective *serene* should be changed to an adverb. And the use of *so…as* instead of *as…as* is awkward.
Choice J is not correct because this comparison should be in the singular to match the singular *lake water*, which appears earlier in the sentence.
Also, in Choices A and D, the use of *so … like* instead of *as … as* is awkward.

19. **(A) Choice A** maintains parallel form by using a series of gerunds (*clinching, slapping, and hitting*).
Choice B is incorrect because *like* is non-idiomatic in this usage.
Choice C is out because it contains nonparallel structure, with a gerund (*clinching*) and two infinitives (*to slap and hit*); it also misuses the comma.
Choice D contains an error in parallelism, meaning that the listing of gerunds becomes inconsistent by not matching *clinching*.

20. **(G) The best answer is G**, because deletion of the phrases *The rough wood* and *the rickety porch railing* would take away from *the setting's rustic nature*, and deletion of *rubbed against my stinging cold hands* would take away from the *coldness* of the setting.
Choice F is incorrect because this sentence does not reveal the author's inner sensitivity.

Choice H is incorrect because deleting this particular sentence would not have the effect of giving the essay, as a whole, *a straightforward pithiness* (clear and concise meaning that has substance).

Choice J is incorrect because deleting this sentence would not result in the essay ending with *more relevant (important or pertinent) detail.*

21. **(B) The correct answer is B** because this sentence describes the natural lake setting about which the author recollects.

    Choice A is incorrect because the description of the lake is not *ominous,* portending gloom or misfortune.

    Choice C is also incorrect; there is nothing wrong with the placement of the sentence as is. Follow this rule of thumb when you revise: Do not fix what is not broken.

    Choice D is also incorrect because the paragraph does not focus on wildlife and birds.

22. **(J) The best answer is J** because this portion is very vivid, descriptive, and creates a frigid feel; therefore, *the reader loses a reminder of how cold it is out by the lake.*

    Choice F is incorrect because it is a stretch to conclude that the reader would gain comfort from the deletion of this phrase.

    Choice G is incorrect because extracting language does not contribute to a more sluggish (slow) pace of the prose.

    Choice H is out because just the opposite is true: the inclusion—not the deletion—of the phrase is likely to cause the reader to feel *more a part of the descriptive scene.*

23. **(D) The best answer is D** because all transitional words are extraneous in this context. None of the other choices listed contributes to the quality and effectiveness of the sentence.

    Choices A and C are incorrect because this sentence is not the concluding statement or result of a story line or explanation, as the word *so* implies.

    Choice B is out because the state-of-being gerund *being* does not make sense here.

24. **(F) The best answer is F** because it is concise and to the point. Choices G, H, and J are unnecessarily wordy.

25. **(D) In Choice D** the quotation marks, comma, period, apostrophe, and exclamation points are all properly placed within this sentence.

    Choice A is incorrect because the comma after *candy* should be placed inside the closed quotation mark. Also, a period should follow *exclaimed* in order to end that independent clause (sentence).

    Choice B is incorrect because a comma should follow *Phillip,* a proper noun used as a name of address. Also, a period should follow *exclaimed,* the final word of the sentence.

Choice C is incorrect because a comma separates two independent clauses (*Phillip, come on* and *we're having candy*), creating a comma splice. An exclamation mark and ending quotation marks should be placed after *candy* to indicate the end of what James exclaimed.

26. **(J) The best answer is J** because the past-tense verb *sprinted* is parallel with the past-tense verb *turned.*

    Choices F and G are incorrect because the present progressive verb (*am sprinting*) and the past progressive verb (*was sprinting*) are not parallel with the past-tense verb *turned.*

    Choice H is incorrect because the present participle *sprinting* cannot stand alone as the verb of a clause.

27. **(D) The best answer is D** because the pronoun *everyone* (like *everybody*) is treated, grammatically speaking, as singular even though *everyone* might make us visualize a throng of people!

    Choice A, NO CHANGE, is incorrect because the plural possessive *their* does not agree with *everyone.*

    Choice B is incorrect because the possessive *hers* does not make sense.

    Choice C is out because the plural possessive pronoun *their* does not agree with the singular *everyone.*

28. **(J) The best answer is J** because *joined* maintains the past verb tense in which the passage is written.

    Choice F, NO CHANGE, is incorrect because it is unnecessarily repetitive to repeat I and because the tense is not parallel.

    Choice G is incorrect because *join* is in the present tense; the other verbs in the passage are in past tense.

    Choice H is incorrect because *will join* is in the future tense.

29. **(B) Choice B** is the most effectively and concisely expressed.

    Choice A, NO CHANGE, is incorrect because *being* is extraneous (unnecessary).

    Choice C is incorrect because it is awkward and diffuse (loosely worded).

    Choice D is incorrect because deleting this portion would not let the sentence flow properly.

30. **(G) The best answer is G** because this sentence contains details that wrap up the scene in a pertinent manner. It serves best as a concluding sentence.

    Choice F is not a good choice because this sentence is rather irrelevant to all that has been narrated thus far.

    Choice H is too abrupt.

    Choice J is rather random; in fact, it is a digression that abruptly veers off-topic.

31. **(D) The best answer is D** because *bandleader* is the most concise choice and because it is parallel to the other two members that appear in the commas series.

Choice A is incorrect because this version demonstrates a lack of parallel structure.

Choice B is a possessive adjective/noun (*their bandleader*) construction, and is not parallel to the list of simple nouns (*clergyman, caterer*) that precedes it.

Choice C is incorrect because the wording is unnecessarily drawn out.

32. **(G) The correct answer is G** because no punctuation is necessary in this sentence. Neither the adverb *ahead* nor the consecutive prepositional phrases that follow (*of time* and *with the hairdresser*) ought to be set off by commas. The adverb and the prepositional phrases modify the action verb *meets;* there is no reason to break the flow between this verb and its modifiers. In fact, the remaining choices (F, H, and J) do not flow smoothly because the commas create choppy and awkward sentences. In Choice H, for example, there is no grammatically sound reason for using commas to set off the prepositional phrase *with the hairdresser.*

33. **(D) Choice D**, *confers*, maintains present tense, and is thus parallel to the present-tense verbs *anticipates* and *meets* in the two prior sentences.

Choice A is incorrect because *conferring* is in the wrong tense and creates a sentence fragment.

The verb phrase in Choice B is too sluggish and drawn out. Neither Choice B nor Choice C maintains parallel structure with the verbs in the two previous sentences. Also, in Choice C, *might of* is not idiomatically sound; we do not speak or write this way. *Might have* is idiomatically correct.

34. **(H) The best answer is H** because the infinitive *to whisper* is parallel to the infinitive *to color*, which appears earlier in the sentence.

Choice F is incorrect because the preposition *in* is unnecessary and creates faulty parallelism.

Choices G and J are unnecessarily wordy and do not flow.

35. **(B) The best answer is B** because *both* is extraneous. Later in the sentence, *as well as* expresses the same essential meaning.

Choice A is incorrect because *both* creates redundancy.

Choice C, *both the two,* is also redundant; this choice is unnecessarily wordy.

Choice D, *even the both:,* sounds very awkward. Also, the colon does not serve a logical purpose.

36. **(H) The best answer is H** because deleting *who are* allows the phrase within the commas to effectively function as an appositive.

Choice F is incorrect because *who are* is not necessary to articulate the explanation provided by the appositive. Choices G (*they are*) and J (*being*) also contain words that are non-essential to the contents of the appositive.

37. **(A)** **In Choice A** the antecedent, *Chet and Laura*, is compound (plural) and therefore the plural-possessive adjective *their* is required.
Choice B is incorrect because *his as well as her,* is awkward and wordy.
Choice C is incorrect because *there* is not in the possessive form, which is required in this case.
Choice D is out because this is a singular construction that does not agree with the plural antecedent (*Chet and Laura*).

38. **(F)** **The best answer is F** because the singular linking verb *is* agrees with the singular subject announcement and because no punctuation interrupts the linking verb and its complement (preview).
Choice G is incorrect because a comma is not needed here.
Choice H is incorrect because in this instance a colon (:) should not be used to introduce the quoted material.
Choice J might sound right because a plural noun (*are*) introduces a compound idea (*festivity and preview*). However, the subject (*engagement announcement*) of this sentence is singular and requires a singular verb (*is*).

39. **(C)** **The best answer is C** because saving money is indeed a practical concern.
Choice A is incorrect because it repeats an idea that was just stated within this same paragraph. Therefore, it is redundant (unnecessary).
Compared to the other choices, Choice B is *practical* (useful, convenient) for neither the bride nor the guests.
Choice D is practical from the point of view of the guests, but not particularly for the bride, to whom this article is geared.

40. **(J)** **Choice J**, embossing, is the only choice that is parallel to the other items in the list (*engraving, lettering, monogramming*).
Choice F, NO CHANGE, is incorrect because *the embossing process* is too wordy and not parallel to the other members within the list.
Choice G is wordy and awkward.
Choice H, *which include embossed,* is incorrect because it is wordy and not parallel.

41. **(B)** **Choice B** is correctly punctuated and expressed in a manner that flows most smoothly.
Choice A, NO CHANGE, is incorrect because it creates a comma splice run-on sentence.
Choices C and D are each incorrect because the part following the semicolons is not an independent clause: the present participle *including* cannot stand alone as a verb.

42. **(J) Choice J**, *should have used*, is idiomatically sound.

Choice F, NO CHANGE, is incorrect because *should of* is non-idiomatic. This is not standard, written English; in fact, *should of* can be considered conversational slang.

Choice G is incorrect because *should've have used* really says *should have have used*!

Choice H is an awkward non-idiomatic language expression.

43. **(D) The best answer is D** because the second-person pronoun *your* is consistent with the rest of the essay and because you need the adjective *handwritten* to describe sentiments.

Choice A, NO CHANGE, is incorrect because you need the adjective form *handwritten* to describe sentiments.

Choice B is incorrect because *they're* (*they are*) *handwriting* sounds awful! Trust your English-speaking ear.

Choice C is inconsistent with the rest of the paragraph because it uses the third-person plural.

44. **(J) Choice J** is the most smoothly and effectively worded choice.

Choice F, NO CHANGE, is incorrect because a comma ought to be used to separate consecutive adjectives (*timeless, elegant*) that could be understood as "timeless and elegant."

Choice G is too drawn out and wordy.

Choice H is incorrect because the plural verb *provide* does not agree with the singular subject *paper*.

45. **(A) The best answer is A** because Sentence 1 directly mentions handwritten sentiments.

Choice B is incorrect because Sentence 2 is more about the paper type and less about what is written on the paper itself.

Choice C is not a good answer because Sentence 3 is more about ink color than about the quality of the stationery.

Choice D is incorrect because this sentence would be relevant to the paragraph.

PASSAGE IV: A HEARTY BREW

46. **(F) Choice F is correct** because the contraction *you're* means *you are*. Contractions are rather casual, but it is acceptable to use one here because this article on cooking a vegetable soup is informal. This pronoun contraction is also consistent with the second-person pronoun *you* that is used earlier in the sentence.

Choice G is out because the verb tense is inconsistent with the rest of the sentence.

Choice H, *your*, is incorrect because the possessive form does not make sense in this context.

Choice J, *someone is,* does not work. The ending of the sentence lets you know that the author is addressing the reader with the use of a second-person pronoun (*you*).

47. **(D)** **In Choice D**, the plural pronoun *they* correctly refers to its antecedent, the plural noun *vegetables.*
Choice A is incorrect because the singular pronoun *it* cannot be used to refer to the plural noun *vegetables.*
Choices B and C are out because the gerunds *being* and *becoming* are not necessary to express this step in the cooking directions.

48. **(G)** **Choice G, *the onions,* is correct** because it is short, contains no unnecessary words, and makes sense.
Choices F, H, and J are incorrect because they are unnecessarily wordy.
Also, in Choice A the use of *they* immediately after *onions* is redundant.

49. **(D)** **In Choice D** all unnecessary wording is deleted and the meaning is clear.
Choice A is incorrect because *this way* is superfluous wording.
Choice B is out because the semicolon is not used correctly.
Choice C is incorrect because it uses unnecessary or superfluous wording and does not flow. The phrase sounds clumsy.

50. **(H)** **The correct answer is H** because *you* is consistent with the second-person pronoun *you* used earlier in the sentence.
Choices F, G, and J are incorrect because they all use third-person nouns or pronouns (*they, he or she, chef or gourmet*); the second-person pronoun *you* was used earlier in the sentence, and the rest of the sentence should be consistent.

51. **(C)** **Choice C is correct** because its future tense makes it parallel to the earlier verb phrase in the sentence, *will blend.*
Choice A is out because *would get tenderized* is not parallel to the prior future-tense verb *will blend.*
Choice B is also wrong because *they tenderizing* is incorrectly and awkwardly worded: the present participle (*tenderizing*) cannot stand alone as a verb. Remember, an *-ing* ending verb cannot be used as the main verb of a sentence.
Choice D is out because it is unnecessarily wordy and drawn out.

52. **(J)** **In Choice J** the colon is correctly used to introduce the list of grain choices.
Choice F is incorrect because a semicolon is not used to introduce a list.
Choice G is out because a hyphen should not be used to introduce listings.
Choice H, *grain,* is incorrect because a comma does not introduce a list of examples.

53. **(D)** Choice D, *coarsely ground black pepper* (adverb–adjective–noun), is the most concise and is most parallel to *grated cheese* (adjective–noun).
Choice A is incorrect because *black pepper that is coarsely ground* (noun–adjective clause) is not parallel to *grated cheese* (adjective–noun).
Choice B is incorrect because *pepper, black and ground coarsely* (noun–adjective phrase) it is not parallel to *grated cheese* (adjective–noun).
Choice C is incorrect because it is awkward and wordy; additionally, it is not parallel with *grated cheese.*

54. **(H) Choice H is correct.** Not only does *and fill you* eliminate *up*, it also is parallel to the earlier verb phrase in the sentence, *warm you.*
Choice F is out because it has the extraneous word *up.*
Choice G, *and also filling*, is incorrect because it does not flow or make sense.
Choice J, *the brew will be filling*, is incorrect because *the brew* is unnecessarily repeated.

55. **(B) Choice B is correct** because *leftovers* is the more specific and fitting word in this context.
Choices A, C, and D are redundant and therefore incorrect.

56. **(F) The correct answer is F** because a quick review of the paragraph's organization reveals that it is soundly organized, with a topic sentence that opens the paragraph and is supported by the sentences that follow.
Choice G is invalid because the focus of the paragraph is not lost at its *midway point.* From beginning to end, the paragraph discusses the soup's various benefits.
Choices H and J cannot be the correct answers because this paragraph is soundly constructed (organized and logically cohesive).

57. **(C) Choice C is correct** because the writer's strategy and purpose in writing this essay is primarily to instruct readers about how to prepare and serve the soup; therefore, the passage is best described as *informative.*
Choice A is incorrect because this passage involves no characters, interpersonal conflicts, or even a plot line.
Choice B is invalid since this passage is not about an individual's life story.
Choice D is unsubstantiated because this passage does not discuss any particular subject matter, and it makes no mention of the soup's origin or history, for example. Nor does it discuss the types of chemical and heat reactions that are integral to the cooking of this soup.

58. **(H) Choice H is the correct answer** because it completes the listing of advantages.
Choices F and J do not work because the subordinating conjunctions *though* and *even though* set up a contradiction, as if it might be difficult to control

the ingredients, portions, and flavorings of something that is homemade—
the opposite of that which the author obviously intends to express.
Choice G does not work because this sentence is not expressing an explanation or result, which the word *Thus* implies.

59. **(A)** **The correct answer is Choice A** because the comma is most effective. The comma is followed by the conjunction *so*. Together, the comma and conjunction separate the two independent clauses that make up this compound sentence.
Choice B is incorrect because the sentence does not contain two independent clauses for the semicolon to separate.
In Choice C the dash is incorrect and not necessary.
Choice D is incorrect because the colon is neither introducing a list nor clarifying a statement or explanation.

60. **(J)** **The correct answer is J** because discussing *specific nutritional benefits of the soup* would best fit the organizational schema of this paragraph. The second sentence of the paragraph (part of the topic statement, really) mentions nutrition.
Choice F is out because it is much less relevant to the topic sentence.
Choice G is out because it does not strengthen the paragraph as a whole: Elaborating on brand types is not particularly pertinent to the value of the soup nutritionally or as a meal option.
Choice H is incorrect because it would not further the intention laid out by the two topic statements that lead off this paragraph.

PASSAGE V: *GOOD EATS*

61. **(C)** **The best answer is Choice C** because *lets* is present tense, and this version includes no unnecessary wording. It is nice and concise.
Choice A is incorrect because *let's* is a contraction that means let us. If you plug *let us* into the sentence, it would not make sense.
Choice B, *is letting*, is a two-word verb phrase (helping verb *is* and main verb *letting*) and, therefore, not as concise as *lets*.
Choice D, *let is*, sounds very awkward; if you plug this alternative into the sentence, you will "hear" that this choice makes no sense.

62. **(J)** **The best answer is Choice J**, *restaurant guides*, because this sentence is comparing this *guide* to other *guides*, not restaurants to guides. The comparison needs to make logical sense.
Choice F, NO CHANGE, is out because this sentence does not intend to compare *restaurants* to guides about restaurants.
Choice G, *types of restaurants*, is wrong because the comparison is between this guide and other guides, not between restaurant types and guides. In addition, *types of restaurants* are not doing the selecting!

Choice H, *guides geared toward selecting restaurants*, is very wordy and makes this sentence read sluggishly.

63. **(D) The best answer is Choice D**, *in which*. Although the wording in Choice D might sound a bit strange, get used to it—it is standard, written English. We may not speak this way (*in which, for which, by which, to whom, for whom…*) but these phrases are idiomatically sound. In other words, these phrases are accepted expressions in standard, written English.
Choice A, NO CHANGE, is incorrect because *whereabouts* is actually an adverb that asks, "at what location or place?"
Choice B is incorrect because *in where* is a faulty expression.
Choice C is out because *regarding that* does not flow soundly within this sentence.

64. **(H) The best answer is Choice H** because *new and trendy spots* is descriptive, to the point, and maintains parallel form.
Choice F, NO CHANGE, is incorrect because the adjectives *new and trendy* create a lack of parallel form. All of the members of the list are noun places: *landmarks, luncheonettes, diners,* and so on.
Choice G, *new as well as being trendy*, is long-winded, awkward, and non-parallel.
Choice J, *new, trendy types*, is vague. Types of what? The ACT prefers language that is precise and clear.

65. **(A) Choice A** is the most concise answer. The ACT adores succinctness!
Choice B, *while they are found*, is wordy and does not flow in context. Trust your ear.
Choice C, *being found*, results in a sentence fragment. Plug it in, and trust your ear to hear the lack of completeness.
Choice D, *they have been found*, is out because *they* is superfluous (an unnecessary word) and the verb tense should be present to match the rest of the sentence. This present perfect tense does not work here.

66. **(G) The best answer is Choice G**, *it has been*, because this version is correctly and clearly phrased. The present perfect tense is needed here in order to be consistent with the verb tense used earlier in the paragraph.
Choice F, NO CHANGE, is incorrect. *It's being* means *it is being*. If you plug this clause into the sentence, you will "hear" how awkward it sounds. Trust your ear and the ouch factor!
Choice H, *being*, is out because this results in a sentence fragment.
Choice J, *it would have been*, is also out because this tense does not match the present perfect tense used at the beginning of the paragraph: *I have always <u>found</u> it easy to find the expensive Long Island restaurants…*

67. **(D) Choice D** correctly conveys the intended idea: houses of several friends. The apostrophe is used correctly here.

Choice A, NO CHANGE, is incorrect because *friend's houses* implies that one childhood friend had two or more houses at which he would have meals. This is most likely *not* the meaning that the author intends to express.

Choice B, *houses belong to my friends*, is unnecessarily wordy. Also, this phrase does not work with the possessive adjective preceding it, *my*.

Choice C, *friends, their houses*, is awkward and choppy; it does not flow easily. Trust how phrasing sounds to your ear!

68. **(G) In Choice G** the plural pronoun *them* correctly refers back to the plural antecedent (pronoun reference) *large cups*.

Choice F, NO CHANGE, is out because the singular pronoun *it* incorrectly refers back to the plural antecedent *large cups*.

Choice H, *the take-out cups*, is unnecessarily wordy and detailed in a redundant manner. We already understand that the coffee is take-out and not brewed at home.

Choice J, *the coffee*, is incorrect because it doesn't make sense to heat up *the coffee* one at a time, as the sentence expresses: *Mom still buys large cups of take-out coffee … and heats the coffee up, one at a time…*

69. **(A)** NO CHANGE (**Choice A**, *by necessity*) is needed to the sentence because it flows logically that this author would eat out at restaurants a great deal. (Remember, his mom is not a cooking enthusiast!)

Choice B (*contradictorily*) and Choice C (*unexpectedly*) are transitional words that do not make sense. In fact, these choices are the opposite of what needs to be expressed here.

Choice D (*unnaturally*) makes the least sense of all. What is *unnatural* about dining out and becoming acquainted with the restaurant scene?

70. **(H) Choice H**, *contributors*, is the most concise and is in plural form, which is correct.

Choice F, NO CHANGE, is incorrect because *of them* is potentially ambiguous. Does *them* refer back to family members, friends, or acquaintances?

Choice G, *of them contributors*, is awkwardly expressed. Can you hear the faulty expression? Trust your ear.

Choice J, *contributing*, is not enough. *Contributing writers* lends clarity to the subject and works more effectively here.

71. **(B) The best answer is Choice B.** A subjective pronoun, *who* is the correct relative pronoun used to refer back to a person (Laura).

Choice A, NO CHANGE, is incorrect because *her who* does not flow; in fact, it sounds clumsy. Grammatically speaking, *her* (a possessive pronoun, as in *her* purse, *her* voice, *her* car, and so on) cannot be used to refer back to a proper noun (Laura).

Choice C, *being those who,* is wordy and awkward. Can you detect the faulty expression with your grammar-savvy ear?

Choice D, *will,* creates an incomplete thought or sentence fragment.

72. **(G) The best answer is Choice G**; indeed this sentence *elaborates* (goes into more detail) *on how Laura has been* supportive to this project.

Choice F is invalid because people who try to *dampen the author's efforts to produce this dining guide* are never mentioned; therefore, juxtaposing (comparing and contrasting) these naysayers with Laura is not possible.

Choice H does not work. This new sentence does not, by any means, *detract* (lessen the value or importance of something by taking something away) *from the prior sentence.*

Choice J is also incorrect. This sentence is *not* filled with *irrelevant details,* and the effect of this sentence is not *to slow the pace* (or make sluggish) *of the dining guide's introduction.*

73. **(D) The best answer is Choice D**, *readers,* because this introduction is from the publisher to his readership.

Choice A is incorrect because *Agents,* is a nebulous (cloudy, vague) term in this context. Exactly to whom is *agents* referring? Freelance writers? Restaurant reviewers contracted for hire?

Choice B is incorrect because *Men and women,* is too limiting. Perhaps teens or young adults are reading this friendly dining guide as well.

Choice C is not the best choice because *People,* comes across as too casual and conversational.

74. **(F) Choice F** is the most succinct and the meaning is clear.

Choice G, *friends living in the tri-state area,* is out because the word *living* is extraneous. If this word is omitted, the meaning remains perfectly clear. The ACT likes wording that is precise and concise.

Choice H, *friends who live in the tri-states,* is incorrect because *tri-states* is non-idiomatic. In conventional written and spoken English, *tri-state* (without the *s*) is used as a compound adjective, as in the *tri-state* area.

Choice J, *friends that are living within the tri-state region,* is also incorrect because the relative pronoun *that* is not used to refer back to people; *who* should be used instead. Also, this version is too wordy.

75. **(C) In Choice C**, *With your input . . . making the next edition of Good Eats even better!,* this concluding line flows nicely from the lines preceding it and from the focus of this ending paragraph as a whole.

Choice A, *This dining guide should inspire reluctant restaurant-diners to eat out more often.,* might be a true statement, but this paragraph—and the passage as a whole—is not about motivating reluctant diners to make reservations.

Choice B, *Please eat at local restaurants more often than at the "big chains" in order to support family-owned businesses.*, is incorrect because this plea seems out of place. When has the author previously mentioned supporting local mom-and-pop establishments? This answer choice is off focus.

Choice D, *Turns out, ambiance and service rank over how the food tastes and what the bill states as the bottom line.*, is an inappropriate choice because the language is too casual and the ideas expressed are not in line with the main focus of the passage.

Reading Test

PASSAGE I: PROSE FICTION

1. **(A) Skim the second and third paragraphs, paying particular attention to how the author is telling her story.** Choice B is incorrect because the author does not use *you* and does not write in the second person. Choice C is incorrect because there are no comparisons and *juxtapositions* (contrasts) between images of weakness and strength. Choice D is also out because, although the author engages in a *nostalgic* (bittersweet memory) tone, she does not use a critical one. **The best answer is Choice A**, for the author does fluctuate between present day and reflection (*my dad's shovels, the ones he used twenty-five years ago*).

2. **(G) Reread the indicated sentence (lines 31–32) carefully, focusing on the rhetorical effect of the descriptive language:** *With a formidable claw and iron clad in industrial orange, it arrived.* Choice F is incorrect. Let's keep our comparisons straight. The strength of the landscaping/constructing mobile (the bobcat) is being emphasized, not that of a cougar! Choice H is off. There is hardly anything "euphemistic" (sugarcoated, intentionally pleasant-sounding) about how the destructive power of this vehicle is described. Choice J is incorrect, since lines 31–32 do not compare the patio project to the work of soldiers. **The correct answer is Choice G**; the bobcat is personified by giving this inanimate (nonliving) object the human-like qualities of having a "claw" (typically a body part of animals or vicious people!) and by being "clad" (dressed) in orange. Is this bobcat making a fashion statement?

3. **(A) Rely on your memory only to an extent. The most foolproof approach to an ALL/EXCEPT question is skimming to find textual evidence for three of the four techniques mentioned.** The author does use Choice B, *stylistic fragments.* See line 2 (*Impossible.*) and lines 22–23 (a rather long gerund phrase) for examples. The author also uses Choice C, *repetition of words and phrases.* For example, in the eighth paragraph (lines 74–87), the author repeats the phrase *a place.* The author does incorporate Choice D,

allusions to historical legends (lines 84 and 85). **The correct answer is Choice A** because the author does **not** pose *rhetorical questions* simply for effect.

4. **(H) Read the indicated phrase (lines 33–34) within its full context and make sure you know the basic literary devices.** Notice how "*like*" is used in the expression: *shredding our newly seeded lawn like cabbage.* The *simile* is a literary device that uses *like* or *as*. Therefore, **the correct answer is Choice H.** Choice F is incorrect, since an *analogy* expresses a similarity between things, or pairs of things, without using *like* or *as*. Choice G, *alliteration*, refers to the repetition of consonant sounds, as in "*Sally sells seashells by the seashore.*" Choice J, *hyperbole*, means *exaggeration*, as in "*I'm so hungry I could eat a horse.*" Lines 33–34 do not contain either alliteration or hyperbole.

5. **(D) Reread lines 44–46 carefully, paying close attention to the words that are underlined:** *Now a wet stonecutter, rented from Frank, became our main* <u>artillery</u>. <u>Armed</u> *with earplugs, waterproof gloves, and goggles, we began.* In this excerpt from the passage, the author's diction (word choice) conjures up images of warfare. (*Artillery* refers to weaponry and armaments.) Therefore, **the best answer is Choice D**, which refers to *warriors* and *a military expedition*. Choice A is not supported by passage evidence. Where in this sentence is the stonecutter described as *old and unreliable*? Financial strain is not suggested here, so Choice B is out. Choice C also lacks passage support. The patio project is being undertaken by the homeowners, so it's illogical to conclude that Frank is asking for their assistance in order to lighten *his* load.

6. **(H) Review lines 47–49 and determine which literary devices are used. The most foolproof approach to an ALL/EXCEPT question is skimming to find textual evidence for three of the four literary devices mentioned.** Choice F is supported. A *simile* is a comparison using *like* or *as*. In this case, "*Chips of paver leaped off the stonecutter, just as charred crumbs jump off burned toast…*" contains a simile using *as*. The entire paragraph includes *imagery*, so Choice G is also supported. Choice J, *onomatopoeia*, is clearly illustrated in these lines: *Zzz . . . Chip! Chip! Zzzz . . . Chip!* Onomatopoeia refers to a single word or a group of words that represents or imitates the specific sound that is being described. **Choice H, *irony*, is the correct answer** because no unexpected twist or paradox is described within the given lines.

7. **(C) Skim the eighth paragraph (lines 74–87), concentrating on detecting the effect or purpose of the author's repetition of the phrase, *the place*.** Choice A is incorrect because it is clear that the narrator is *not* attempting to *baffle* (confuse, befuddle) the reader. Choice B is also incorrect, because the author is not trying to carry out hypnosis; to an extent, one might consider this an extreme (and therefore unreasonable) answer choice. Choice D, to *lull the reader by imitating the repetitive lyrics of a chorus*, might ring true because repetition does appear in Paragraph 8. Still,

it is a stretch to liken the narrator's description to the lyrics (words) of a chorus (the part of a song that tends to be repeated). **The correct answer is Choice C**, *emphasize how much pleasure the patio offers*, since the eighth paragraph lists many examples of how the narrator and her family enjoy the patio.

8. **(G) Reread lines 79–85, paying particular attention to the concrete details that the author includes. Your inventory of specific details might look something like this:** *sweet-smelling honeydew, tamari almonds, terra-cotta votives, fragrance, "na-nilla" ice cream, apple pie.* Choice F is incorrect because *allusions (references) to the carefree pastimes of most children* would not necessarily include gazing at terracotta votives or eating tamari almonds. Choice H is way off the mark because the author is obviously reveling in the outdoors, so she does not convey *detached interest* (apathy, remoteness) in spending time with her family on the patio. Choice J is also out, since this part reads very descriptively and not in the more serious style of a *cultural commentary.* **The correct answer is Choice G** because these lines do *appeal to the senses of smell* (sweet-smelling honeydew and tamari almonds, tropical fragrance), *sight* (gaze, trail of... ice-cream cone), *and sound* ("na-nilla").

9. **(B) Consider lines 88–95 while focusing specifically on the contrast between the patio and the half wall:** *I love the solidity of our patio ... The feel of stone beneath my bare feet is strengthening, enduring like the antiquity of old English cobble. With a girth of three inches, the blocks promise the longevity of ages. We had thought of building a half wall of brick around the patio. I'm glad we didn't. Like Humpty Dumpty, walls eventually fall down.* Choice A is only partially correct: Although *transience* (not lasting) is a characteristic of the half wall, *belligerence* (a warlike quality) is not characteristic of either the patio or the half wall. Choice C is also invalid: Neither the patio nor the half wall is described in terms of its *beauty* or *fancy* (whimsicality, creativity). Choice D (*durability and stability*) rings true, but solely for the patio. Based on passage evidence and process of elimination, **the correct answer is Choice B**. *Longevity* means "long life" or "durability" and applies to the patio; *evanescence* means "fleeting" or "short-lived" and applies to the half wall, since *walls eventually fall down.*

10. **(H) To draw a general conclusion, you need to have absorbed and digested the passage as a whole. Thoughtfully reflect on what you have read.** Choice F is not supported, since the passage gives no reason why the author would not tackle another project. After all, the closing paragraph expresses how much satisfaction she has reaped from this project. Choice G lacks solid verification: The author does love the patio and all it has to offer, but this sweeping generalization about preferring the outdoors over the indoors is not adequately supported. Choice J is also off-the-mark; negative emotions about working with her husband, her father-in-law, and Frank the mason are

not expressed. **The best answer is Choice H**, for there is plenty of proof that the author *prefers things that are durable (long-lasting) to those that do not endure for long.*

PASSAGE II: SOCIAL SCIENCE

11. **(B) To answer words-in-context questions, read—at a minimum—the entire sentence in which the word appears:** *A speech-language pathologist can* <u>adapt</u> *a storybook to incorporate the communication board by using symbols to represent words.* Choice A, *acclimate*, does not quite fit because to acclimate is to become accustomed to; this substitution does not flow logically. Choice C is also incorrect since *camouflage* means to hide or conceal; this would result in an unfavorable obscuring of meaning. Choice D, *familiarize*, is also out because this word's meaning (*to closely acquaint*) suggests something too intimate or friendly for the reading of a storybook. **The best answer is Choice B**, *modify*, because *modify* (to change to an extent, even slightly) best fits the context of "altering" the experience of reading a storybook by integrating an aid such as a communication board.

12. **(H) Return to the passage and reread until you have a clear sense of the distinction between "unaided" and "aided" symbols.** Choice F is invalid since *shapes made with the hands* would not represent an "aided symbol" because these manually drawn shapes do not make use of *picture communication symbols, line drawings, and tangible objects.* (See lines 10–13.) Choice G, *gesturing combined with lip movement,* also does not fit the category of "aided symbol." Choice J is incorrect because *full and dramatic body movements* imply "gestures" and therefore exemplify an unaided method. **The correct answer is Choice H** because *colorful flash cards with drawings on them* fit into the category of aided symbols. At the end of the first paragraph, the passage clearly states that *aided* symbols include picture communication symbols, line drawings, and tangible objects. Since flash cards can be held and manipulated, they are "tangible."

13. **(C) To answer words-in-context questions, read—at a minimum—the entire sentence in which the word appears:** *AAC focuses on people with severe and expressive communicative disorders, and attempts to* <u>compensate</u> *for the speech that they lack either temporarily or permanently.* Plug in the word choices; which flows best and makes the most sense? Choice A is out; to *compound* the speech they lack is to add to it or make this deficit worse. Choice B, *befriend* (make friends with), makes no logical sense. Choice D is incorrect also. In other usages, compensate can mean to reimburse or *pay back*, but not in this context. **The correct answer is Choice C:** The passage discusses how AAC helps people with communicative disorders learn to communicate—in other words, how to *make up* for the speech they lack.

14. **(J) Use the line references to hunt for the objects indicated. Reread these areas of the text to get a sense of the client's role in using the Macaw and the Dynavox.** Choice F is unsupported since neither tool requires the client to *manipulate* (*maneuver, handle*) *objects.* Choice G is incorrect since neither the Macaw nor the Dynavox requires the client to sketch pictures. Choice H implies the ability to operate electronic and mechanical devices, which is not required. **The best answer is Choice J,** *utilize the sense of sight to recognize pictures and/or objects.*

15. **(A) Reread the portion that discusses "*zero exclusion criterion*" (lines 40–41). Try paraphrasing this description of the criterion.** Choices B and C are incorrect since the passage supports neither *avoiding the use of AAC* except under dire (*extreme, urgent*) circumstances nor *using AAC as a last resort.* Choice D is also incorrect because it implies that AAC services might not be beneficial—a suggestion that this reading selection does not support. **The best answer is Choice A** since it best summarizes the criterion, focusing on a speech-language pathologist's measurement of a client's abilities and determination of the most suitable AAC methods.

16. **(G) ALL/EXCEPT questions require the use of process of elimination and skimming the line in which the word appears, as well as the surrounding lines that may offer clues as to the word's meaning:** *Because it has numerous <u>settings</u>, it allows for many pictures to be incorporated, giving the clinician a longer, more versatile lesson.* Choice F, *volume,* is reasonable since the previous sentence refers to the Macaw as a *communication system that allows multiple levels for recording one's voice.* Certainly, volume can be construed as a voice setting. Choice H, *images,* is supported by the evidence that *many pictures can be incorporated.* Choice J, *a mixture of sounds and pictures,* is also sensible because the passage tells us that the various settings ultimately provide a *versatile lesson.* (A blend of image and sound certainly qualifies as versatile.) **The correct answer is Choice G** because the passage offers no suggestion that the Macaw has anything to do with *body temperature.*

17. **(B) To answer words-in-context questions, read—at a minimum—the entire sentence in which the word appears:** *Alternative strategies are implemented to <u>hone</u> the skills needed to comprehend the information.* Choice A is out since *memorize* misses the mark; the alternative strategies do not seek to help the client memorize skills as much as they strive to effectively use or *sharpen* (the correct answer!) them in order to process . . . literacy information, as indicated in the preceding line in the passage. Even though *tone* rhymes with *hone,* Choice C is incorrect. Sometimes rhyming answers can be tempting, especially when our concentration begins to wane. To *harness* skills is to capture or bind them (not very effective), so Choice D is also out. **The correct answer is Choice B,** *sharpen.*

18. **(H) This is a global question based on information presented within the entirety of the passage.** Skim lines 47–54, which discuss the inclusion of various related service providers. Choice F is a close contender but not the best answer. While *obtaining a large group of professionals and opinions* may enhance the likelihood of a client's success, it is not the ultimate goal expressed for involving multiple service providers. Although remembering people's names (Choice G) may occur as a desirable side benefit, it is definitely *not* the main objective. Choice J is also invalid; facilitating *pragmatic (practical, sensible) concerns* like scheduling—although important—is not the main point. **The correct answer is Choice H**; it is true that with all of the professionals' input and expertise, all areas of a client's functioning will be assessed to ensure a device that is appropriately evaluated and improved.

19. **(A) Skim the final paragraph, focusing on the context surrounding the specific skill of "print awareness."** Although Choices B, C, and D all sound like worthwhile language-building activities, only Choice A, *working with the therapist, using a device with aided symbols*, is supported by the sentence, *The therapist draws attention to print using aided systems such as a <u>communication board</u> . . .* (lines 108–110), which is textual evidence. While taking the ACT Reading Test, you need to leave your creativity and great ideas behind, and simply focus on what the passage says. **The correct answer is Choice A.**

20. **(G) This question requires you to understand key concepts about methods that are described throughout the passage as well as to ascertain the particular uses of various communication tools.** The lack of line references can make this question challenging. Pay careful attention to the key word in this question—*least. The Macaw* and *the Dynavox* (Choices F and J) are devices that are largely computer-operated, so the easeful and skillful use of one's arms and hands is not critical. In other words, these tools would be appropriate for students who could not speak and who had limited use of their hands and arms. Choice H should be crossed off as well; like the Macaw and the Dynavox, *a communication board* would be helpful to a student with these limitations. **The correct answer is Choice G**, *sign language*; of all the answer choices, this modality (manner or way of doing something; method or form) particularly necessitates both sight and broad gesturing of the arms and hands.

PASSAGE III: HUMANITIES

21. **(C) This is a tricky point of view/narrative perspective question.** The question asks you to select the answer that best reflects the author's point of view. Choice A, *depicting the most desirable type of fame that all of modern humankind seeks*, is incorrect as it attempts to lump *all humankind* into one mindset with regard to conceptions of fame. Cross off Choice B, *examining various concepts of fame from across times and cultures*, as the scope of this choice is too broad for the ideas about fame discussed in the passage.

Choice D, *touting his ability to create fame for himself in various ways*, is also incorrect because the author is not bragging about or flaunting (touting) his self-created versions of fame. **The best answer is Choice C**, *surveying his students' notions about what types of fame are most desirable.*

22. **(G) This is a holistic question that asks which conclusion is best supported by the passage.** Cross off Choice F, *Fame is defined primarily by money and social status*, as status and affluence are not emphatically stressed throughout the passage. Likewise, eliminate Choice H, *Fame is among mankind's most deleterious enemies* because fame is not predominantly characterized as harmful or pernicious (deleterious). Cross off Choice J, *Fame is an undesirable state of being.*, as this blanket statement does not express the gist of the excerpt. **The best answer, therefore, is Choice G**, *Fame that lasts indefinitely is more prized than that which is ephemeral.*

23. **(D) This is an inferencing question, requiring higher-order thinking skills.** The question asks about the meaning of lines 52–57 ("If I hold . . . quickly"). Carefully reread the referenced lines to glean a sense of their meaning, as expressed by Achilles:

> If I hold out here and I lay siege to Troy,
> my journey home is gone, but my glory never dies.
> If I voyage back to the fatherland I love,
> my pride, my glory dies . . .
> true, but the life that's left me will be long,
> the stroke of death will not come on me quickly.

Cross off Choice A, *Only a fool would sacrifice a long life for honor*, because honor through battle for one's country is not being dismissed as foolish. While Choices B and C may be alluring *An individual's sense of immortality is tested only when he or she goes to war*, and *In battling for one's country, one can only attain a fleeting sense of fame*, the word *only* makes it incorrect. Beware of red flag words, such as *only, never, always, no, all*, and *so forth*. **The best answer is Choice D**, *Dying in battle can yield a type of eternal fame*, for Achilles says, "my glory never dies" in imagining dying in battle for his fatherland.

24. **(H) This word-in-context question asks about** the word *grappled* in line 15. Use trial and error and your ears. Plug each choice into the sentence and "listen" to see which action verbs fit and flow most seamlessly. The sentence reads, *It focused not on individual personalities, but on the long line of thinkers who have* grappled *with the meaning of fame.* Eliminate Choice F, *faced*, as this word reads awkwardly in the context of the given sentence. Plugging words in for a good fit with regard to semantics and syntax leads us to eliminate Choices G, *collided*, and J, *handled*, as well. **The best answer is Choice H**, *wrestled*, which is this case has less to do with winning over your

opponent on the mat, and more to do with struggling to understand the concept of fame.

25. **(B) This is a challenging type of reading question type because it has to do with varying degrees, as represented in the answer choices.** Although Choice B, *What inspired Emily Dickinson to write her poem about fame, "Fame is a bee . . . it has a wing."*, may be tempting, the passage does not directly address Dickinson's source of inspiration. Cross off Choice C, *For how long did this course run at the college?*, as clear evidence to answer this question is lacking. Also eliminate Choice D, *What type of fame do most college age students seek today?*, as specific types of fame are not substantiated by the passage evidence. **The best answer is Choice B**, *Who designed the form and content of the course taught at The College of New Jersey?*, as the text evidence most directly answers this question. The passage states that the author "prepared a course" and that his "aim was to build a course." (form and content are implied)

26. **(J) This holistic question features answer choices in pairs, making it more challenging.** The question asks which pair *represents sources of fame that are most likely to endure the passage of time.* Eliminate Choices F, *battle victories and bravery*, and G, *slavery and humility*, as these conditions are not stressed as keys to long-term fame. Also, cross off Choice H, *public service and political writing*, as there is a lack of textual evidence to show these endeavors provide enduring fame. **The best answer is Choice J**, *art and poetry*, as encapsulated in the passage's closing lines, "Hundreds of years after the Iliad . . . without a poet of Homer's skill, his fame would be more transitory than that of his hero Achilles."

27. **(A) This is a straightforward word-in-context question about the use of** the word *reservations* in line 72. Reread the entire sentence. *The Greeks had significant* reservations *about fame, which, for many students, resonated with their own.* This is the topic sentence of Paragraph 7, so skim the paragraph to get the gist of what it's about. Cross off Choices B and C because, *plans* and *hindrances* do not fit and flow, given the discussion of the paragraph. Also, cross off Choice D, as *territories* does not fit the meaning of the sentence or the relevant paragraph. **The best answer is Choice A** because *qualms* are doubts or misgivings, which makes sense in the fuller context of the paragraph.

28. **(H) This inference question (cued by the key word "suggests") requires a broader context, beyond the sentence in which the word "discussions"** appears. *My aim was to build a course that could defamiliarize fame by exploring its roots in the ancient world. I wanted students to see that fame was not always associated with glamor and excess. I wanted them to appreciate how previous cultures had integrated fame into treasured stories about virtue, character,*

mortality, and public life. But like Dickinson's bee, our **discussions** *took flight and frequently landed us in fields far removed from antiquity. In the end, my students discovered the remoteness of the past; what they taught me is its unmistakable presence today.*

Eliminate Choices F, *predictable and mundane*, and G, *unfounded and myopic*, as there is little commonplace (mundane) or myopic (narrow-minded, limited in vision and scope) about discussions taking "flight" and alighted in "fields far removed from antiquity." Cross off Choice J, *unprecedented and arbitrary*, as the text certainly does not validate that these discussions are new or novel (unprecedented), as if they have never before been explored. **The best answer is Choice H**, *expansive and reflective*, as this pair of adjectives aptly characterizes the sense and feel of these discussions, as the textual evidence above confirms.

29. **(A) This question asks about the effect of a rhetorical or literary device—in this case, the simile in lines 85–88:** "Like a contemporary politican complaining about his press coverage, Alexander grumbled ... ." Skim the context in which this simile (a comparison using "like" or "as") appears: *Hundreds of years after the Iliad, Alexander the Great recognized the importance of art in keeping his conquests alive. As designed by his favored sculptor, statues of Alexander relied on certain trademark features (the curl of his hair, the cast of his eyes) that identified him for posterity. Like a contemporary politican complaining about his press coverage, Alexander grumbled that, without a poet of Homer's skill, his fame would be more transitory than that of his hero Achilles.*

Choice B, *deprecating Homer's skill as an author and poet*, is out: there is nothing deprecating (disapproving, derogatory) about this sentence in terms of putting down Homer's writing ability. Likewise, Choice C, *exaggerating the effect that art can have on one's posterity*, cannot be substantiated by the textual evidence. There is no sense of hyperbole with regard to how an individual's art (in terms of writing, painting, or otherwise) affects future familial generations. Choice D, *contradicting Dickinson's notions about fame as expressed in her poem*, is also incorrect, as the author's statement does not refute Dickinson's concepts of fame. **The best answer is Choice A**, *emphasizing Alexander's desire for everlasting fame through the pen of a skilled author*, as Alexander yearns for a great poet, like Homer, to write about him so that his name and fame can endure and not be transitory (fleeting, short-lived).

30. **(H) This is an ALL/EXCEPT question. It can sometimes be time-consuming because you have to find evidence for three, and then the answer choice lacking evidence is the correct answer.** The question asks, according to the author, which answer choice is not a characteristic of the meaning of fame.

In the third paragraph, the author writes, "Fame itself may be fleeing," so cross off Choice F, *fleeting nature*. Eliminate Choice G, *enduring pleasure*, as Dickinson's poem expresses how fame can change its course and change its effect and not always be about everlasting pleasure. The poem captures Dickinson resigning herself to how ephemeral fame can be, how effortlessly it moves from one person to the next, pleasing, wounding, and deserting them as it travels across the earth. Cross off Choice J, as *individual stardom* can be construed as a meaning of fame attributed to "individual personalities," as exemplified by Beyoncé, Madonna, and Bruce Springsteen. **The best answer is Choice H**, as *eternal anonymity* is reasonably an antithesis to the characteristics of fame explored in this passage.

PASSAGE IV: NATURAL SCIENCE

31. **(D) To answer diction questions, reread the sentence in which the word appears to achieve its effect:** *The greatest burden from this infection falls* <u>*squarely*</u> *on the shoulders of women of reproductive age and women as the primary child caretakers.* Even though Choice A is true in that women do endure great difficulty in caring for themselves and their sick children, the word *squarely* emphasizes more that the brunt of this diseases falls fully/flatly/directly on the shoulders of women. Choice B is incorrect; even though it is true that this sentence *undermines* (weakens) the extent to which men are affected by the disease, the statement does NOT support men's *flatly disregarding the destructive potential* of the disease; the selection does not portray men in this light. While Choice C may be true, the sentence does not *underscore* (accentuate, stress) the *unfairness of health policies that do not adequately protect victims of malaria*; more important, the use of the word *squarely* does not underscore this point. **The correct answer is Choice D**; the statement does *emphasize the extent to which the burden of this particular disease rests (resides with) with women.*

32. **(H) Skim the article to find where this point is addressed; given what is said in this sentence and in the other sentences in the paragraph, ask yourself, "What is the most likely effect of malaria cases *not* being reported?"** While Choice F seems likely to occur, nothing in the passage supports the idea of limiting *the resources and manpower* and resources to fight malaria. Astute critical readers answer questions based exclusively on passage evidence. While Choice G also sounds like a reasonable effect, *funds and fiscal matters* are not mentioned in or around this line. Choice J is most unlikely, given the fact that throughout the entire article no mention is made of *doctors and researchers* who are skeptical about the negative effects of malaria. **The correct answer is Choice H**, since the phrase *leading to an unimaginable toll of global mortality and morbidity* (lines 24–25) reasonably support the idea expressed in this answer choice: *the potential for the scale of misery and fatalities caused by malaria loom even larger in people's minds and imaginations.*

33. **(D) Reread around the topic of sub-Saharan Africa to pick up on as many details and as much descriptive information as you can; this way, you will be in a strong position to answer the question accurately.** At the very least, reread and reconsider most of the second paragraph (lines 26–52). Choice A, *a region immune to the particular effects of the diminution* (*decrease, lessening*) *of the farming industry*, is too rose-colored and hopeful, particularly since the author clearly mentions *the decline of agriculture and green spaces* (lines 36–37) as a negative consequence of urbanization. Choice B is off target: the paragraph does not mention *rapid economic growth* (*business, commerce*) *and prosperity.* Choice C, *marked by the convergence of cultures,* is supported by lines 33–34; however, the author does not go on to say or imply that this convergence will *illuminate* (*shed light on, bring about insight*) *the various value systems that are held by peoples worldwide.* Like Choice A, Choice C is reading the passage through rose-colored glasses. **The correct answer is Choice D**, for the second half of the second paragraph (lines 34–52) supports this picture: *regions with higher occurrences of displaced families, a decline of untouched greenery, and increasing rates of malaria.*

34. **(J) This is a time-consuming question that requires you to refresh your memory about the prospect of each of these four geographical areas. Go back to the passage, hunt for these locations, and skim around them to determine which location is most promising. Be a smart test taker. Be a page-flipper, and do not rely on your memory alone.**
    Choice F, *sub-Saharan Africa,* is incorrect because the line that follows the reference to countries of sub-Saharan Africa says that *these . . . locations comprise the greatest burden of malaria infections.* This choice is out because this statement is *not* promising. Choice G is also out because in the passage Kawempe is plainly referred to as *the largest shantytown in Kampala, the capital of Uganda.* There's nothing optimistic about that description. Choice H, *the outskirts of cities,* is incorrect because of the lengthy, grim portrayal that spans lines 42 to 47. Reread this section of the passage to prove to yourself that the future of these *outskirts* does not seem hopeful:
    As families have become displaced economically from their customary forms of livelihood they are invading <u>the outskirts of cities</u> desperately looking for employment, where they often find themselves in "black holes of social exclusion." Castell terms this shared reality . . . world's "ghettos" as the fourth world. These "outposts of powerlessness" . . .
    The correct answer is Choice J, *Rio de Janeiro.* A great amount of textual evidence, spanning lines 85 to 95, supports this answer choice as the most promising of all: *. . . cities such as <u>Rio de Janeiro</u> have dramatically cut transmission [of malaria] . . . by implementing environmental health strategies.*
    Malaria control in <u>Rio de Janeiro</u>, Brazil, utilizes a visionary multi-pronged strategy: field sanitation technicians visit outlying communities, spraying insecticides in breeding areas, removing standing water, increasing easy access to clean water as well as taking blood samples to treat persons suffering from malaria.

35. **(D)** **To answer this question, you need to grasp the author's overall perspective and attitude regarding future prospects of malaria. It is to your advantage to answer this question once you have digested the entire passage.** Choice A, *is despairing (lacking hope) and pessimistic,* is incorrect because it is extreme and very negative. The author cites positive action that is being taken to prevent the spread of malaria. Choice B is also incorrect because it too is overly negative: *has resigned himself to … steady, worsening doom.* Choice C is out because no textual evidence supports the idea that the author thinks in terms of *fantasy.* **The correct answer is Choice D**; the author *envisions the possibilities for human efforts to result in significant positive outcomes.* In lines 70–71, he optimistically states, *prevention and control are possible in these settings* and in the fourth paragraph (lines 72–88), he mentions several actions that humans can take to curb the spread of malaria: increased surveillance, insecticide-treated bed nets, and access to clean water.

36. **(H)** **To answer this question in an educated fashion, return to the passage to review the article. To what does the phrase *current estimates* refer? Do not rely on your memory because then you are likely to become distracted by invalid answer selections.** Be a prudent test taker, and revisit the paragraph (lines 53–71) that begins with the sentence *Current estimates predict that half of the African population will live in urban settings by the year 2025.* Choice F, *women will likely pursue higher levels of formal education,* is unsupported by the text surrounding *current estimates.* While Choices G and J are appealing due to their positivity, nothing in this portion of the passage states or suggests that *future migrants . . . will learn to better protect themselves against infection* or that *urban populations will thrive.* Supported firmly by the second half of the paragraph, **the correct answer is Choice H**, which presents a grim picture: *more and more people will live in urban areas characterized by unsanitary, cramped living conditions that will, in turn, breed more cases of malaria.*

37. **(C)** **Return to the text and plug in each answer choice for *poses* in the sentence *For these reasons, malaria poses a very serious environmental health effect, but prevention and control are possible in these settings.* Select the choice that fits and flows *best.*** Choice A, *portrays* (describes), does not quite work. This term is effective for description, even dramatic description; however, it would not be correct to say that malaria describes a serious environmental health effect. Choice B, *stands for,* does not flow in this sentence; after all, malaria is being addressed as itself and not as something *else*; it does not stand for a serious environmental health effect. Choice D, *impersonates,* is incorrect, since malaria is neither being personified nor being compared to an actor! Using process of elimination of incorrect answers and astute interpretation of the passage, you can see that **Choice C (*causes*) is the best answer.**

38. **(H) ALL/EXCEPT questions can be time-consuming because they require you to find proof for three of the four answers listed. Counterintuitively, the choice that lacks support from the passage is the correct answer.** You can eliminate Choice F because the *abbreviation* ACT is defined in lines 75–76. Choice G is incorrect because *a metaphor* (a direct comparison between humans and a reservoir) appears in lines 100–101: *as infected humans are the prime reservoir of future infections.* Choice J is not correct because *a specific example followed by supporting details* appears in lines 89–95, where the author mentions a *multi-pronged strategy*, then proceeds to list several examples that comprise this strategy. **The correct answer is Choice H** because no *vivid flashback* appears in this paragraph.

39. **(B) For words-in-context questions, remember to return to the text and substitute each answer choice for the verb in question. Select the action verb that fits and flows *best* in the sentence** *Each community has a health office where people who <u>suspect</u> they are infected can come for an examination and treatment with ACT.* Choice A does not work because *scrutinize* means to examine closely. Choice C, *doubt*, is not correct either; even though people who are *suspect* (used as an adjective in this case) may *doubt* a particular situation, the sentence within the passage requires a verb. While Choice D, *conclude*, might be an acceptable answer, it is not the best one. *Conclude* implies the following of a process or series of steps, which is not the case in this context. **The correct answer is Choice B**, *believe*; it flows and makes sense in this sentence.

40. **(F) As a prudent test taker, you should reread or skim (depending on your timing) the final paragraph (lines 102–110) to determine its overall effect. Summarize its purpose and effect to yourself before you consider the answer choices.** The savvy test taker knows that it is usually more effective to think for oneself first; reading answer choices first can be distracting and/or misleading. Choice G does not make sense, for the paragraph does not *contradict several points that the author made earlier.* Choice H is also invalid; the author does not *excessively exaggerate the current and potential harms of malaria worldwide.* Choice J is unsupported as well; the closing paragraph does not have the effect of spreading *doubt upon the main points the author has expressed throughout the article.* **The correct answer is Choice F**; the author does *summarize key points* (increased globalization, rise of malaria cases, risk of women and children, environmental health threat) and *put forth a plea to restrict (slow down) the spread of malaria (need for control measures).*

DIAGNOSTIC CHARTS
ACT English Test

45 MINUTES—75 QUESTIONS

<u>Note</u>: For the purpose of this self-assessment test, there is flexibility among these subdivision categories: writing strategy, organization, author's style. English is an art, not a science, so some questions overlap to a degree. On the ACT, you will have to answer 40 questions pertaining to usage and mechanics and 35 questions pertaining to rhetorical skills.

Skills	Questions	Possible Score	Your Score
Usage/Mechanics			
Punctuation	1, 7, 25, 26, 32, 38, 40, 41, 52, 59	10	
Grammar and Usage	6, 10, 12, 27, 33, 37, 42, 43, 46, 50, 61, 66	12	
Sentence Structure	8, 14, 16, 19, 28, 29, 31, 34, 36, 47, 49, 51, 53, 54, 63, 64, 65, 71	18	
Rhetorical Skills			
Writing Strategy	5, 13, 15, 21, 22, 39, 57, 67, 68, 70, 72, 74	12	
Organization	4, 11, 20, 23, 30, 45, 56, 58, 60, 69, 75	11	
Author's Style	2, 3, 9, 17, 18, 24, 35, 44, 48, 55, 62, 73	12	

Total: 75

Percent correct: _____

ACT Reading Test

40 MINUTES—35 QUESTIONS

Passage Type	Referring	Reasoning	Possible Score	Your Score
Prose Fiction	1, 2, 4, 7	3, 5, 6, 8, 9, 10	10	
Social Studies	11, 13, 17	12, 14, 15, 16, 18, 19, 20	10	
Humanities	21, 22, 25	23, 24, 26, 27, 28, 29, 30	10	
Natural Science	32, 33, 37, 40	31, 34, 35, 36, 38, 39	10	

Total: 40

Percent correct: _____

Score Conversion Table*

English Raw Score	Reading Raw Score	Scaled Score
70–75	34–40	31–36
61–69	27–33	25–30
46–60	20–26	19–24
31–45	12–19	13–18
14–30	4–11	7–12
0–13	0–3	1–6

*Note: This chart is designed to give you a general approximation of the number of questions you need to get right to fall into a general score range on the actual test. It is *not* designed to give you an exact score or to predict your actual ACT score. The variance in difficulty levels and testing conditions can affect your score range.

Overview and Format of the ACT

1

- English Test
  - Format
  - Timing Plans
  - English Skills Assessed
- Reading Test
  - Format
  - Timing Plan
  - Reading Skills Assessed
  - Types of Reading Passages
  - Reading Test Tips
- Writing Test
  - Format
  - Timing Plan
  - Writing Skills Assessed

ENGLISH TEST

Format

- 5 Passages, 75 questions, 45 minutes
- Standard usage and mechanics skills
- Rhetorical skills, Diction, Punctuation
- Logical sequence of ideas
- Placement of words, phrases, sentences

Question Topics and Their Percentages

- Punctuation   13%
- Grammar and Usage   16%
- Sentence Structure   24%
- Organization   15%
- Strategy   16%
- Author's Style   16%

Timing Plans

How you spend your "down time" when at home is a matter of preference. Similarly, how you pace yourself on the ACT is a matter of personal style. The chart on the following page illustrates three different timing plans. Experiment with the Self-Assessment Test and Practice Test in this book, and see which of the suggested timing plans works best for you. To further experiment with your timing style, consult Barron's *ACT* review book, which contains a diagnostic test plus five additional practice ACTs. Sharpen your pencils, roll up your sleeves, hunker down, and block out time in your calendar that you can dedicate to ACT practice.

Let's review the numbers: There are *five* English passages, *seventy-five* questions (an average of *fifteen* questions on each passage), and *forty-five* minutes to work. Set a wind-up timer, a microwave oven timer, a stopwatch, or any other timing device to determine which timing plan works best for you:

Timing Plan A	**Timing Plan B**	**Timing Plan C**
I will spend about 9 minutes on each passage. This will entail both reading the passage and answering its corresponding questions.	I will spend about 5 minutes reading each passage (5 minutes × 5 passages = 25 minutes total). Then, I will devote about 20 minutes to reading and answering the 75 questions at a pace of about 4 minutes per passage.	I will spend about 1½ minutes *skimming* through each passage, then I will spend about 30 seconds answering each of the 75 questions. If I answer the questions more quickly, I will spend the remaining time allotted to this test reviewing my work and returning to the questions that I found most difficult. I will also make sure that my answer sheet is clearly marked — no smudges, no ambiguous markings.

English Skills Assessed

- **Punctuation:** accentuating how punctuation affects meaning; internal punctuation marks (semicolons, colons, commas, dashes, hyphens, quotation marks) and end marks (periods, exclamation points, question marks)
- **Grammar and Usage:** agreement between pronouns and their antecedents; agreement between subjects and verbs; correct expression of various modifiers, verb forms, pronoun case, comparative and superlative forms of adjectives; expression of sound English idioms according to standard usage
- **Sentence Structure:** parallel form; correct placement of modifying words, phrases, and clauses; independent and subordinate clauses; run-ons, comma splices, fused sentences, fragments, and sound sentences
- **Organization:** understanding coherence and the ordering of ideas as they are presented; passage form, development, and unity
- **Strategy:** developing and supporting a cohesive idea; when to add/revise/delete sentences and phrases; the use of effective opening, transitional, and concluding sentences, such as topic sentences of paragraphs
- **Author's Style:** understanding how to determine as well as maintain the author's tone and writing style; avoiding ambiguous pronouns; avoiding redundancy, verbose language, empty phrasing, colloquial language, and slang

READING TEST

Format

4 passages, 40 questions, 35 minutes

⏱ Timing Plan

Allot about nine minutes per reading selection; these nine minutes would comprise reading the passage and answering the corresponding set of ten questions. For example, spend five minutes reading the passage and then about four minutes answering the ten questions that follow. Adjust this flexible timing plan according to your personal reading pace: If you read the passage in four minutes, for instance, then you will have five minutes to read and answer the questions.

Of course, 9 × 4 (4 passages) = 36 (minutes), but let's keep the timing simple. You actually have 8.75 minutes per reading passage.

Reading Skills Assessed

- Understanding what is directly stated
- Recognizing statements with implied meanings
- Finding the main idea
- Drawing comparisons
- Making generalizations
- Recognizing cause-and-effect relationships
- Evaluating author's writing method and voice
- Comprehending the sequence of events
- Ascertaining the meaning of words and phrases in their specific contexts

Types of Reading Passages— Four Genres/Four Flavors:

- **Prose Fiction:** excerpts from short stories, novels, novellas, and memoirs; may be written in the first-person narrative style, using the pronouns "I" and "me." This genre of writing can be referred to simply as fiction.
- **Social Science:** writing on topics such as anthropology, archeology, biography, business, economics, education, geography, history, political science, psychology, and sociology. This section is sometimes referred to as Social Studies.
- **Humanities:** excerpts from personal essays and memoirs; writing on topics such as architecture, art, dance, ethics, film, language, literary criticism, music, philosophy, radio, and theater.
- **Natural Science:** writing on topics such as anatomy, astronomy, biology, botany, chemistry, ecology, geology, medicine, meteorology, microbiology, natural history, physics, technology, and zoology.

> **SMART PREP**
>
> To sharpen your skills and your performance on the Reading Test, regularly read articles in quality periodicals and newspapers that span a broad range of genres and topics.

Reading Test Tips

READ the entire passage in one sweep, or read it in halves. Do not break down the passage into too many chunks (stopping after each paragraph, for example, to see if there is a question you can answer pertaining to that particular paragraph) because, unlike on the SAT, the questions on the ACT do not necessarily appear in order of the material presented in the reading passage. ACT questions are randomly, haphazardly arranged, for the most part.

This lack of order within the question set can be annoying at first, but as you work through the practice tests you will get used to this "haphazard" presentation of questions. Most test takers find that it is to their advantage to read and absorb the entire passage at once, or to digest the passage in two halves. Either method can work fine; experiment to determine which modus operandi (approach) is most effective for *you*.

REFERENCE the passage, as needed, to help you answer the questions. Our memories are not always reliable (excuse the platitude, but for many of us they are like sieves or porous buckets!)—particularly under timed testing circumstances. So, make it a habit to refer to the reading selection for passage evidence as you narrow in on the best answer choice. Test takers who "flip pages," going back and forth from the questions to the text, have the right idea. Keep in mind, however, you may only move around the specified section within which the proctor asks you to work. Otherwise, your test score will be disqualified.

CONSIDER all answer choices before you choose the one you think is best. Do this methodically, working at an efficient pace: not too fast that you risk making careless errors, not too slow that you risk spending too much time on any one question or passage. Use process of elimination to cross off answer choices that are invalid or only partially valid. Keep in mind that 75 percent of what you encounter as you read through the answer choices is bogus: unsubstantiated, off-topic, or merely partially correct. Strive to pick the best, not second best, since no partial credit is given for "runner-up" answers.

 Time-Saver

If you find yourself pressed for time, try a de-stressing technique called Outline Reading.

Are you a tortoise or a hare? It's a good idea to take many practice tests and time yourself (under testing conditions) to get a sense of your speed. If you find it tricky to get through the passages, try outline reading.

THREE SIMPLE STEPS TO OUTLINE READING:

OUTLINE READING

Outline reading saves time and is a great de-stressing technique for many students who may have trouble concentrating when taking tests with time constraints.

STEP 1 Carefully read any **introductory material** that precedes the passage. Here you will usually be told the name of the author and the topic. And, read the **entire introductory paragraph**. If the introductory paragraph is skimpy (just a few lines or so), then read all or most of the second paragraph as well. Focus on the thesis of the introductory paragraph, which is typically the last sentence of the introduction.

STEP 2 Carefully read the **topic sentences** (first sentences) of each body paragraph and then, in a skimming fashion, read the rest of each paragraph.

STEP 3 Carefully read the **concluding paragraph**. (The author's main idea, tone, and overall purpose are often reinforced in this important paragraph.)

Outline reading not only saves you time but also effectively provides you with an overall understanding and sense of the passage. In addition, this shortcut reading technique gives you a "framework" or structure for how the information is organized and presented within the passage. This way, when you embark on answering the questions and go back to the passage as a reference, you will have a better sense of where to find the information and supporting details you are looking for.

WRITING TEST
Format

1 essay, 40 minutes
4–6 paragraphs suggested

Timing Plan

Prewriting	2–3 minutes
Writing	35 minutes
Revising/Editing	2–3 minutes

This timing plan is merely a suggestion. Experiment with writing your essay within this forty-minute time frame, and determine for yourself which timing plan allows you to pace yourself most effectively.

Writing Skills Assessed

 Express your opinion by taking a standpoint on the topic presented in the writing prompt.

Stay focused on the issue throughout your essay; refrain from superfluous information and asides; do not get sidetracked as you write.

Use specific examples, supporting details, and coherent reasoning to develop your point of view; be sure that your examples do not contradict each other but contribute coherently to your position on the issue.

Organize your ideas in a way that makes logical sense; keep your lines of reasoning moving from beginning to middle to end; refrain from taking "big leaps" in logic that leave your reader befuddled and wondering, "How did he (the author) get from point A to point B?" Beware the ESP factor: Do not assume that your readers know what you are thinking or where you are coming from.

Use effective and clear language that adheres to the conventions of standard, written English; avoid colloquialisms, slang expressions, and anything that sounds talky. To be even more prudent (careful and conscientious), avoid contractions such as wouldn't, isn't, didn't, and won't. This is a college-entrance exam, so put your best foot forward and write as properly as you can. Remember, this essay is about standard *writing*, not casual speaking!

Chapter Summary

Now that you've read this chapter, you are in-the-know; you have informed yourself with a clear and thorough sense of what to expect when you take the ACT. It is human nature to feel more at ease when we know what's coming up. The numbers have been clarified for you in this chapter: the number of verbal subtests within the ACT, the number of passages, the number of skills being assessed, the number of questions, and the number of minutes allotted. The chapters that follow cover the contents of the ACT with greater comprehensiveness and detail.

Be a Class ACT on Test Day

2

- Advanced Prep Plans
- How to Be a Class ACT on Test Day
- ACT Timing Tips
- ACT Testing Tips
- What to Bring to the Test Center
- What *Not* to Bring to the Test Center
- What to Expect at the Test Center
- What to Expect During the Test

ADVANCED PREP PLANS

Beyond applying all of the valuable tips within the bevy of checklists provided in this handy chapter, this chapter explains how **advanced preparation** for the ACT comes in three main types:

ADVANCED PREP PLAN 1:
Read Far, Wide, and Deep

Make it a habit to read all good material you can get your hands on. No need to tell anyone that you're doing ACT prep. Think of this as covert prep. Simply declare to yourself that you are a voracious, insatiable reader and act on it! Peruse (read attentively or leisurely) the *New York Times,* the *Wall Street Journal, Scientific American, National Geographic,* and your local newspaper. Refrain from reading the paper's back pages only, though; a sports passage on the ACT is a rarity. Don't hesitate to pick up *Time* magazine and digest an article or two. If you prefer, you can read local, national, and international news coverage online.

Think of schoolwork as ACT prep. Read all of your assigned novels for school and read your textbooks with the ACT in mind: In other words, while you read keep your eyes peeled for sentence structure, punctuation usage, word choice, author's style, and overall organization of the material. Read books for pleasure. For now, put aside the DVDs and CDs, and replace them with a stack of good reads on your bedside table.

This type of reading commitment will edify you in several ways. You will be a more interesting person to talk to: informed, up-to-date, and in-the-know. You might find yourself taking credit for invigorating dinner conversations. You will be a sought-after conversationalist at family parties and gatherings. You will be able to participate in discussions about current events in your social studies class, while at the same time you will be sharpening your skills in preparation for the English, Reading, and Writing Tests found on the ACT. What more could you ask for?

Advanced Prep Plan 2:
Do a Number of Practice Tests; Time Yourself

A bag of tricks . . . a secret code . . . answer key patterns . . . foolproof testing techniques . . .

Even though some test takers wish there were some top secret strategies for acing the ACT, the truth is: There is no better preparation than working through lots of practice ACT tests and ACT-related material. Be sure to do the Self-Assessment Test, the Quick-Drill exercises, and the full-length Practice Test found in this workbook. Keep in mind that these tests and exercises cover only the English Language Arts/ Verbal sections of the ACT—English, Reading, and Writing (this is an optional test).

Use a stopwatch, your cell phone, or the timer on your microwave oven (if you are testing in the kitchen) to time yourself as you work through the various forty-five-minute, thirty-five-minute, and thirty-minute verbal sections.

This practice plan includes thoughtfully reading over the answer explanations, which are provided for each test. Even if you get an answer right, reading the explanations that detail why other choices are wrong can illuminate an aspect of English or grammar that may have been unknown or rusty for you.

NOT ALL PRACTICE IS PERFECT

When you put the time in for ACT practice, you should make your time really count. Be smart by preparing yourself for the actualities of test day. Here are some work habits I routinely observe during my private tutoring sessions. Over time, I encourage my students to remove these habits, as they are not proper for test day. If you have these types of habits when doing your practice work, slowly and steadily wean yourself off of them and your preparation hours will prove the adage, "Practice makes perfect!"

Counterproductive Preparation Habits

- ✗ Listening to music or wearing headphones while working through the English and Reading passages.
- ✗ Tapping the test booklet with a pencil; strumming on the desk with your fingers.
- ✗ Humming while reading "silently."
- ✗ Reading passages and questions aloud.
- ✗ Taking breaks in between the individual passages of either the English Test or the Reading Test. Breaks are given between some of the five tests (English, Reading, Science, Math, Writing) that comprise the ACT, but breaks are not given in between the passages themselves that appear within a given test.

✗ Mouthing the words while reading (lip reading).

✗ Watching television, checking your phone, and cruising Facebook while working through your practice questions.

In the short term and long run, these types of test-prep habits are counterproductive. Such habits bring impediments to your preparation, preventing you from achieving the best score of which you are capable.

ADVANCED PREP PLAN 3:
Consider Your Schoolwork ACT Prep

TIME-SAVER

Schoolwork as ACT Prep

This preparation plan lets your schoolwork serve double duty and lets you *save valuable time.* The premise is that the written material in your textbooks is grammatically sound and sensibly organized. With this being the case (and hopefully it is) you become a proficient multitasker. Your schoolwork time and study time double in purpose: Not only do you read the material to comprehend it so that you can score high on your next AP Euro or English test, but you also read the material to notice grammatical conventions. As you read your textbooks, Internet articles, handouts, and research materials, make it a point to notice and think about multifarious language-related aspects like these:

• The pronoun *them* stands in for *political policies.*

• The pronoun *it* stands in for *government agency* (even though you may picture a bunch of people when you read the word *agency,* this noun must function as singular—yes, a collective singular—that takes the singular pronoun, *it* and the possessive *its*).

• The two *independent clauses* of this sentence are separated by a *semicolon* (;)—yes, this construction builds a compound sentence. If you swap out the ; for a comma (,), a run-on comma splice occurs!

• A comma is used to introduce quoted dialogue; other punctuation marks that are part of the dialogue appear *within* the closed quotation marks.

• The author discusses each bill in *chronological order,* then at the end of each paragraph, he *reflects* on a disadvantageous circumstance that existed before this bill. (As you read, this type of awareness builds your sense of how authors structure and organize their writing.)

• The author *repeats certain phrases and words* over and over; the effect of this intentional *style element* is to markedly emphasize the main points. This is an example of a literary or figurative device.

• The author *contradicts himself* in the last paragraph of the article by providing evidence for an antithetical point of view.

See how much can be gleaned about grammatical conventions and writing style just by making a conscious effort to notice these types of things? So, while you are reading a chapter in your history text or while you are reading an essay written by a particular scientist, explorer, or literary master, you can likewise garner (gather) insights into the author's writing style, tone, use of rhetorical devices, and the more general uses of standard, written English.

ADVANCED PREP PLAN 4:
Improve Your Vocabulary: A Major Key in Reading, English, and Writing Test Preparation

Both verbal tests contain a good deal of vocabulary. Not knowing certain words—or simply being confused about the precise meanings of words—can make the difference between answering a question correctly or incorrectly. In my private tutoring practice, most recently I have had students whose confusion about words appearing on the ACT have cost them questions. Some of these words include: *balk*, *scarcity*, and *whet*.

Here is a sampling of words that appeared in the Reading and English Test passages of actual online practice ACT exams, listed in order of their appearance:

English Test: preceding, clamor, feat, skeptical, wield, ambiguous, depicted, distinct, engrossed, immersed, incorporating, constituted, relevant, gourd, allusion

Reading Test: contours, feign, dissolution, attributed, dismay, sustainable, burgeoning, devoid, listless, perplexity, enunciation, hymned, indissoluble, ministering, fleeting, invariably, voraciously

It goes without saying that a varied, strong, and fitting vocabulary will improve your Writing Test score as well. Demonstrating your vocabulary skills will help to make your essay more engrossing and effective.

HOW TO BE A CLASS ACT ON TEST DAY

Call to mind this original acronym—**A**ttitude, **C**oncentration, **T**echnique—to help you focus on three vital aspects of **ACT** test taking that can really make a positive difference in your preparation and performance.

> **A**ttitude
>
> **C**oncentration
>
> **T**echnique

Attitude

As you prepare for and think about this test, keep a positive attitude. An upbeat outlook works wonders on your test preparation efforts and, certainly, on your testing performance on the actual day of the test. Adopt positive "self-talk" as you prepare. Regularly say the following types of things to yourself, and you will feel your mindset become stronger, buoyant, and more focused. Positive rhetoric and an encouraging mindset also help to alleviate anxiety and before-the-test jitters.

SELF-AFFIRMATIONS

☺ I am participating in a win-win situation because there is no penalty for incorrect answers on the ACT. This is a test-taker's dream! I will always make an educated guess because—once again—I will not be penalized for incorrect answers. I am savvy about the scoring of this test: I know not to and will *not* omit any questions. *Note:* Consider this hypothetical worst-case scenario: You have five questions left and forty seconds on the clock! What do you do? Just fill in those bubbles neatly and firmly on your answer sheet. You have nothing to lose, literally, and the potential to gain some additional last-minute points.

☺ I have what it takes to do very well on the ACT.

☺ I am preparing in a way that is effective and thorough.

☺ I am good at finding and setting aside ample time to read and work through this book. I have organized a study schedule for myself that is manageable for me.

☺ I can build up my reading, English, and writing skills by working through this book and by letting my schoolwork serve double duty. (See page 73, Advanced Prep Plan 3.)

☺ I am thankful for having the opportunity to take the ACT as one of my college entrance exams because this is a test on which I can shine and achieve a strong score.

☺ Taking the ACT is a win-win situation, for I have the prerogative (choice) to decide if I want to report my scores to the colleges.

☺ If there are principles of grammar, English, reading, or writing that I don't understand at this point, I will master them before test day.

As you keep your attitude up, banish negative self-talk that can only bring you down. If you catch yourself speaking or thinking any one of the following, make every effort to rid this junk from your rhetoric and from your inner thoughts. Banish these types of statements and questions from your mental dialogue. All of the following are examples of negative self-talk:

☹ I'm not looking forward to or—*I'm dreading*—the ACT.

☹ I'm not going to do well on this annoying test.

☹ Why do I even have to take this test?

☹ I can't believe how long the ACT is and that there are so many subject-specific subtests!

☹ It's impossible for this test to show what I know and how I'm capable of doing in college.

☹ Uggh! I just don't want to take this test.

Concentration

Including the Writing Test (which is optional) and including the Science and Math Tests, the ACT assessment in total is about three and a half hours long. In light of this fact, developing concentration is one key to your success.

Practice developing concentration at home when you work on the Quick-Drills offered in this book, when you read through the instructional material in this book, and when you work on the Self-Assessment Test. As a supplement to this book, which focuses a great deal on strategy and substance, pick up a book such as Barron's *ACT*, which contains a diagnostic test as well as three full-length practice tests. Do these practice tests under testing conditions and work on the various tests according to the time allotted. Doing practice tests regularly—once or twice a week, for instance—will build up your concentration level so that you are sharp and ready on test day.

CONCENTRATION BUILD-UP

The first time at the gym, even the best-intentioned exerciser does not tackle the entire circuit training loop. He might start with a handful of repetitions on a few machines. At the next visit, he might do more reps and then add a weight machine or two. The process is a gradual build-up that—over time—will have that exerciser doing three sets of fifteen on every machine in the circuit. Before you know it, he lifts those weights full throttle, works out for two hours, and lifts to the point of muscle fatigue. Well, let's not go overboard.

Likewise, you can build up your stamina in terms of concentration. The following are suggestions about how you may go about gradually building up your concentration level:

Timing Plan—Level A

Pick up a three-pound dumbbell. Time yourself on just *one* of the five English test passages. Give yourself about **9 minutes** to read the passage and answer the fifteen accompanying questions.

Timing Plan—Level B

Pick up a seven-pound dumbbell. Time yourself on *three* of the five English test passages; give yourself about **27 minutes** to read the passage and answer the forty-five corresponding questions.

Timing Plan—Level C

Next, pick up that fifteen-pound body bar and do some squats. Time yourself on the entire English Test: **45 minutes**, seventy-five questions. You can do it *and* remain focused!

Timing Plan—Level D

Interval training! After three reps of twenty squats with that body bar across your shoulders, do a bunch of crunches with a heavy weight resting on your chest. Sharpen your pencils, and do an entire English Test (**45 minutes**) plus add, for example, *two* Reading Test passages, which will tack on an additional **17–18 minutes** of testing time. Alternatively, you can add on the Essay (**30 minutes** more) at this point, if you opt to take the Writing Test.

Little by little, you will build up to the three and a half hours of total testing time, without straining any muscles (like your brain!) or running out of steam. You have now built up test-taking stamina!

Real-life testing conditions are never perfect, so the testing conditions that you try to duplicate at home do not have to be perfect either. In fact, as you take your diagnostic test, your practice test, or as you work on the Quick-Drills, let your younger brother's radio play in his bedroom, let the hum of the clothes dryer drone on, let the hot-air corn popper make its raucous noise, let your dog wrestle with her chew toy at your feet, and let the noise of the family room television travel up to your bedroom. Do *not* listen to your iPod, take breaks to play a handheld video game, or fiddle with your cell phone because these types of electronic devices are not permitted at the testing center.

Concentration is built best under less-than-perfect conditions. No matter what anyone tells you and no matter what you have heard, we assure you that less-than-perfect conditions exist at all testing facilities. One or more of the following may *try* to distract you: The heater or air conditioning hums and makes strange noises; the test taker sitting in front of you beats his toes on the floor or taps a pencil on his desk; the proctor organizes the complete contents of her purse; the student sitting next to you sucks on a cough drop as if it's a triple-scoop ice-cream cone; and there is construction going on in the adjacent courtyard. Could that be the sound of jackhammers breaking up concrete?! Don't be surprised.

No worries—you can deal with all of these distractions because you have worked to sharpen your level of concentration. Your head doesn't turn with every new noise or movement. You are not concerned about what page the person next to you is working on, or what question the guy across from you is up to. Your head is down, your shoulders are squared off and forward, your eyes are fixed on the page, and your pencil is moving purposefully.

Technique and Timing

Once you have absorbed and digested the contents of this book, you will have a wealth of test-taking techniques to apply to the Reading, English, and Writing portions of the ACT. Chefs apply various techniques to their cooking: how they slice zucchini on the bias, how they tenderize flank steaks before marinating them, or how they season a vegetable medley before roasting. Just as top chefs are edified by special methods, so you will have the know-how to apply to the three distinct verbal exams.

Following is a slim *sampling* of the techniques you will know how to apply once you've internalized the substance of this book.

READING TEST

- How to read the passages using a time-efficient process called outline reading
- How to anticipate the types of questions that you are likely to encounter in this section
- How to use your pencil as a test-taking tool as you read by writing brief notations in the margins next to the reading passages

ENGLISH TEST

- When to use a comma, semicolon, or colon when given a particular portion of text
- How to navigate through the various numbers (boxed, bracketed, subscripted) that appear throughout the English passages
- How to decide which portions of text to add, re-situate, or omit

WRITING TEST

- How to break down the thirty minutes allotted to write the essay into a timing plan that works for you
- How to make the most of the minutes you set aside for revising and editing
- How to organize your essay so that it flows logically and maintains coherence

The **checklists** that follow provide valuable keys to success. These handy checklists put you in the best possible position for achieving your personal best score on test day.

ACT TIMING TIPS

 ## Timing Tip: Jot a 9 at the Top

On test day, the proctor is not required to tell you how much time you have for each passage. The proctor is also not required to tell you when to move on to the next passage. In other words, the proctor will not help you allocate enough time to work on all five English Passages and all four Reading Passages. Pacing yourself throughout the test is completely up to you.

Simply jot down a 9 at the top of each and every English Test and Reading Test passage. In your test booklet, your big handwritten 9s will stand out, giving you visual reminders of how much time you can "safely" spend on that passage. On the English Test, the math works out seamlessly: 45 minutes, five passages . . . 9 minutes per passage. Perfect.

On the Reading Test, however, the math gets a little fuzzy: 35 minutes, four passages . . . 8.75 minutes per passage. For the sake of ease in remembering your time allocations, simply jot 9s at the tops. When 7 to 8 minutes have passed, you should be thinking about wrapping it up and moving on (in a minute or two) to the next passage. When you are approaching the 16–17-minute mark, you should be thinking of moving on soon to the next passage, and so on.

 ## Time-Saver: Choose One Passage for Guessing

This strategy is geared toward the ACT student who tends to be hard-pressed to get to the last passage of the ACT verbal tests. This time-saving technique works on both the Reading Test (four passages total) and English Test (five passages total). Here's how it works: if you are a stronger math/science student, you would choose to guess on either the Prose Fiction or Humanities passage on the Reading Test. These passages tend to deal with topics pertaining to the arts and literature. Experiment with different approaches to see which one works best for you.

This approach allows you to spend more time on the remaining three reading passages and the remaining four English passages. Only use "Choose One Passage for Guessing" if you have practiced several Reading and English tests and you—consistently—do not have enough time to address the final passage of each test. If you have a few months of preparation time before test day, then keep practicing using the time allotted per each test: 45 minutes for the English Test; 35 minutes for the Reading Test.

Do not simply adopt this strategy (as appealing as it may be . . . yes! Skip a passage!) without a good deal of timed practice first. You do not want to shortchange yourself.

One caveat: do not omit the questions that correlate with the passage you will be "skipping." Instead, bubble in answers for all ten questions of

> **TIMING TIP**
>
> Jot a 9 at the top of all passages, reminding yourself how much time to allocate to each.
>
> On test day, you are in charge of your pacing.

> **TIME-SAVER**
>
> Choose one passage for "guessing."

> **READING TEST TIP**
>
> Start with your favorite passage type.
>
> Natural Science?
>
> Prose Fiction?
>
> Humanities?
>
> Social Science?
>
> The choice is yours.

the Reading Test passage or all fifteen questions of the English Test passage. Based on "guessing" alone, you will earn two or three correct answers on the reading passage and around three or four questions right on the English passage. "Guessing" becomes educated guessing, however, when you have a few minutes to devote to this passage. Use your remaining time wisely by skimming the introductory and closing paragraphs and trying to answer as many questions as you can—and as time permits—before you move on to simple guessing.

Beyond this, you can pick the passage you want to start with. If you're a fan of fiction, start with the prose passage—that was a cinch because Prose Fiction is always the first passage type anyway. Let's try again. If you're a Natural Science buff, start with that passage, which is the last in line of the four. Just be sure to bubble in the correctly numbered ovals on your answer sheet. Answer ovals for the Natural Science passages are numbers 31–40 *not* 1–10.

ACT TESTING TIPS

☑ **Rest up** with extra zzzzz's the night before the test and—if possible—get to bed early for three or four days leading up to the test. Extra shut-eye will ensure that you are sharp and ready to apply yourself fully on the day of the test. Your body experiences a wonder of repair and restoration while it sleeps. Give yourself what you need to do your very best on test day by giving your body what it needs (sleep, rest!) to perform at its best.

☑ **Be a breakfast person.** If you don't already make time for breakfast, start making breakfast part of your morning routine during the months and weeks leading up to the test. For a steady energy release, try to include some type of protein in your morning meal such as cheese, yogurt, eggs, milk, or all-natural peanut butter. Whole grain toast, all-natural muffins, and fiber-rich cereals also contribute to a balanced breakfast that sustains your energy level. Other good choices include unrefined, unsweetened oatmeal and French toast made with whole grain bread.

Be open-minded and adventurous with your morning meal. Move aside that old cereal box and experiment with various healthy breakfast options. Ever try unsweetened yogurt topped with fresh berries, a spoonful of flaxseed meal, and a drizzle of honey? Try a cool, morning smoothie: Blend together ice, vanilla yogurt, honey, berries, all-natural orange juice, and a banana. Smoothies are fun because the variety of healthful concoctions is endless. Ever try blueberry-buckwheat pancakes? Go easy on the powdered sugar and syrup, though—beware the energy slump midway through the ACT. Mom and Dad are right: Breakfast is the most important meal of the day. As the adage says, "Eat breakfast like a king or queen."

☑ **Don't show up without a clue.** Give yourself the benefit of a good dose of advanced preparation and know-how. Months, or at least weeks before the test, become familiar with the directions for the English, Reading, and Writing sections. Also, familiarize yourself with the contents of each of the three tests and the types of questions you will be asked.

- ☑ **Be ready** with all of the supplies that you will need to work through the test. Bring at least three soft, lead #2 pencils with good erasers (no smudgy ones) to the testing center. Do not use pens or mechanical pencils.

- ☑ **Read and underline** is your best modus operandus. Read each question carefully, and get into the habit of underlining the key words within the question itself. Savvy test takers realize that identifying and knowing your precise task is as important—if not more important—as attempting to accomplish your task. If you're not into underlining, then circle key words.

- ☑ **Pace yourself.** Skillful test takers know not to spend too much time on any single reading selection or question.

- ☑ **Answer every question.** Multiple-choice tests are based on the number of questions you answer correctly. This is a win-win situation when it comes to scoring. There are no demerits for incorrect answers!

- ☑ **It's not nap time** if you have four minutes left over after you complete a particular test. Lift your head off the desk and review your work. Before time is up, always go back and check your work—after all, you are trying to achieve your personal best score.

- ☑ **No smudges!** Mark the bubble sheet neatly. If you erase an oval that you had filled in, be sure to erase completely and cleanly. Otherwise, the electronic scoring system may mark a correct answer as wrong because your actual choice cannot be unequivocally determined. If your pencil eraser tends to smudge, then bring along a clean gummy eraser to do the job flawlessly.

- ☑ **Respect timing limits.** Do not mark ovals, erase ovals, or change any ovals on your answer sheet or continue working on the Writing Test after time is up. If you do any of these things, you risk being disqualified from the test.

- ☑ **Take a stroll in the park, then walk uphill.** All questions on the ACT earn the same number of points, so answer the easy questions first and then answer the more difficult ones. For each reading selection, the questions tend to start off easy, then get harder. Regardless of this ascending order of difficulty, you determine which questions are accessible and which questions are challenging. Therefore, feel free to skip around a bit, answering the ones you find easier first. Remember to skip the ovals on your answer document for the more difficult questions that you want to return to at a later time. You can jump to a different passage within a given test, but you cannot jump to a different test section altogether.

- ☑ **Don't underestimate process of elimination.** Though this technique is sometimes underrated and underused, it is very effective, especially on the more difficult questions. Just start with what you know doesn't work by crossing off as many incorrect answers as you can. Make an educated guess among the remaining choices.

PACK A FEW DAYS BEFORE

True, ACT Test day is no vacation but, still, don't wait until the morning of the test to gather your supplies.

Give yourself an edge by packing your admission ticket, sharpened #2 pencils, calculator, water bottle, sweatshirt, and so on, at least the night before—better yet, two or three days before—so that you are calm and so that things are "under control" on the morning of the test.

Being prepared ahead of time lessens test day anxiety.

☑ **Be confident.** Psyche yourself up to rank on this test! Adopt a confident and geared-up mindset that says, "I am ready to show them (the test makers and evaluators) what I know!" instead of, "Oh no, they're gonna get me . . ." Your mind is a powerful center; use it to your advantage.

WHAT TO BRING TO THE TEST CENTER

Rushing around like a chicken-without-a-head on test day is never a good idea. Set your alarm for bright and early, and get up at least a half hour sooner than you need to. This way, you can get ready in a calm and relaxed fashion. Last but not least, give yourself an extra ten to twenty minutes of travel time. This way, you can leisurely stroll into the test center a few minutes early, as calm and cool as a decaf iced cappuccino.

It's a great idea to make a practice run to the test center the week before so that you are crystal clear about how to get there and where to park if you are driving yourself. Make a note of how much time you will need to travel from your home to the test center.

☑ **Your admission ticket (not needed for standby students)**

☑ **A calculator** (a back-up calculator is optional) and extra batteries. Make sure that your particular type of calculator is permitted. Check with your teachers or contact the testing center directly. Remember those back-up batteries! You may help yourself out of a pickle or be able to help a friend whose calculator dies.

☑ **Identification:** a non-expired, current, official photo ID, as issued by city/state/federal government (a passport or a driver's license), or by your school, or by your employer. Your legal name and photo must appear on the ID. Acceptable identification also includes a school transcript or letter, which should be typewritten on official letterhead. (Refer to *www.actstudent.org* for more details on acceptable IDs.)

☑ **Supplies, supplies, supplies!** At least three #2 pencils (it never hurts to be over-prepared), a large gummy eraser, and a calculator (for the math section only). You may even want to bring a handheld pencil sharpener in case the one available in the testing room is defunct. Also consider bringing tissues or wipes.

☑ **Comfy, versatile clothing:** A zipper-down sweatshirt and layered clothing are recommended; comfortable pants. Flip-flops are not recommended.

☑ **Snack Time!** Bring a couple of energy-sustaining snacks, juice, and/or water (some test sites allow water at your seat; others do not). It is a long test; you want to keep up your energy and stamina.

☑ **Verification of special testing accommodation:** In some cases, you may want to bring your paperwork as verification of your special testing accommodations, such as extended time. In fact, you may take the ACT in a separate testing area. You, your parents, and your guidance counselor should determine—well ahead of test day—exactly what the special accommodations are, whether the test center administrators and proctors are clearly informed, and whether you should bring copies of your paperwork to the test center on test day. In fact, you should look into test centers that may not be among the most local to your school or home, as certain centers may offer you better test-taking conditions. This research is well worth it.

✔ Bring a watch that does not have an audible alarm. A clock might not be in the testing room, or it might not be working.

WHAT *NOT* TO BRING TO THE TEST CENTER

✘ **Paper:** Scratch paper, lined paper, post-it notes or sticky notes, a notebook—any kind of paper (except for your admission ticket, of course) is a no-no!

✘ **Books:** dictionaries, reference books, pleasure reading novels, notebooks, prior ACT score reports. No books—period.

✘ **Colored pens or pencils, highlighters:** Here's a rhyme to help you remember what writing utensils you need on test day: *If it's not a soft, lead pencil #2, it shouldn't go to the test center with you.*

✘ **Correction fluid or tape:** Neither of these items is permitted for use, so leave them at home.

✘ **Electronic devices:** This is not a day at the park or the beach, so leave devices such as cell phones, pagers, timers, beepers, headphones, laptops, cameras, iPods, iTouch music players, and handheld camcorders at home.

✘ **Food, water, snacks:** These items are typically not permitted into the testing room. Your test supervisor, however, may allow you to keep these items outside of the testing room so that you may have a snack or a drink of water during breaks. One way to find out these particulars is to ask an older schoolmate if he or she was permitted to have water or a snack during breaks. Or, try calling the test center.

✘ **Timing devices:** Cell phones, oven timers, and stopwatches might have been very helpful to you when you were taking your practice ACT Tests at home. On test day, however, your proctor will be the official timekeeper, most likely using the clock on the classroom wall. Sometimes, however, testing centers have large digital clocks that they use, similar to the ones you might see at an intramural basketball game. Your proctor may write the start and end times on a blackboard or dry-erase board. Many proctors will let you know when half of your allotted time is up, and they are supposed to give you about a 5-minute warning toward the end of each test.

✘ **Negative attitude:** Check this at the door. A negative mindset will only undermine your performance, so adopt a mental outlook of confidence and courage instead. Use optimistic, positive self-talk like, "I'm here, my pencils are sharpened, and I am ready to show them what I know. I will do great!"

WHAT TO EXPECT AT THE TEST CENTER

- **Early bird gets the worm:** Expect to arrive at your test center at, or a little bit before, the time indicated on your admission ticket, which is normally at 8:00 in the morning. If you arrive earlier than 7:45 A.M., you may have to wait outside until the test center opens and the proctors are ready to sign you in.
- **Chill time! Rest time! Down time!** Whatever you call it, a brief respite is yours after the first two tests. During this mini-break of "free time," you can stretch your legs, use the restroom, rest your eyes, sharpen your pencils, stare into space, or just chill.
- **Snack time?** Depending on your testing site and your testing proctor and supervisor, you may be able to take a quick nibble during the break. No club sandwiches or meatball heroes, just small and quick snacks like a cheese stick, a cereal bar, dried nuts, or fruit . . . you get the idea. Check with your test center the week before to find out whether you are permitted to bring a small snack or drink.

WHAT TO EXPECT DURING THE TEST

- **A slow start:** Once everyone is checked in, seated, and settled the sluggish start begins. One or all of the following may take place: filling out answer sheets, collecting standby registrations, learning about particular rules set forth by your proctor, and listening to a lengthy reading of instructions about procedures during and after the test.
- **Reality check:** Testing centers are usually not perfect, quiet, and calm. Sometimes there's construction in the courtyard outside your testing room window. Sometimes proctors talk with each other. Sometimes a proctor may be pushing paper, and making distracting "ruffling sounds." Learn to tune out this static by practicing at home under less-than-perfect testing conditions. In other words, don't close your bedroom door, but let the sounds of your home invade your "quiet" testing conditions: the dog barking, the bird squawking, the shower running, the television humming, the kitchen fan whizzing. With practice, you will gradually learn to tune out this influx of white noise, the static, and to concentrate even under nonideal circumstances.
- **Weather forecast:** It may be cold, it may be balmy. The temperature will vary depending on when the heater or air conditioning finally kicks in, or depending on whether or not someone decides to open the windows. So, to prepare for comfort, wear layers and bring a zip-down sweatshirt.
- **Fewer tricks, traps, and decoys:** Many consider the ACT to have fewer tricks or "false positives" than the SAT has. With this in mind, follow this process: First eliminate answer options that you confidently feel are incorrect. Next, trust your logic to select the best answer from the choices remaining. More often than on the SAT, ACT questions can be answered on a direct level rather than on an inference level.

- **Never omit!** This is an ACT golden rule. Since there is no penalty for guessing (to be construed as "educated guessing with your thinking cap on") *never* leave an answer blank on your answer document. In other words, be sure to fill in each and every oval.

Chapter Summary

Congratulations! Kudos! Now that you have read through this chapter, you will be a class ACT on test day. You have learned about several options for preparation for the ACT. You can try one or more of these Advanced Prep Plans and see which is most effective for your particular learning style and weekly schedule. Now you know the ins and outs of the ACT. You are in-the-know about general ACT testing tips, such as these two important ones: *Never omit!* And *No points lost for incorrect answers!*

When you show up to take the ACT, you will have pep in your step. You will be prepared to do your personal best because you know exactly what to bring to the test center. Your backpack or tote bag will be packed and set to go with everything you will need to register at the test center and take the ACT with calm and confidence. You will not forget a thing because you have your checklist on which to rely. On the flipside but equally important, you are now well versed about what *not* to bring to the testing location.

Reading through this chapter has also given you a twofold reality check: You know details about what to expect at the test center and key information about what to expect during the test itself. Refer to this chapter and its checklist whenever you wish to reacquaint yourself with the realistic basics of taking the ACT exam.

English Test

3

- English Skills in Closer Focus
- **ACT** English Principles
  - **A** **A**uthor's Style
    Accuracy in Grammar, Usage, and Sentence Formation
  - **C** **C**onciseness
    Coherence, Unity, and Focus
    Commas, **C**olons, Semi**C**olons, and Other Punctuation
  - **T** **T**echnique: Strategy and Organization
    Tone Used by the Author
- No Sweat Points: Things You Won't Be Tested On
- A Note About Vocabulary and Spelling
- Quick Drills
- Making Sense of the Double-Column Format
- The *Ouch!* Factor
- Test-Taking Tips
- Practice Mini-Passage

ENGLISH SKILLS IN CLOSER FOCUS

You wear many hats as you work on the ACT English Test: grammarian, proofreader, English teacher, test taker, reviser, editor, and attentive reader.

One Test, Three Scores! You earn three scores for the English Test: a total score and two subscores (see the table on page 88).

There are a multitude of errors that you will need to detect and correct on the English Test. Good news: You do not need to *name* these errors like a die-hard grammarian! Just spot and fix them.

As you work through the 75 questions of the ACT English Test, concentrate on the key **ACT Principles**, which are presented in detail in this chapter.

This chapter uses **ACT** as an **acronym** and as an **organizational tool** to present the main English principles that are tested on the exam. First, the letter **A** addresses aspects of English composition, such as **A**uthor's style and **A**ccuracy as it pertains to the multifarious rules of grammar, usage, and sentence formation. Second, the letter **C** addresses the important elements of **C**onciseness and **C**oherence, which is another term for the unity or focus that a paragraph or passage maintains. **C** also delineates the various usages of **C**ommas, **C**olons, and semi**C**olons, as well as other important marks of punctuation. Third and last, the letter **T** presents instructional material pertaining to the author's stylistic devices of **T**echnique and **T**one. This acronym is not one that the test maker has devised. Again, it is used to present the English grammar material in an original and organized fashion. You can memorize the meaning of the acronym, but it is not essential that you do. What is far more important is that you understand these aspects of standard, written English, and how to accurately answer such questions that appear on the exam.

Total Test Score	Based on all 75 questions	Includes both Skills Sets listed below
Usage/Mechanics Subscore	Based on 40 questions	Skills Included: **punctuation** (how punctuation like semicolons, colons, commas, hyphens, etc., affect meaning); **grammar and usage** (verb tense, pronoun case, idiom, subject–verb agreement, etc.); **sentence structure** (sound sentence formation without fragments, run-ons, and comma splices; placement of modifying phrases and clauses; arrangement of subordinate and independent clauses)
Rhetorical Skills Subscore	Based on 35 questions	Skills included: **author's writing strategy** (topic development, revising and editing decisions, relevancy or lack of); **organization** (overall organization plan used to develop passage; use of introductory, transitional, and closing sentences); **author's style** (diction and imagery, consistency of style and tone, lack of ambiguity, verbosity versus economy of language, and redundancy)

ACT ENGLISH PRINCIPLES: PRESENTED AS AN ORIGINAL ACRONYM

A

Author's Style
Accuracy in Grammar, Usage, and Sentence Formation

C

Conciseness
Coherence, Unity, and Focus
Commas, **C**olons, Semi**C**olons, and Other Punctuation

T

Technique: Strategy and Organization
Tone Used by the Author

ACT ENGLISH PRINCIPLES: PRESENTED IN GREATER DETAIL

A

Author's Style

Fashion style is all about the look: elegant or trendy, classy or gaudy, sporty or dressy, too much or too little. Fashion style is about the feel of various colors, fabrics, and cuts. Writing style is a blend of many facets. It's defined by the collective feel of the words, the phrases, and the author's references and how they contribute to an overall effect.

Style can also be thought of in terms of how easily the piece is to "get into." Think of it this way: For the majority of readers, would you say that a particular passage—regardless of whether it's natural science, social science, humanities, or fiction—is accessible and easy to slice, like a piece of banana-cream pie? Or, is reading the passage like trying to saw a chunk off a block of granite? If the passage is like pie, then the style is *straightforward* and *comprehensible*. If the passage is like granite, then the style could be called *obscure*, *opaque*, or even *impenetrable*.

To pick up on author's style, ask yourself questions like: Is this author *wordy* and *redundant*, or is this author *economical*, using just the right amount of words? Does the author's writing have or lack *clarity*—in other words, is the meaning clear and *straightforward*, or murky and *ambiguous*?

To further investigate the author's writing style, you can ask yourself these additional questions: Does this author use *word forms* that make sense or is the author's *diction* (choice of words) rusty, confusing words like affect/effect, insinuate/intimate, indefinite/indecisive, or delude/denude? Does the author's writing style seem *consistent*, or is it all over the place and disjointed, making you wonder if the author has a multiple personality?

More questions that can help you detect particular categories of the author's style include:

- Is the author's style *erudite* (scholarly, learned), alluding to great works of literature, philosophers, and groundbreaking scientific discoveries?
- Is the author's style *pedantic*, exhibiting unimaginative teaching instruction about something, or is the author light years removed from a lecturing tone?
- Is the author's style *florid* or *ornate*, writing with lavish descriptions, evoking colorful imagery, and including numerous and intricate metaphors and similes?

Narrative point of view comprises another aspect of the author's style. Is the author writing in the first-person, using personal pronouns like *I, me, we,* and *us*? Is the author writing in the less-often-used second-person, addressing the reader as he uses the pronoun *you*? Or, is writing in the popular third-person narrative perspective, using pronouns like *he, she,* and *they*? To further define narrative point of view as an important element of style, consider whether the author is *omniscient*, that is, seeming to know the inner workings and contents of the characters' minds and hearts.

Accuracy in Grammar, Usage, and Sentence Formation

Good writers don't just express it well, they write it soundly. Their sentences flow seamlessly and they accurately uphold the conventions of standard, written English. As you keep your eyes peeled for *accuracy*, keep in mind these *golden grammarian rules*:

SUBJECTS AND VERBS SHOULD AGREE Words and phrases that may come in between—or interrupt—the subject/verb pair do not matter. Interrupting language may include prepositional phrases, appositives, subordinating clauses, or modifiers. No matter what interlopes between the subject and the verb, they still must agree (go together).

Sometimes the subject and verb are flip-flopped or in inverted order. Even in this case, when the verb precedes the subject, they still must agree. In the examples that follow, the subjects and verbs are in italics:

- (subject–verb lacking agreement) The potted red *geraniums* that line the driveway *blooms* all summer long.
- (subject–verb in agreement) The potted red *geraniums* that line the driveway *bloom* all summer long.

GRAMMAR NOTE: This subject–verb pair is interrupted by the subordinating clause *that line the driveway*. This clause functions as an adjective because it modifies the plural noun *geraniums*.

- (subject–verb lacking agreement/interrupting prepositional phrase) The *basket* of dried fruits, nuts, and carob chips *were* passed around the patio table several times because all of the guests relished this sweet and crunchy snack.

- (subject–verb in agreement/interrupting prepositional phrase) The *basket* of dried fruits, nuts, and carob chips *was* passed around the patio table several times because all of the guests relished this sweet and crunchy snack.

GRAMMAR NOTE: *of dried fruits, nuts, and carob chips* is an adjectival prepositional phrase that modifies the noun *basket*.

- (subject–verb lacking agreement/inverted order) Around the bases of the baseball diamond *runs* (action verb) the *soccer players* (plural subject), conditioned athletes whose speed and agility attest to their training.
- (subject–verb in agreement/inverted order) Around the bases of the baseball diamond *run* (action verb) the *soccer players* (plural subject), conditioned athletes whose speed and agility attest to their training.

GRAMMAR NOTE: These sentences start off with two consecutive prepositional phrases, *Around the bases of the baseball diamond.*

PRONOUNS SHOULD AGREE IN GENDER AND NUMBER WITH THEIR ANTECEDENTS (THE WORDS THEY REFER BACK TO): Pronouns and antecedents are in italics.

- (pronoun–antecedent lacking agreement) At the break of dawn the *newscasters* review *her* script for the morning broadcast.
- (pronoun–antecedent in agreement) At the break of dawn the *newscasters* review *their* script*s* for the morning broadcast.

GRAMMAR NOTE: Even though *their* is a possessive pronoun, it still must agree in number (plural to match with *newscasters*) with its antecedent. Notice how, in the corrected version, script becomes script*s* so that we have plural consistency throughout the sentence.

- (pronoun–antecedent lacking agreement) Justin, Tyler, and Christian eat scrambled eggs or French toast in the morning, for not *one* will start off *their* morning meal with a bowl of steel-cut oats topped with berries.
- (pronoun–antecedent in agreement) Justin, Tyler, and Christian eat scrambled eggs or French toast in the morning, for not *one* will start off *his* morning meal with a bowl of steel-cut oats topped with berries.

GRAMMAR NOTE: Even though this compound sentence starts off with a plural subject (Justin, Tyler, and Christian), after the comma–conjunction (*, for*) the subject becomes singular (*one*) and so the possessive pronoun *his* must also be singular.

- (pronoun–antecedent lacking agreement) The pop *singers*, who have trained extensively in classical opera, have taken *its* place on the central platform.
- (pronoun–antecedent in agreement) The pop *singers*, who have trained extensively in classical opera, have taken *their* place*s* on the central platform.

GRAMMAR NOTE: Even though the singular noun *opera* appears before the possessive pronoun, the pronoun must agree with its plural antecedent, *singers.* Notice how place changes to place*s* to maintain plural consistency within this sentence.

POSSESSIVE PRONOUNS SHOULD BE USED BEFORE GERUNDS Just as it is correct to say "My sense of fun delights her," so it is also correct to say "My knowing how to fix things around the house delights her." (*My knowing* illustrates a possessive pronoun correctly preceding a gerund.)

- (incorrect pronoun usage) *Us* letting the dog lounge on the family room couch is a decision we regret.
- (correct pronoun usage) *Our* letting the dog lounge on the family room couch is a decision we regret.

GRAMMAR NOTE: "Us" is a group of people and not a decision that is regrettable. "Our letting . . . couch" is the regrettable decision.

- (incorrect pronoun usage) *Him* biting the sleeves of his T-shirts is a habit that Mother could hardly bear.
- (correct pronoun usage) *His* biting the sleeves of his T-shirts is a habit that Mother could hardly bear.

GRAMMAR NOTE: It's not that Mom couldn't stand "him," but that Mom couldn't bear "his biting" his T-shirt sleeves.

- (incorrect pronoun usage) *She* having a multitude of after-school commitments has put a strain on her and her family.
- (correct pronoun usage) *Her* having a multitude of after-school commitments has put a strain on her and her family.

GRAMMAR NOTE: It's not that the girl herself ("She") puts a strain on her family, but that "Her having" so many commitments is a heavy load for the family to carry.

PRONOUNS SHOULD BE IN THE CORRECT CASE—OBJECTIVE OR SUBJECTIVE English teachers like to use mysterious terms like "subjective case pronouns," "objective case pronouns," "demonstrative case pronouns," and even "nominative case pronouns." Such terminology sounds more like a detective story and less like a grammar lesson. To demystify the terms "objective case" and "subjective case" (which are the ones most tested on the ACT), simply remember that *subjective* case pronouns are those that can function as subjects. So, by default, if a pronoun *cannot* function as a subject, then it must be an objective pronoun. You can think of objective pronouns as pronouns that receive the action of the verb.

Do these simple tests to see if a particular pronoun can function as a subject:

_____ eat(s) a meatball hero.

or _____ run(s) around the track ten times!

If the pronoun makes sense on the lines above, then it can function as the subject of the sentence and is in the subjective case. It's as simple as that. For those of you who like visual representations like tables and charts, the following chart splits up the two types of pronouns.

Subjective Case Pronouns	Objective Case Pronouns
I You She, He It We Who They	Me You Her, Him It Us Whom Them

Subjective Case Pronouns

1. **I** was delighted to take a walk along the beach boardwalk with my boyfriend.

2. **You** are one of the most unusual characters **I** have ever hung out with.

   Are **you** the team players for the Vipers?

3. **He** cordially returned Caroline's phone call, even though **he** was not interested in pursuing a relationship with her.

   When **she** began dating him, **she** wasn't quite sure if he was the one for her.

4. "**It** is on the kitchen table, just where **you** left **it**," Mom replied.

5. **We** will meet at The Hideaway for lunch at 11:30 tomorrow morning.

6. **Who** is at the front door?

7. After fifteen years of loving marriage, **they** enthusiastically renewed their wedding vows at their hometown church.

Objective Case Pronouns

An **objective personal pronoun** means that the pronoun is acting as an *object* of a *verb*, *compound verb*, *preposition*, or *infinitive phrase*.

In the sentences below, the **boldfaced** words function as objective case personal pronouns:

Sandy stole Lela's heart, so she felt joyfully compelled to marry **him**.

Above, the objective personal pronoun "him" is the object of the preposition "to."

After skimming the flyer, Nina tossed **it** into the trash can.

As used above, the pronoun "it" is the direct object of the verb "tossed."

The eager apprentice walked up to the master silversmith, stared him in the eye, and confidently replied, "I will consider your offer and contact **you** by the end of the month."

In the sentence above, the pronoun "you" is the direct object of the action verb "contact."

Regina and Teresa will join **us** at the café in Sea Cliff that just opened.

Above, the objective personal pronoun "us" is the direct object of the compound verb "will join."

Refer your client's friend to **me**.

Above, the objective personal pronoun "me" is the object of the preposition "to."

I don't know if my colleague has the time to work with **you** at this juncture.

Above, the objective personal pronoun "you" is the object of the preposition "with."

Linda was happy to see **her** at the bus stop.

Above, the personal pronoun "her" is *not* functioning as a subject, so it must be in the objective form.

This gift is for **whom**?

Consider these examples:

- (incorrect pronoun case) Gina and *him* are the school's most popular couple.
- (correct pronoun case) Gina and *he* are the school's most popular couple.

GRAMMAR NOTE: Subjective pronouns (like *he*) precede the main verb of the sentence.

- (incorrect pronoun case) Stop telling Henrietta and *I* what to do with our free time!
- (correct pronoun case) Stop telling Henrietta and *me* what to do with our free time!

GRAMMAR NOTE: The objective pronoun *me* receives the action of the verb *telling*. In this sentence, the subject is the invisible "you." Think of "you" as the one being addressed by this command.

No Sweat Points

Positive Pronoun News! You will not be asked to label a pronoun (heaven forbid!) as one of these following types: personal-possessive, interrogative, demonstrative, nominative, or relative. In addition, you will not be asked to define the antecedents of pronouns, although it is always helpful to understand what person, thing, place, or concept a pronoun is referring to so that you are able to clearly comprehend what you are reading.

SENTENCES SHOULD BE WRITTEN IN PARALLEL FORM Parallel form (also called parallelism) is a grammatical term. However, you can think of parallelism as *balancing* parts of a sentence so that they are expressed in the same way. This skill will not only help you make decisions about how portions of text are worded on the ACT English Test, but a sense of parallelism will also help you to write in a logical, grammatically sound way. Consider the examples below as you gain the feeling for what makes a sentence parallel:

- (not parallel) Reading, cooking, and interior decor are three of Barbara's favorite pastimes.
- (parallel) Reading, cooking, and interior decorating are three of Barbara's favorite pastimes.

Did you pick up on the faulty parallelism in the first sentence? To be parallel or balanced, every member of the comma series within the sentence must be expressed with an *–ing* ending.

- (not parallel) The homeowners planted two weeping flowering cherries to flank their front door and two thundercloud plum trees, which flank the backyard entranceway.
- (parallel) The homeowners planted two weeping flowering cherries to flank their front door and two thundercloud plum trees to flank their backyard entranceway.

Did you sense the lack of parallelism in the first sentence? If not, try the next few examples. With practice, you will develop a mindset for parallel form and become more sensitive to sentences that lack it.

- (not parallel) While relaxing on the patio lounge chairs, the family spotted two hawks circling above, a chipmunk resting in the shade, and they noticed two birds who were pulling at a piece of string.
- (parallel) While relaxing on the patio lounge chairs, the family spotted two hawks circling above, a chipmunk resting in the shade, and two birds pulling at a piece of string.

Can you detect the difference in balance between the two sentences above? The second sentence is parallel because each of the three members of the comma series contains an animal(s)/an *-ing* verb/some elaboration in the form of an adverb (*above*) or a prepositional phrase (*in the shade*), or two prepositional phrases in succession (*at a piece of string.*)

- (not parallel) Some highlights of their summer were hitting balls at the driving range with friends, hoops in the pool, and playing baseball at night under the City Stadium lights.
- (parallel) Some highlights of their summer were hitting balls at the driving range with friends, shooting hoops in the pool, and playing baseball at night under the City Stadium lights.

Did you pick up on the parallel form error in the first sentence? To be parallel, every member of the comma series within the sentence must be expressed as a gerund (*-ing* ending).

SENTENCES SHOULD BE SOUND—THEY SHOULD NOT BE RUN-ONS OR FRAGMENTS After the boys played wiffle ball in the side yard, they jumped in the pool and played basketball using a hoop that is mounted at the pool's edge. (sound sentence/a complex sentence because it contains a subordinate clause)

Note: Run-on sentences run rampant on the ACT English Test. Keep your grammarian eyes peeled for them! Run-ons are the messy, non-standard "sentences" that occur when two sentences collide without the proper punctuation between them. There are myriad ways to prevent and remedy run-ons. For this test, however, the rules are simple: Independent clauses must be divided by a semicolon (;) or by a comma followed by a conjunction, such as *, and* or *, so.* If the two independent clauses (simple sentences) are strung together with only a comma, then a run-on results (a comma splice). If the two independent clauses just flow one right into the next without any punctuation at all, then a run-on also results (a fused sentence). The examples that follow illustrate these two types of run-on sentences:

- (run-on/fused sentence) The boys played wiffle ball in the side yard next they jumped in the pool and played basketball using a hoop that is mounted at the pool's edge.
- (run-on/comma splice) The boys played wiffle ball in the side yard, next they jumped in the pool played basketball using a hoop that is mounted at the pool's edge.
- (fragment/incomplete sentence) The boys playing wiffle ball in the side yard next jumping in the pool playing basketball using a hoop that is mounted at the pool's edge.

An *-ing* ending or gerund forms of verbs cannot be used as the main verbs of a sentence, unless they are accompanied by helping verbs. If gerunds are used as the main verb, a sentence fragment results.

C

Conciseness

Short, sweet, and to the point is the essence of conciseness. This includes avoiding unnecessary redundancy and repetition. Conciseness matters when you write papers for school, it matters when you deliver a timed speech, and it matters when you write newspaper headlines, leads, and captions. It matters a great deal on the SAT, and it matters as much on the ACT English Test. With practice, you will develop sensitivity to the feel of conciseness—also called *brevity, succinctness,* or *pithiness*—in order to spot the places where the language needs to be tightened up. As real-world practice that serves to also inform you about our world, read the leads of articles and headlines in the *New York Times,* the *Wall Street Journal,* and other well-written newspapers and periodicals. Headlines and article leads are typically pithy and, therefore, exemplify models of conciseness. Notice how the flabby parts have been excised from the sentences below:

- (wordy and flabby) The imaginary aquatic creature, whose made-up name is the Electric Skrab, makes his ocean habitat in the deep temperature ocean, which is where he lives.
- (flab crossed out) The imaginary aquatic creature, ~~whose made-up name is~~ the Electric Skrab, makes his ~~ocean~~ habitat in the deep temperature ocean, ~~which is where he lives~~.
- (concise) The imaginary aquatic creature, the Electric Skrab, makes his habitat in the deep temperature ocean.
- (wordy and flabby) In the early nineteenth century, 1809, is when Miss Penny Ross began to write in her diary, her first entry being made in that year.
- (flab crossed out) In ~~the early nineteenth century,~~ 1809, ~~is when~~ Miss Penny Ross began to write in her diary, ~~her first entry being made in that year~~.

- (concise) In 1809, Miss Penny Ross began to write in her diary.
- (wordy and flabby) In the summer months of June, July, and August, the Camara family uses their pool a great deal during day and night, all day long.
- (flab crossed out) In ~~the summer months of~~ June, July, and August, the Camara family uses their pool a great deal during day and night~~, all day long~~.
- (concise) In June, July, and August, the Camara family uses their pool a great deal during day and night.

Coherence, Unity, and Focus

Oddballs, black sheep, and sore thumbs—as you read through the English passages, be on alert for sentences and phrases that stick out like they just don't belong. These oddball sentences do not belong because they stray from the overarching tone or purpose of the essay, or because they stray from the topic sentence of a particular body paragraph. If you spot one of these sentences, chances are there will be a question that asks you something like, "Which sentence should be omitted to maintain coherence in the essay or in the specified paragraph?"

Unity and focus are other terms for coherence. You might find *unity* or *focus* substituting for the word *coherence* in the sample preceding question.

Commas, Colons, Semicolons, and Other Punctuation

COMMAS

Do not be comma phobic. Do not be comma happy! Sentences overloaded with commas are awkward and choppy to read. Some writers don't use commas enough; others overuse them. Let's go over some basic rules so you do not have to guess about when to use a comma.

☑ Use commas to set off items in a list.

NASA provides information about earth science projects relating to air, Earth's crust, tropical rainfall, and thunderstorms.

One version of Ezekiel bread blends four whole grains and four beans that may include the following: lentils, hulled millet, organic spelt, pinto beans, and red kidney beans.

One popular and convenient store in Amagansett sells, rents, and repairs bicycles, kayaks, surfboards, boogie boards, and skateboards.

☑ Use commas to separate the names of cities and states as well as days and years.

Michelle Licousi was born and raised in Poughkeepsie, New York, which is the home of Marist College.

Boston, Massachusetts, is a hopping college town, unlike the sleepy town of Vestal near Binghamton, New York.

On December 31, 1999, the world said goodbye to the momentous twentieth century and joyfully greeted the twenty-first century!

☑ Use commas to set off subordinating or dependent clauses.

Even though their nephew works in the Norwalk, Connecticut, branch of the chain store, Alex and Linda are given a twenty-five percent family discount at the store's Long Island, New York, location.

Although June wedding festivities will be held at the well-known Gurney's Inn in Montauk, most guests will be staying overnight at the Beachcomber Resort, which is located just a few minutes down the scenic and historic Old Montauk Highway.

Despite Mother's offering fruits and vegetables several times a day, the children infrequently would help themselves to these foods on their own volition.

☑ Use commas to introduce and set off quotes.

Mulling over John F. Kennedy's famous words, Dexter asked himself, "Should I think more about what my country can do for me, or should I think more about what *I* can do for my country?"

There is much depth and truth in Ralph Waldo Emerson's words, "Life consists in what a man is thinking of all day."

"Please transfer the clean clothes from the washer to the drier," Mom pleaded. "This way, the outfit you want to wear to the party tomorrow will be ready."

Note: Notice how the comma after *drier* is situated within the closed quotation mark.

☑ Use commas to set off appositives (nouns, noun phrases, or noun clauses that follow nouns or pronouns and rename or describe them).

Jacques Cartier, a well-known French sailor and explorer, is given credit—by some historians—for settling the territory that is now modern-day Montreal, Canada.

An American painter who exhibited her work with the Impressionists and whose famous works include *Woman Reading in a Garden* and *Mother and Child*, Mary Cassatt studied art at the Pennsylvania Academy of Fine Arts in Philadelphia, traveled throughout Europe, and ultimately settled in Paris in 1874.

Sandro Botticelli, a Florentine early Renaissance painter who worked as a goldsmith's apprentice, created the spirited *Birth of Venus* and *Primavera*.

☑ Use commas after addressing a person by name.

Justin, did you like our social studies unit on World Explorers, or did you prefer our more recent unit on Colonial America?

Ms. Fine, what would you say is the single most important administrative strength that you could offer this school district?

How many times have I asked you, Ernest, to please lower the volume on the television?

✔ Use commas to set off interrupting words or phrases.

If gas prices climb, heaven forbid, to $6.00 per gallon, taking leisure rides to the beach or taking a ride for ice cream after dinner will become rare treats.

She drove to the dry cleaners, begrudgingly, just to pick up one shirt that her boyfriend wanted to wear that night.

I tried several times, like you suggested, to download the photos from the digital camera to the computer program on the desktop, but I just couldn't get it to work.

✔ Use commas after introductory prepositional phrases and after other types of introductory subordinating phrases and clauses (groups of words that cannot stand alone).

In the middle of the night, she awoke to the soft yet persistent cries of her two-month-old son.

During the fifteen-minute intermission, the couple shared a large buttered popcorn and a diet soda.

Extending 775 miles from Mexicali in the north to Cabo San Lucas in the south, the Baja California peninsula separates the Pacific Ocean from the Sea of Cortez.

✔ Use commas to separate adjectives that modify the same noun.

Grandma's traditional taralle cookies contain anise, vanilla, and lemon flavors of extract.

The Labrador retriever and poodle mixed breed has a long, tight, curled tail.

Tony wiped down his large, round, stainless steel, wood-burning stove.

✔ Use commas along with conjunctions (connector words) to separate independent clauses when forming a compound sentence.

Many living creatures have the ability to camouflage themselves in order to elude predators, *and* many of them also have two or more means of self-defense.

Saltwater systems are recommended for backyard pools because they are gentler on swimmers, *and* they offer superior algae control without the use of harsh chemicals.

The flesh of a mango is smooth, juicy, and moist, *yet* stringy fibers spread out from the large kidney-shaped seed.

COLONS (:)

☑ Use colons to introduce a list.

At Wild Fig Market I bought: asparagus, red bell peppers, vine ripe tomatoes, and three mangos.

Which is your favorite flavor of gelato (Italian ice cream): nocciola, panna, straraciella, or ciocolatta?

If money were no object, which of the following sports cars would you most desire: Lamborghini, Maserati, or Ferrari?

☑ Use colons to separate independent clauses and to provide emphasis.

His reason for moving to Miami was straightforward: this Florida city quickly became his favorite vacation spot.

Halloween is her favorite annual celebration: the best part of this holiday is the unlimited supply of chocolates, candy novelties, and other sugary treats.

☑ Use colons to introduce a clarification or an explanation.

Let me clarify for you what I mean by "living thing": any supposed plant or animal that exhibits *all* of the essential characteristics of life.

When the beautician says natural-looking fingernails, this is what she means: nails that are clean, trim, uniformly-shaped and painted in a pale pink, sheer, or off-white shade of nail lacquer.

☑ Use colons to introduce quotations.

He always believed in the age-old saying: "To give is better than to receive."

Growing up, my mother would tell me over and again: "It's nice to be nice."

SEMICOLONS (;)

☑ Use semicolons to separate independent clauses (groups of words that contain a subject and verb and can stand alone as complete sentences).

I prefer dark chocolate with a very high cocoa content; she prefers milk chocolate.

The Magic Kingdom is a pristine, fairytale paradise; Animal Kingdom is an exotic, peaceful journey through nature.

One of the older brother's favorite fiction books is the convoluted murder mystery, *The Westing Game*; one of the younger brother's favorite books is *The Wide Window*, from Lemony Snicket's *A Series of Unfortunate Events*.

☑ Use semicolons to separate items in a list, in which each "item" already contains a comma; this is sometimes referred to as a semicolon being used as a "super comma."

They have lived in Clearwater, Florida; Weston, Connecticut; and Lancaster, Pennsylvania.

As of this moment in time, the most significant days of their lives include June 28, 1992; January 23, 1995; and March 7, 1997.

Your upcoming dental appointments are April 28, 5:30 P.M.; May 10, 4:00 P.M.; and June 18, 10:00 A.M.

OTHER PUNCTUATION

☑ Use apostrophes (') to show ownership or possession.

The examples below show the addition of an 's. This convention is followed even if the singular form of the word ends in –s, as in Jansons, which is the name of the family that appears in the third example below.

No one could believe that Mia's radio was stolen at the beach.

Those seven movies are Donna's DVDs; I borrowed them from her last weekend.

The Jansons's newly-renovated home turned out simply beautiful.

☑ Use an apostrophe only (') at the end of plural nouns that already end in –s:

The neighbors' landscapers added rich, black mulch to the bases of trees and to the flowerbeds.

Janice couldn't decide which of her three girlfriends' sleepover parties she should attend.

The two poodles' favorite outing was a trip to the dog run at Christopher Morley Park.

☑ Use an apostrophe (') and –s ('s) at the end of compound or hyphenated words, again to show ownership or possession.

Their brother-in-law's newsmagazine column was very touching.

A newcomer to the summer theater stage, this diamond-in-the-rough's star quality and potential amazed everyone in her debut performances in *Oklahoma* and *Godspell.*

They greatly appreciated the father-in-law's gift of sanding and painting the wrought iron railing that surrounds their bluestone patio.

☑ Use an apostrophe (') and –s ('s) at the end of the last noun to show joint possession, at the end of each noun to show separate possession.

Located just a few blocks from the ocean shore, Mark and Gina's beach home gives them and their family a great deal of pleasure.

Located just a few blocks from the ocean shore, Mark's and Gina's beach homes give them and their families a great deal of pleasure.

Tina, Sam, and Joe's summer plans include a trip to Paris and leisurely weeks of lounging along the Mediterranean shoreline.

Tina's, Sam's, and Joe's summer plans include trips to Paris, Rome, and Athens, and leisurely weeks of lounging along the Mediterranean shoreline.

Mom and Dad's recipe for success includes rising early, working hard, and persevering courageously through even the most challenging of times.

✔ Use dashes (—) to separate words that are situated in the middle of a sentence; when using dashes, no space should come between the words that appear right before and right after the dash.

Note: As you most likely recall, commas also can be used to set off words and phrases that appear in the middle of a sentence. Setting off the phrase with dashes, however, gives more emphasis to the intervening words. Furthermore, you can even set off full sentences with dashes. Commas cannot do this! Use dashes sparingly; otherwise, they could lose their special luster.

Laura Jean—a brilliant and talented attorney—earned her law degree with honors from Harvard Law School.

Jeannette's prescription for optimum health—eating raw foods, walking for an hour every day, and drinking green tea—seems to be working for her because she epitomizes (represents) vigor and vitality.

Big Logan Mayer—his classmates refer to him as the schoolyard bully—is actually an insecure loner who wishes he had more friends.

The lack of pleasure reading among today's grade school children—English Department Chair Evelyn Benz calls the situation a literary travesty—is perhaps a consequence of too much time spent playing video games and surfing the Net.

Note: Using dashes as shown in the two prior sentences allows one sentence to serve double duty. You actually write a "nested" sentence construction or a sentence within a sentence. Merging sentences in this way stresses the relationship between the ideas and focuses your attention on the sentence within the dashes.

✔ Use dashes (—) to add words to the end of a sentence; you can do this when there is a logical and clear "break" in the flow of the sentence.

Typically, children have taste buds that cry out for sweets—sometimes, though, there are children who prefer apples to donuts, yogurt to ice cream, and carrots to lollipops!

The student–athlete will be unable to attain each and every scholarship for which he has applied—unless, of course, the Midas touch is his!

All of the boys in the fourth-grade class prefer spooky novels and mysteries—except Jake, who consistently chooses biographies over thrillers and who-done-its.

✔ Use hyphens (-), which are shorter than dashes, to connect numbers and words (regardless of whether the numbers are written out or in numeral form), as in *thirty-eight-year-old man* or *320-foot tail of the kite*.

The seven-foot-tall man could barely pass through the old stone archway that led into the cathedral.

The sunbathers who were reading and lounging leisurely at the beach were shocked to witness the 50-foot wave.

The middle-aged man became so ornery that he was acting like a two-year-old.

☑ Use hyphens (-) to spell the names of *great-* relatives, as in *great-great-grandfather* or *great-Uncle Emil* and in-laws: *brother-in-law, mother-in-law.*

His great-uncle, Donald Prescott, used to live in Brazil for six months out of the year.

Great-aunts and great-uncles contribute to the richness of extended family.

The mother-in-law and her daughter-in-law get along great since they are more alike than different in a multitude of ways.

☑ Use hyphens (-) when forming a compound word that starts with the prefix *self-*, as in *self-directed* and *self-awareness.*

To boost a child's self-esteem, tell him often how proud you are of his actions and words.

Self-loathing is the extreme antithesis to self-adoring.

Michaela is so pitifully self-possessed that her daily agenda continues to focus around her wants, needs, and inclinations.

☑ Use hyphens (-) to form combination words that include a prepositional phrase, such as *Jack-of-all-trades, bundle-of-energy,* and *stick-in-the-mud.*

When you want something done, call Alex; he is truly a Johnny-on-the-spot.

Lift your chin off the floor; you look as if you're down-in-the-dumps!

When it comes to loyal friends who would walk over hot coals for you, Janine is truly one-in-a-million.

☑ Use hyphens (-) to spell out fractions, such as *two-thirds majority* and *one-sixth of the pie.*

Drake wanted to eat the entire pizza pie, but Mother would only allow him a two-eighths portion.

Although she was on the move all day, she didn't even accomplish three-fifths of what she intended to get done.

She missed the Presidential Academic Award because her grade point average lagged by a one-tenth percentage point!

T

Technique: Strategy and Organization

As you read, ask yourself, "*How* is this author developing his essay or narrative?" Is he trying to persuade readers to believe or support a certain position or perspective?

Is he using dates and presenting the information in *chronological* order? (Be aware that sometimes authors may present their material in *reverse-chronological* order.)

Is she discussing his past and, therefore, being *reflective*? Is he opening with a thesis and then supporting his position with examples?

Is she devoting one main *example* or *type* to each paragraph in an effort to steadily build an argument?

Is he composing the passage by describing one particular viewpoint and then offering a counterviewpoint?

Is he describing a setting followed by his experiences associated with that setting?

Tone Used by the Author

Since questions about author's tone, mood, or attitude are popular, make it a habit to try to pick up on the author's writing style or tone as you read. This way, when a question pops up that relates to tone, you'll be well prepared. Since tone is not something that is directly stated, determining tone can be challenging. Instead, you must infer the tone based on various elements such as diction (author's choice of words) and phrasing. You may also think of tone as the author's "persona," the personality that he would most likely project if he were delivering the text in a public forum.

- Is the tone *nostalgic*—longing for the past?
- Is the tone *expository*—describing or explaining in detail?
- Is the tone *censorious*—critical?
- Is the tone *personal-anecdotal*—based on a vignette (sometimes comical) from the author's life?
- Is the tone *indignant*—reflecting the author's anger toward the subject and/or his audience?
- Is the tone *casual*—the author sprinkles some conversational expressions, even slang, into the essay?

TECHNIQUES FOR TUNING INTO TONE

Use your imagination and inner sense as you employ these creative techniques that can greatly help you to pick up on the author's overall tone.

Imagine yourself "listening" to the author's voice as he reads his piece of writing to you. How would you define the quality of his voice? What might the pauses in between his words and sentences tell you? What might be revealed by his voice inflection and cadence (rhythm)? Which words and phrases does he emphasize or understate as he speaks?

Imagine yourself "watching" the author as he delivers his piece. What do his bodily movements look like? His gestures? How would you characterize his facial expressions? Do you picture his eye contact as being steady, piercing, shifty, or erratic?

Your insights and conclusions about tone will help you later when answering questions; keep your eyes and ears peeled for tone, and you'll be ahead of your game. On the ACT, some tone questions are based on specific words, phrases, and sentences that are underlined in the passage. Others are based on a longer section of the passage or on the reading selection as a whole. Once you have selected your answer, reread the sentence (keeping in mind its larger context within the passage) to ensure that your selected answer is the best version offered.

VOCABULARY OF TONE

Aloof—detached

Apologetic—saying sorry; admitting fault

Assertive—strongly stating

Cautious—hesitant

Confrontational—argumentative

Contrite—remorseful

Cynical—seeing worst in people

Defensive—protecting your point of view

Derisive—ridiculing

Empathetic—feeling for others

Emphatic—stressing your points

Entreaty—begging, pleading

Explanatory—explaining

Inquisitive—asking questions

Nostalgic—remembering the past

Penitent—remorseful

Reflective—remembering the past

Sardonic—sarcastic

Scathing—harsh

Scholarly—intellectual, cerebral

Sensationalistic—exaggerating emotions

Skeptical—doubtful

Tentative—hesitant

Understated—mildly suggested; unstressed

Wry—cynical in a comical manner

VOCABULARY OF MOOD

Amusement—humorous

Bemusement—puzzlement

Detachment—lack of concern

Disdain—scorn

Disparagement—belittlement

Indignation—anger

Ironic—unexpected

Mockery—poking fun at

Objective—based on fact; no opinion

Optimism—positive thinking

Pessimism—negative thinking

Smugness—feeling self-satisfied; complacent

ACT TRANSITION VOCABULARY

On the English Test of the ACT, several questions require students to determine which transition language would work best in a particular context. This transitional language might be a single word (*however, indeed, moreover*) or a phrase (*to these ends, for instance, in other words*). To answer this question type accurately, students need to read and understand the reasoning of the sentence in which the underscored part appears, as well as both prior and post sentences for fuller context.

What follows is a complete listing of the transition words and phrases found in the answer choices of the three practice tests in *The Official ACT Prep Guide 2017*. Some words (*however* and *instead*, for example) may appear on more than one test; this listing gives a sense of the frequency with which the words appear on the English Test questions. All transitions in boldface are accompanied by examples.

> **TRANSITION TIP**
>
> When you read the sentence in which the transition question appears, mentally vocalize "blank" for the transition word or phrase in lieu of the answer choices (*however, indeed, thus, likewise, for example*) so that your thinking does not get skewed.

TEST 1

However—although, in spite of that, on the other hand

For instance—for example, taken as an example

Baja California Sur is home to some of the most picturesque settings and dining experiences; **for instance**, Sunset Mona Lisa boasts extraordinary Mediterranean fare and stunning water views.

Cabo Adventures offers fun and adventurous excursions to their guests; **for instance**, guests can take camel riding tours, go zip-lining, or take desert tours on all-terrain vehicles.

As always—as ever, as expected, once again

By now—up until this time, at this time

Instead—on the other hand, contrary to the aforementioned

On the other hand—instead, looking at something from another perspective

Meanwhile—at the same time

At Flora Farms, some guests strolled the tranquil grounds and lingered by the pool; **meanwhile**, others visited the goats, roosters, and puppies that lived on the property of this farm-to-table dining establishment.

At John F. Kennedy Airport travelers sat on the plane, which was being inspected for an apparent start valve malfunction in the right engine; **meanwhile**, passengers were offered water, pretzel rods, and almonds while they waited for the mechanics to complete the engine repair.

In other words—to explain in a different manner, another way of consideration

When it comes to sports and eating, Luke exhibits ambidexterity; **in other words**, he shoots a soccer ball with his right foot and cuts steak with his left hand.

Mia's daily to-do list takes on a life of its own; **in other words**, tasks and responsibilities inevitably develop even when she doesn't see them coming or have them written down.

Therefore—as a result, consequently, thus

Instead—on the other hand, in place of what was mentioned before

TEST 2

However—although, in spite of that, on the other hand

For example—taken as a specific illustration, for instance, specifically

One time—on this particular occasion, once

Instead—on the other hand, in place of what was mentioned before

Specifically—provided as a specific illustration or example of something more general that was previously stated or discussed, precisely

Ultimately—in the end, finally

Instead—on the other hand, in place of what was mentioned prior

Thus—consequently, for example

Beatrice sticks to a regimented study schedule and, **thus**, she rarely has to cram for an exam.

Natural science is fascinating for James; **thus**, he enjoys reading about animals, geology, and earthquakes.

Coincidentally—resulting from chance, unexpectedly, unpredictably

Similarly—likewise, in the same fashion, in line with aforementioned

The weather in Cabo San Lucas is dry and pleasant: **similarly**, the climate in San Jose, California, is enjoyable and conducive to spending time outdoors.

Hayden is a fitness enthusiast; **similarly**, Dustin is an avid yogi.

Besides—as well, in addition to, what's more, more to the point

By all means—certainly, at any cost, without fail

Hilde is determined to eat nutrition-packed salads more regularly; **by all means**, a salad called "Thrive" is an ideal choice, for this popular menu item contains lentils, cilantro, peppers, green apple, couscous, and Romaine lettuce.

Every year, Gwen strives to fulfill an item on her bucket list; **by all means**, a full body aromatherapy massage in a tent at the beach allowed Gwen to cross-off an item on her wish list!

For example—provided as a specific illustration or instance

Gretta enjoys writing mystery stories; **for example**, last week she completed her fifth in a mystery series titled *Who Has the Golden Key?*

During their trans-Atlantic flight, the frequent flyers enjoyed games on the touch screen above their food tray; **for example**, they played bingo, French solitaire, and backgammon.

In contrast—contrary to, on the other hand, with regard to the opposite

Jacob has a short fuse; **in contrast**, Nikko is level-headed and calm in nature.

Yolanda is long-winded in speech but her sister, **in contrast**, is terse, a young lady of few words.

Thereafter—afterwards, then, subsequently

Hilde used to keep her papers in a disorganized fashion until one day she spent hours and hours looking for certain documents; **thereafter**, she devised a folder system and stuck to it religiously.

Once Duncan had tried his first rainbow sushi roll, he **thereafter** made a point to have sushi once a week.

TEST 3

For example—provided as a specific illustration or instance

Pasquale possesses some of the most admirable of human traits; **for example**, he is honest, kind, and gentle.

Julianna enjoys a cold, slushy-like smoothie; **for example**, one of her favorites is vanilla protein blended with chunks of fresh pineapple and mango.

On the other hand—in contrast, to illustrate an opposite point or point of view, contrarily

Swimming with whale sharks is relatively safe; **on the other hand**, swimming with regular sharks in the open seas is significantly risky.

Travel can be exhilarating, cultural, and mind-opening; **on the other hand**, it can be exhausting.

Just in case—in the event that something does or does not occur

Thus—therefore, as a result, consequently, hence, accordingly

Instead—on the other hand, in place of what was mentioned prior

Furthermore—also, additionally, moreover, to explain or elaborate

However—although, in spite of that, on the other hand

Also—moreover, additionally, plus

Keanna has a passion for Chinese language and culture; she has **also** visited the country three times over the past several years.

Although Heidi is a boisterous comedian, she is **also** a sober conversationalist when it comes to global social issues.

Furthermore—also, additionally, moreover, to explain or elaborate

The party of twelve is looking forward to their dinner at Flora Farms in Baja California Sur this January; **furthermore**, they are excited about their pre-dinner guided tour of Flora's beautiful farm and gardens.

Kim has declared an interdisciplinary major in Chinese studies and communications, as she intends to pursue international journalism as her career; **furthermore**, she may consider earning her Juris Doctor degree, as she also finds law to be an intriguing field.

Therefore—as a result, consequently, thus

Likewise—similarly, also, equally, in a similar fashion, by the same token

Sofia feels blessed with close family ties; **likewise**, she feels grateful for her long-lasting friendships.

Henry enjoys the dynamics and intricacies of international law; **likewise**, he enjoys fine dining and travel.

No Sweat Points

THINGS YOU WON'T BE TESTED ON

☺ You will not be asked to *define*, in complete sentences, the various rules of grammar. You will not be asked to *name* the grammar rule, even though rules are given names in this prep guide, for example: parallel form; subject–verb agreement; standard, written English; idiom; and so on.

☺ You will not be asked about the meanings and subtleties found within the reading selections that comprise the English Test. There are no reading-between-the-lines and inference-level questions on the ACT English Test. Remember, this is a test about language, grammar, and standard usage—not critical reading.

☺ No worries—no hard-and-fast, direct grammar questions will be posed either. To make this clear, you will not be asked to answer daunting grammar and punctuation-type questions like the straight-up ones listed below. These questions could even make an English teacher's hair stand on end!

☒ Is a semicolon used exclusively to separate independent clauses?

☒ Must a subordinating clause always be set off by commas?

☒ Are all nonrestrictive clauses automatically set off from the rest of the sentence by commas?

☒ Describe and give an example of an arcane usage of the semicolon.

☒ Do prepositional phrases only come in two types: adverb phrase or adjective phrase?

☒ Should end marks always appear within quotation marks?

☒ Can an interrogative sentence express strong emotion?

☒ Could restrictive and nonrestrictive clauses both appear in a complex sentence?

Also—breathe a sigh of relief:

☺ You will not be asked to define a list of vocabulary words; there is no vocabulary matching, fill-in-the-blank questions, or defining of word roots and prefixes either . . . *phew*!

☺ You will not be made to choose the correctly spelled word among a bunch of misspelled, tricky spelling demons. However, you may be asked to pick an appropriate homonym.

A NOTE ABOUT VOCABULARY AND SPELLING

Vocabulary and spelling are not centerpieces of the ACT English Test; still, it makes perfect sense that the stronger your vocabulary, the easier time you will have on the reading sections of the test, where vocabulary does come into play to a considerable extent (see Chapter 4).

In addition, although there is no vocabulary-matching section or choose-the-right-word section, a strong vocabulary will make you better equipped to correctly answer questions on both the Reading and English Tests. Some questions ask you to choose the most appropriate word, based on the surrounding context.

Last but not least, a command of spelling and vocabulary will make you look good on the essay portion of the ACT Writing Test. The official Scoring Rubric for the ACT Essay indicates the following for essays that score a 6, which is the best score that an individual evaluator can give to an essay: "The essay shows a good command of language. Sentences are varied and word choice is varied and precise."

QUICK DRILLS

Quick Drill: When to Use Commas

Insert commas, where needed, in the following sentences.

1. Beth Fine the District-wide Coordinator of Special Education is one of the most talented and dynamic administrators the school district has ever had.

2. Luke please put your dirty socks in the hamper and do not leave them on the couch any more.

3. The delicious and refreshing fruit salad contained four types of berries: clam shell blackberries blueberries strawberries and raspberries.

4. Before walking out the door Lana turned to Jack and said "Drive safely and take good care of yourself."

5. The ACT unlike the SAT has no sentence completion questions or long double-passage reading selections.

6. Luca did you leave your pool towel at your friend's house earlier today?

7. Growing up I frequently would be reminded of my well-intentioned mother's favorite words of wisdom "Waste not want not" and "The early bird gets the worm."

8. Before leaving for the four-hour car ride the family worked together to prepare and pack sandwiches snacks and a cooler filled with fruit and cold drinks.

9. Now married for decades of marvelous years the couple met on September 9 1989 at Bar Beach–Hempstead Harbor Park in Port Washington New York.

10. Situated at the end of the road the white brick colonial which is the largest house in Forest Court boasts over 5,500 square feet of interior living space.

ANSWERS

1. Beth Fine, the District-wide Coordinator of Special Education, is one of the most talented and dynamic administrators the school district has ever had. (Rule: Commas are used to set off appositives.)

2. Luke, please put your dirty socks in the hamper, and do not leave them on the couch any more. (Rule: Commas are used after addressing a person; commas are used with a conjunction to separate independent clauses in order to form a compound sentence.)

3. The delicious and refreshing fruit salad contained four types of berries: clam shell blackberries, blueberries, strawberries, and raspberries. (Rule: Commas are used to separate items in a list.)

4. Before walking out the door, Lana turned to Jack and said, "Drive safely and take good care of yourself." (Rule: Commas are used after introductory prepositional phrases; commas are used to introduce a quotation.)

5. The ACT, unlike the SAT, has no sentence completion questions or long double-passage reading selections. (Rule: Commas are used to set off interrupting words or phrases.)

6. Luca, did you leave your pool towel at your friend's house earlier today? (Rule: Commas are used after addressing the person to whom you are speaking or writing.)

7. Growing up, I frequently would be reminded of my well-intentioned mother's favorite words of wisdom, "Waste not, want not" and "The early bird gets the worm." (Rule: Commas are used to set off introductory phrases—in this case, the gerund phrase *Growing up*.)

8. Before leaving for the four-hour car ride, the family worked together to prepare and pack sandwiches, snacks, and a cooler filled with fruit and cold

drinks. (Rule: Commas are used after introductory prepositional phrases. Commas are also used—as in the latter part of this sentence—to separate items in a list.)

9. Now married for decades of marvelous years, the couple met on September 9, 1989, at Bar Beach–Hempstead Harbor Park in Port Washington, New York. (Rule: Commas are used to set off introductory phrases. Commas are also used between the date and year and between the city and state.)

10. Situated at the end of the road, the white brick colonial, which is the largest house in Forest Court, boasts over 5,500 square feet of interior living space. (Rule: Commas are used to set off subordinating clauses—in this case, the adjective clause that describes the brick colonial.)

Quick Drill: When to Use Colons and Semicolons

Insert colons or semicolons, where needed, in the following sentences.

1. Hilary loves field hockey Corey is more into lacrosse.

2. The play show times are Thursday, 7:30 P.M. Friday, 8:00 P.M. and Saturday, 8:30 P.M.

3. The Quaker family owns five varieties of pets dogs, turtles, cats, birds, and chinchillas.

4. Ms. Jones went to the potluck dinner and brought the following green bean casserole, a loaf of raisin bread, and a pumpkin pie.

5. Miranda puts four types of berries in her fruit salad strawberries, raspberries, blueberries, and blackberries.

6. Perplexingly, the treasure hunt map indicated three destination points Laurel Lane, 3 miles east of Hillside Maple Court, 2 miles north of Marcus and Nassau Road, 7 miles west of Serpentine.

7. "The early bird gets the worm" works nicely along with one of my other favorite sayings "no use being a day late and a dollar short."

8. Video games often get a bad rap, but some can argue that they have three redeeming benefits providing an outlet for downtime, encouraging game dialogue when not "in play," and exercising eye-hand coordination.

9. Only buy beverages that contain natural flavorings avoid beverages that contain artificial sugars, color enhancers, and chemical additives that are hard to pronounce.

10. Her words rang true to me it is a gift for one to know what he is and is *not* good at doing.

ANSWERS

1. Hilary loves field hockey; Corey is more into lacrosse. (Rule: Use a semicolon to separate independent clauses.)

2. The play show times are Thursday, 7:30 P.M.; Friday, 8:00 P.M.; and Saturday, 8:30 P.M. (Rule: Use semicolons to separate items in a list, in which each "item" already contains a comma; this is sometimes referred to as a semicolon being used as a "super comma.")

3. The Quaker family owns five varieties of pets: dogs, turtles, cats, birds, and chinchillas. (Rule: Use a colon to introduce a list.)

4. Ms. Jones went to the potluck dinner and brought the following: a green casserole, a loaf of raisin bread, and a pumpkin pie. (Rule: Use a colon to introduce a list. In this particular case, the list contains adjectives and nouns.)

5. Miranda puts four types of berries in her fruit salad: strawberries, raspberries, blueberries, and blackberries. (Rule: Use a colon to introduce a list.)

6. Perplexingly, the treasure hunt map indicated three destination points: Laurel Lane, 3 miles east of Hillside; Maple Court, 2 miles north of Marcus; and Nassau Road, 7 miles west of Serpentine. (Rule: Use semicolons to separate items in a list in which each "item" already contains a comma; this is sometimes referred to as a semicolon being used as a "super comma.")

7. "The early bird gets the worm" works nicely along with one of my other favorite sayings: "no use being a day late and a dollar short." (Rule: Use a colon to introduce a quotation.)

8. Video games often get a bad rap, but some can argue that they have three redeeming benefits: providing an outlet for downtime, encouraging game dialogue when not "in play," and exercising eye-hand coordination. (Rule: Use a colon to introduce a list, even if the list is made up of gerund phrases.)

9. Only buy beverages that contain natural flavorings; avoid beverages that contain artificial sugars, color enhancers, and chemical additives that are hard to pronounce. (Rule: Use a semicolon to separate clauses and provide emphasis.)

10. Her words rang true to me: it is a gift for one to know what he is and is *not* good at doing. (Rule: Use a colon to introduce an explanation or clarification.)

Quick Drill: When to Use Apostrophes, Dashes, and Hyphen Marks

Insert apostrophes, dashes, and hyphen marks, where needed, in the following sentences.

1. Dianas father in law prepared a delicious Mediterranean egg salad that everyone enjoyed at the anniversary brunch, which was celebrated in honor of Diana and Davids five year wedding anniversary.

2. Foolishly, freshman Gus signed up for whichever classes met late in the day so he could sleep in clearly, his priority was partying and not studying.

3. Tango Mango and Green Worm are the fourth grade boys favorite crayon colors.

4. Cotton candy flavored lollipops and chocolate flavored licorice sticks were Grant and Zachs favorite snacks while watching action adventure movies.

5. Melissa Blanca one of the most amiable girls at the middle school always offered a sweet smile and friendly word to her friends.

6. It has been said that one mans trash is another mans treasure recycling belongings among friends testifies to the truth behind this saying.

7. The chorus body movements, hand motions, and facial expressions made us feel like we were watching an off Broadway show not just listening to a bunch of youngsters singing!

8. Getting ready for next weekends ski trip, Justina first borrowed Mias gloves, then she borrowed Paulas scarf one can't help but wonder what Justina will borrow next?

9. Hannahs recipe for thick, cake like brownies is much better than Linas recipe Linas brownies always turn out rather flat, gooey, and stick to the touch.

10. A traditional summer sleeping late, taking a ride to the beach, hanging with neighborhood friends is what most appeals to the family this year.

ANSWERS

1. Diana's father-in-law prepared a delicious Mediterranean egg salad that everyone enjoyed at the anniversary brunch, which was celebrated in honor of Diana and David's five-year wedding anniversary. (Rules: Use apostrophes to indicate possession and hyphens (-) to spell the names of *great*-relatives, as in *great-great-grandfather* or *great-Uncle Emil*, and in-laws, as in *brother-in-law*, or *mother-in-law*, and to indicate adjective forms.)

2. Foolishly, freshman Gus signed up for whichever classes met late in the day so he could sleep in—clearly, his priority was partying and not studying. (Rule: Use dashes (—) to add words to the end of a sentence; you can do this when there is a logical and clear "break" in the flow of the sentence.)

3. Tango Mango and Green Worm are the fourth-grade boy's favorite crayon colors. (Rule: Use hyphens (-), which are shorter than dashes, to connect numbers and words—regardless of whether the numbers are written out or in numeral form.)

4. Cotton candy-flavored lollipops and chocolate-flavored licorice sticks were Grant and Zach's favorite snacks while watching action-adventure movies. (Rule: Use hyphens (-) to separate words that make up a compound adjective.)

5. Melissa Blanca—one of the most amiable girls at the middle school—always offered a sweet smile and friendly word to her friends. (Rule: Use dashes (—) to separate words that are situated in the middle of a sentence. The dashes emphasize these intervening words.)

6. It has been said that one man's trash is another man's treasure—recycling belongings among friends testifies to the truth behind this saying. (Rule: Use dashes (—) to add words to the end of a sentence; you can do this when there is a logical and clear "break" in the flow of the sentence.)

7. The chorus' body movements, hand motions, and facial expressions made us feel like we were watching an off-Broadway show—not just listening to a bunch of youngsters singing! (Rule: Use dashes (—) to add words to the end of a sentence; you can do this when there is a logical and clear "break" in the flow of the sentence.)

8. Getting ready for next weekend's ski trip, Justina first borrowed Mia's gloves, then she borrowed Paula's scarf—one can't help but wonder what Justina will borrow next? (Rule: Use dashes (—) to add words to the end of a sentence; you can do this when there is a logical and clear "break" in the flow of the sentence.)

9. Hannah's recipe for thick, cake-like brownies is much better than Lina's recipe—Lina's brownies always turn out rather flat, gooey, and stick to the touch. (Rule: Use dashes (—) to add words to the end of a sentence; you can do this when there is a logical and clear "break" in the flow of the sentence.)

10. A traditional summer—sleeping late, taking a ride to the beach, hanging with neighborhood friends—is what most appeals to the family this year. (Rule: Use dashes (—) to separate words that are situated in the middle of a sentence; when using dashes, no space should come between the words that appear right before and right after the dash.)

MAKING SENSE OF THE DOUBLE-COLUMN FORMAT

As you may already be aware, an odd-looking, double-column format is used on the English Test. Now's the time to make sense of these columns (herein referred to as the "left column" and "right column") and their features; otherwise, you might find yourself a bit befuddled on test day.

Left Column	Right Column
Numbers in brackets: 　　[1] [2] [3] [4] [5] Sometimes you will see numbers in brackets like the ones above. Only some of the English passages feature bracketed numbers. When they do, bracketed numbers may be used in one of two ways: 1. to divide the passage into sections (usually paragraphs) by centering the bracketed number above each new paragraph break, for example. Numbers in brackets is a clue that you will have some questions that refer to specific paragraphs or sections of the passage. 　　For example, you might be asked about rearranging the order of paragraphs, or about inserting information in between paragraphs, or about omitting particular sentences or examples from paragraphs 　　The bracketed numbers are practical in that they provide a road map so that the question maker can easily refer the test taker to specific areas of the reading selection. 2. to divide a paragraph into sentences; in this case, each sentence of the paragraph is preceded by a bracketed number, as in the paragraph below. These bracketed numbers are smaller than the ones that denote paragraphs or larger sections of the passage. *[1] Laura Halperin advises using simple stationery so that <u>your handwriting</u> sentiments stand out. [2] Traditional paper in ivory, ecru, or white <u>is a timeless elegant choice</u>. [3] Use navy or black ink to maintain a classic style. [4] A simple satin ribbon may be all that is needed to add an elegant, finishing touch.* [45]	**Fifteen questions per passage:** Questions are numbered 1 through 75. They will appear in the left column most often as small numbers situated under an underlined portion of text and sometimes in a box at the end of a sentence or paragraph. See 45 in the italicized example in the left column. **Four answer choices per question:** (Note that the SAT has *five* answer choices per question, but the ACT has only *four* answer choices per question, indicated by letter sets A, B, C, D or by F, G, H, J. See example below.) (A) (B)　　A, B, C, D are the letter choices (C)　　for odd-numbered questions (D) or: (F) (G)　　F, G, H, J are the letter (H)　　choices for even-numbered questions (J) <u>NO CHANGE</u>: If NO CHANGE is offered as an answer choice option (which it is for the vast majority of questions), it will always appear as the first answer choice listed, either A or F. *Note:* You may find gaps—chunks of white space—in between questions in this right column. The test questions are formatted and spaced out in this way so that the questions are as adjacent as possible to the left-column text that the questions refer to.

Left Column	Right Column
Numbers in square boxes: Numbers in boxes (as in number 45 on the previous page) also allow you to locate sections of the passage. A boxed number might refer you to the entire sentence that precedes it, eliminating a good amount of underlining. ⬜1 ⬜2 ⬜3 ⬜4 ⬜5 **Small numbers beneath underlined text:** ‾‾hesitantly‾‾ ‾‾confidently‾‾ ‾‾casually‾‾ 1 2 3 These types of numbers are the most common form you will see in the left-hand column. Each passage has fifteen corresponding questions and, quite often, there are fifteen sections of text underlined. You are to reread and consider the underlined portion in order to answer the corresponding question. **Gaps (white space) that break up the passage:** Uniform line spacing does not exist in the left column. At first look, it appears that the line spacing is haphazard or that it was done by a sleep-deprived typesetter. There is a reason for this quirky line spacing, however: The test maker wants to align (as best as possible) the question in the right column with the corresponding text in the left column. So, try to ignore the random, all-over-the place spacing that breaks up the lines of the left-column passage. Focus on the question numbers and corresponding numbers in the passage instead.	

THE *OUCH!* FACTOR

You will have an amazing test-taking tool with you as you sit down to take the ACT: *your ears!* As you read through the four versions provided in the answer choices of the English Test, simply "listen" to detect what sounds good and what doesn't. For many test takers, it's as simple as that. You do not have to name the grammatical rules. You do not need to comment upon the intricacies of sentence syntax. You do not need to label parts of speech or (Heaven forbid!) sketch multi-level sentence diagrams. You just have to listen . . . carefully.

Assuming that you have been surrounded by family members, neighbors, friends, coaches, and teachers who speak English well, your native English-listening ears will help you determine what is most proper. Keep your ears tuned to a higher level of language, however, because the English Test is about how we *write* in standard, written English—not simply how we may speak. If it sounds chatty or "talky," cross it out!

TEST-TAKING TIPS

The following are additional testing tips that apply to the English part of the ACT. Think about the aspects of writing that appear in each underlined portion of the passage. Several questions ask you to base your decision on some particular feature of writing, such as tone.

Not all questions refer to underscored parts of the passage. In these instances, you will be asked questions about specific paragraphs or portions of the passage or the passage in its entirety.

- **Like a detective at a crime scene**, scrutinize answer choices with a close eye. At first glance, a couple of answer choices might look exactly alike. Keep your eyes peeled—notice how each answer choice is different. Sometimes the words within two answer choices are *identical,* but one might have a semicolon, dash, or comma that the other lacks. You really need to keep your focus in order to notice these slight variations.

  Think about each and every feature of a particular answer choice. One comma, one colon, *one letter* can make the difference. For example, *reflects* and *reflect* differ by one letter only (s), but the former is a singular verb; the latter, a plural verb. Notice the slight difference between Choices G and J, below:

  (F) Bruce, the boxing champ, responded.
  (G) Bruce the boxing champ responds.
  (H) Bruce responded, being a boxing champ.
  (J) Bruce the boxing champ, responds.

  On ACT English, every letter and every punctuation mark counts!
- **Always read with style**—the author's *writing style*—in mind. *Style comes in many varieties,* including: nostalgic, scholarly, objective, casual, and so on.

  Is the author's writing flowery—filled with description, similes, imagery—or is it more straightforward and austere? Noticing style will help you to select answer choices that are consistent with the style that the author has "set up." The ACT English Test, unlike your English class at school, does not offer you opportunities to be creative. The grammar has to be sound and standard; the style and tone have to be fitting and on par with the rest of the passage.

- **Don't sell yourself short** by picking the first answer you come across that sounds pretty good. "Pretty good" might not cut it when it comes to earning points. Don't take shortcuts; stick it out and consider all four of your options—A . . . B . . . C . . . D or F . . . G . . . H . . . J—until you have carefully contemplated each and every answer choice.
- **Don't settle for second best.** Determine the *best* answer; second best earns you nothing, not even partial credit.
- **Plug in your selected answer**, and reread the sentence to make sure that it flows and makes sense both semantically and grammatically.

Time-Saver: Zoom In and Zoom Out

For some test takers, reading every paragraph with time and attention slows them down, preventing them from adequately addressing the fourth and fifth passages of the English Test, which comprises five passages in total. To manage your pace and to answer questions with greater accuracy, approach English Test passages in this step-by-step fashion:

1. **Zoom In**: Read the passage **title**.
2. **Zoom In**: Read the **first paragraph or two**, carefully, using your best concentration and most vivid visualization.
3. **Zoom In** to the **underlined portions** among the body paragraphs and read the corresponding **questions**.
4. **Zoom Out** about a sentence prior to and following the underlined portion, enabling you to **absorb a broader context** and answer questions with greater **accuracy**.
5. **Zoom In**: Read the **concluding paragraph** carefully.

TIME-SAVER

Zoom In and Zoom Out to work at an effective pace and to absorb broader contexts for accuracy.

TIP

Use an Active Pencil to mark grammatical elements in the broader context of the underlined portions.

Test takers naturally tend to focus on the underlined portions of the English Test. However, it is just as important—often more important—to focus on the non-underlined portions that are in the vicinity. I call this "the broader context."

Zoom out to absorb a broader context, by skimming a line or two before *and* after the underlined portion of the passage. This technique prompts you to notice and pick up on a variety of written elements, such as author's style, verb tense, tone, and whether the surrounding nouns are plural or singular. As you skim the broader context, in your zoom-zoom fashion, keep your pencil active. Mark these types of elements that appear in the broader context. You can mark in any way you like: underline, circle, or jot x's under words and phrases in the context that deserve your attention. Remember, the great majority of English Test questions require you to make the underlined portions consistent in grammar and the author's tone and style.

Let "zoom-zoom" remind you to skim the context rather quickly so you can work through the questions at a time-effective pace.

Time-Saver: Use Caret Symbols for Placement Questions

Some English Test questions ask you to determine the most effective placement for a word, phrase, or sentence. Like an editor, use a caret symbol (∧) to keep track of your placement options. A caret is an editor's mark used to show where missing text should be inserted.

To improve your accuracy in answering questions, use caret marks to indicate where the word or phrase may go, as indicated by the four answer choices. Placement questions tend to be among the most challenging for test takers. Using caret marks is particularly well suited for visual learners who benefit from the picture cue provided by the caret mark.

Here are examples of such questions:

14. Upon reviewing Paragraph 6 and determining that some information has been left out, the writer composes the following sentence:

    He remotely programs the lights to turn on at a time when his neighbor will be stopping by.

    The most logical placement for this sentence would be:
    (A) before Sentence 2
    (B) after Sentence 2
    (C) after Sentence 3
    (D) after Sentence 4

As a focused and disciplined test taker, jot a caret in each of those four locations and—using trial and error, your English-speaking ear, and your reasoning skills—determine the most effective placement for this sentence. Placement questions can be time-consuming. Caret marks, however, are your quick and easy place markers that save you time; they prevent you from having to repeatedly go back and forth from answer options to passage. Caret marks are time-savers!

Here's another version of a placement question:

70. The best placement for the underlined portion would be:
    (F) where it is now
    (G) after the word "them."
    (H) after the word "luncheon."
    (J) after the word "grounds" (ending the sentence with a period).

Rest assured, caret marks hold your placement options, allowing you to read through the placement choices in context with greater ease. What follows is an illustration of how carets are used in the context of a sentence from an English passage:

Choice G	Choice H	Choice J

… [4] One of them ∧ was for seniors a weekly luncheon ∧ at the beach picnic grounds ∧.
70

Here is another example of how to use carets in placement questions:

35. For the sake of the logic and coherence of this paragraph, Sentence 1 should be placed:
    (A) where it is now.
    (B) after Sentence 3.
    (C) after Sentence 4.
    (D) after Sentence 5.

Again, use caret marks to clarify your placement options.

Tackling Top-Heavy Questions

Most English Test questions simply comprise the four answer options indicated by the set of letters ABCD or by the letters FGHJ. (I have yet to figure out why vowels are not included.) Other questions on the English Test have specific questions that precede the answer choices. I call these top-heavy questions: questions that define one or more revision tasks for you to accomplish by choosing the correct alternative of the four choices given.

Sometimes, top-heavy questions can even present three revision tasks in just one question. To increase your test-taking accuracy, always underline the **revision task**(s) that the top-heavy question asks you to accomplish.

Here is an example with *two* revision tasks underlined:

37. Given that all the choices are true, which one would <u>best conclude this sentence</u> so that it <u>demonstrates Miguel's carpentry skills</u>?
    (A) NO CHANGE
    (B) he used tools commonly used by amateur woodworkers
    (C) his clients could easily book his services
    (D) he perfected symmetry, contour, and craftsmanship in his work

Here is another top-heavy English Test question with the key revision task underlined:

TIP

Underline revision tasks in top-heavy questions to focus *precisely* on what your revision alternative needs to accomplish.

23. At this point, the writer wants to add a sentence that would further <u>describe</u> the <u>interior walls</u> of the <u>pool house</u>.
    Which of the following sentences would best accomplish this?
    (A) I guess the sweeping brush pattern is supposed to resemble marble but it doesn't.
    (B) Varnish provides protection for some painted wood surfaces.
    (C) To me, I'd say that peppermint green is a strange choice for an interior wall color.
    (D) I would think that the person who selected that color and effect must be an unusual individual.

Chapter Summary

All of this chapter's reading, studying, and work is done, and now you are more grammatically savvy than ever before! You have been briefed on the **ACT English Principles**, which include elements of author's style; accuracy in standard, written (not spoken!) English; grammar; and usage. You have also gotten the scoop on sound sentence formation; conciseness; coherence; and correct use of commas, colons, semicolons, and other pertinent punctuation. You have learned about an author's technique in three specific areas: strategy, organization, and tone.

Icing on the cake: You have taken your new knowledge for a test drive by working through a bevy of **Quick-Drill Exercises** pertaining to standard, written English and the conventions of grammar. You do not want any surprises on test day, and you don't want to find yourself asking, "What in the world is this? These double columns are hard to figure!" So, you've learned how to make sense of the quirky, inscrutable **Double-Column Format** ahead of time so you'll know the drill on the day of the test.

On an uplifting note, you've been given a list of **No Sweat Points**: all the aspects of English usage and grammar that you will *not* be tested on so you don't have to worry about. Now that's a plus! You have learned the truth about the role of **Vocabulary and Spelling** on the ACT English Test. You have been given an extra dose of **Test-Taking Tips**, for good measure, and several key **Time-Saver Strategies**. Now you are ready to embark on several **Practice English Mini-Passages** that conclude this chapter. You have also put the icing on the cake by carefully reading the **Answer Explanations** just to sharpen your grammatical skills a bit more.

Practice Mini-Passage

"My Locker"

Click, Clack . . . "Hey, Phil!" I'm walking down the hallway, looking down at <u>the floor, three</u> <u>minutes</u> to class and I'm at my locker. "I'm in good <u>shape," I say</u> to myself.

21–5–36 Cling! My locker opens. I could feel the sharp sting of the metal against my hand. My locker is very wide, with a deep maroon color inside. The net of the basketball hoop that I mounted inside rattles, like it has a mini-earthquake inside. Then I <u>am seeing</u> my gym clothes from last week, and believe me, it's not a pleasant sight or smell.

Next I check the time on the <u>mini, shiny silver,</u> <u>clock</u> in my locker once again. The clock is stuck to the inside of my locker with a magnet; the Discovery Store has the coolest things. I check the digital display: two minutes to class—need to hurry up!

1. (A) NO CHANGE
   (B) the floor, having three minutes
   (C) the floor—three minutes
   (D) the floor with three minutes

2. (F) NO CHANGE
   (G) shape", I say
   (H) shape," as I say
   (J) shape," I am saying

3. (A) NO CHANGE
   (B) have seen
   (C) see
   (D) saw

4. (F) NO CHANGE
   (G) mini, shiny silver clock
   (H) mini shiny silver clock
   (J) mini, shiny, silver clock

As I try to find my art binder on the top *shelf,* I quickly, in a snatching motion, put one book in and take one out. "My bookshelf is really working," I say to myself, happily. "It's sturdy and hasn't fallen apart yet!" I glance at the clock. ⑤ Without thinking, I grab my favorite Z-grip pen and a mechanical pencil. I slam the locker shut, BAMM! As soon as the locker snaps closed, the bell rings, and I sigh.

5. At this point, the author is considering adding the following sentences:

> The locker shelf I had before was plastic, and it wasn't sturdy at all. In fact, it cracked in two places.

Should the writer insert these new sentences here? Why, or why not?

(A) Yes, because the sentences give the reader more descriptive details.

(B) Yes, because this essay is largely built on contrasts.

(C) No, because this sentence is irrelevant to the substance of the prior two paragraphs.

(D) No, because this sentence just slows down this paragraph with details that are not important to the action of what's taking place.

Answer Key

1. **C**   2. **F**   3. **C**   4. **J**   5. **D**

Answers Explained

1. **(C)** The original version, Choice A, creates a run-on construction known as a comma splice.

   Choice B is incorrect. . . . *having three minutes to class* sounds awkward and the sentence is cluttered with commas.

   Choice C, *the floor—three minutes,* **is the correct answer** because the dash correctly sets off two independent clauses that relate to each other.

   Choice D is awkward and unclear; it sounds as if the prepositional phrase, ". . . *with three minutes,*" is positioned to modify "the floor."

2. **(F) The original version, Choice F, NO CHANGE, is the correct answer.**

   Choice G, *"shape", I say,* is wrong because the comma is outside of the closed quotation mark.

   Choice H is also incorrect because the word "as" is not needed.

   Choice J is not bad, but it is not as concise as the original version.

3. **(C)** The original version, Choice A, NO CHANGE, is incorrect because the verb phrase "am seeing" is not as straightforward or as concise as the simple past tense, "saw."

   Choice B is also wrong because "have seen" is not in the simple past tense like the verbs within the two preceding sentences.

   Choice C is the correct answer because the action verb "see" is in the present tense, just like the two verbs from the preceding sentences: "is" and "rattles." Choice D is wrong because it shows an unnecessary tense shift from present to the past, "saw."

4. **(J)** The original version, Choice F, NO CHANGE, is incorrect because a comma is missing between two consecutive adjectives.

   Choices G and H are also missing commas that belong in between the adjectives that all modify "clock."

   The correct answer is Choice J, *mini, shiny, silver clock,* because the comma placements are correct.

5. **(D)** It is best not to include these sentences, so answer Choices A and B are out. Choice C is not the best answer. Talking about different types of shelves is not totally irrelevant, but **Choice D is the best answer** because inserting this sentence would indeed weigh down and slow down the paragraph with details that are not terribly vital.

Reading Test

4

- Reading Strategies: Preview, Focus, Read, Answer
  - *Quick Drill:* Underlining Key Words in the Reading Questions
  - Be a Page Flipper!
- Five Levels of Concentration and Comprehension
- Reading Skills in Closer Focus
  - Finding the Main Idea
  - Locating and Interpreting Details
  - Recognizing Events in Sequence
  - Drawing Comparisons
  - Understanding Cause and Effect
  - Grasping Meanings in Context
  - Formulating Generalizations
  - Examining Author's Voice and Method
- Vocabulary
- Practice with a Prose Fiction Passage
- Practice with a Social Science Passage
- Practice with Humanities Passages
- Practice with a Natural Science Passage
- Practice with Comparative Reading Passages

One Test, Three Scores! You earn three scores on the Reading Test: a total score and two subscores.

Total Reading Test Score	Based on all 40 questions	Scaled subscore range
Social Studies/Sciences Subscore	Based on 20 questions relating to Social Studies and Natural Science passages	1–18
Arts/Literature Subscore	Based on 20 questions relating to Prose Fiction and Humanities passages	1–18

READING STRATEGIES

PREVIEW ➡ FOCUS ➡ READ ➡ ANSWER

PREVIEW the questions first if you find that this preliminary step works for you. Previewing is *not* reading the questions with intense concentration and attempting to memorize what they are asking. Memorizing the questions is too time-consuming, plus it's very hard to recall what all *ten* questions (per passage) are asking of you.

Previewing as a preliminary step is a matter of personal preference. It is meant to be done quickly and is more like *skimming* the questions (rather than *reading* them) in order to get a "general sense" of what you'll be asked. There are no hard and fast rules when it comes to peeking at the questions first or just going straight for the passage.

To preview or not to preview the set of questions (ten questions per passage) is a matter of personal test-taking style. Some test takers find previewing helpful; others don't. Experiment with previewing questions and then reading the passage, or try simply diving straight into the passage. See which method of attack is most effective for you.

A CLARIFICATION OF PREVIEWING

Let's clarify previewing a bit more. Previewing the questions is not about reading each and every one of the ten reading questions (per passage) very carefully in entirety. Also, it is not about taking risky shortcuts: trying to answer the questions by hunting down the information *without* reading the passage. Previewing is a skillful approach with a single goal: skim the questions to try to get a "heads up" about what, in particular, the questions will be asking. In a nutshell: previewing is skimming astutely.

Here's an added touch for the skillful test taker: Underline the crux—the central point—behind each question. Underlining the key ideas within the question keeps you focused on what you're looking for, and is helpful later on (after you've read the reading selection) when you go back to actually answer the questions. If people are mentioned, simply underline their surnames (last names) because that is how they will most likely be referred to throughout the passage and the answer choices. If a time frame is mentioned—at first, midway, ultimately—make it a habit to underscore those key words as well. Underlining key words such as <u>not</u>, <u>all/except</u>, <u>true</u>, <u>false</u>, <u>initially</u>—among others—is also a pragmatic (sensible, practical) test-taking strategy.

Sharpen your pencil and underline the key ideas and key words in the sample questions that follow. Subjectivity is involved in selecting key words: some test takers will underline more or fewer words.

1. The narrator draws which of the following comparisons between the old storytellers and Evan's grandparents?

2. According to the passage, Benjamin Franklin believed that societal change should include all of the following EXCEPT:

3. It can be reasonably inferred from the passage that the narrator regards her initial discovery of the actual circumstances surrounding the competition among her neighbors as:

4. The main function of lines 44–48 in terms of the fifth paragraph (lines 45–47) as a whole is to:

5. Which of the following questions is NOT answered by the information in the passage?

6. According to the narrator, which of the following statements was untrue about Harriet at the moment when she first arrived at the university?

7. It can reasonably be inferred that toward the end of the research process Thomas and William conducted the study of the presumably extraterrestrial meteorites with an attitude of:

ANSWERS

The answers that follow are suggestions that illustrate minimal underlining. As you'll notice, some questions require more underlining than others, depending upon their length and substance.

1. The narrator draws which of the following <u>comparisons</u> between the <u>old storytellers</u> and <u>Evan's grandparents</u>?

2. According to the passage, Benjamin <u>Franklin</u> believed that <u>societal change</u> should include <u>all</u> of the following <u>EXCEPT</u>:

3. It can be reasonably inferred from the passage that the narrator regards her <u>initial discovery</u> of the actual circumstances surrounding the <u>competition</u> among her <u>neighbors</u> as:

4. The <u>main function</u> of lines <u>44–48</u> in terms of the <u>fifth paragraph</u> (lines <u>45–47</u>) as a whole is to:

5. Which of the following questions is <u>NOT</u> answered by the information in the passage?

6. According to the narrator, which of the following statements was <u>untrue</u> about <u>Harriet</u> at the moment when she <u>first arrived</u> at the <u>university</u>?

7. It can reasonably be inferred that toward the <u>end</u> of the <u>research process Thomas and William</u> conducted the study of the presumably extraterrestrial <u>meteorites</u> with an <u>attitude</u> of:

FOCUS most closely on the most pertinent parts of the reading selections. This approach amounts to smart reading. These significant parts include: the first two paragraphs of the passage (here is typically where you will find the main idea and where you will pick up the general lines of reasoning that run through the entire passage), the first sentence or two (topic sentences) of each body paragraph, and the concluding paragraph. Concentrating on the significant parts does not mean that you bypass the others. Instead, you skim the other sections or read them in a more casual fashion.

The ACT reading selections can be long (typically eighty-five to ninety-five lines), so knowing where to *focus* and knowing where to *skim* can help you get through the lengthy selections in a time-smart fashion.

> **PREVIEWING AND UNDERLINING: A WINNING COMBINATION**
>
> As you preview the reading questions, underline the crux of each question. What, specifically, is the question asking? Underline the key words and/or topics within the questions to help you focus on the essential information when the time comes for you to answer the questions.

READ through the entire passage. Now you know where to *focus* and where to *skim*. Beware of shortcuts that promise big returns like, "Don't read the passage, just read the questions and then hunt down the answers," or "Skim the entire passage, then just answer the questions based on what you remember; there's not enough time to go back to the passage to rekindle your memory or to find backup for answers." These types of shortcuts will put you at a big disadvantage.

An alternative to reading through the entire passage at once is to read the piece in halves or thirds. Once you've read about a third, for example, check out the questions to determine which ones you can answer based on what you've read so far. Then read the next third. Again, check out which questions you can answer at this point. Read the final third of the passage and answer the remaining questions.

Some test takers find reading in halves or thirds more comfortable than reading the entire passage in one sweep. This technique breaks down the reading selections, making this section of the test less intimidating. As you prepare for the ACT, try these different methods—reading in thirds, reading in halves, reading it all at once—and see which one works best for you. The test preparation process allows you the time and opportunity to experiment with different approaches. Trying out various methods and deciding on the one that is most effective for you personally will give you a big advantage on test day!

Read with your mind's eye open and active: As you read, use your powerful mental canvas to visualize what is being described by the text. Mindless reading will not pull a high score. Instead, *react and respond* to what you are reading. In other words, let the author's ideas affect you and prompt a response in you. Reacting and responding occur during a quiet, inner dialogue that you have with yourself as you read. Practice this type of active reading every time you read an ACT passage, a textbook passage for school, or a newspaper article. Do not mumble out loud! Do not move your lips considerably as you read! The proctor will wonder what's up with you, and the other test takers may glare at you contemptuously for disturbing their concentration.

For example, if you're reading a natural science passage, you might say to yourself, "I never knew of the theory that says 'Mars' atmosphere was blasted away by . . . asteroids and comets.' Imagine that!" Or, when reading a social science passage, you might think to yourself, "Who would've thought that Thomas Jefferson was repeatedly accused of *plagiarism*!" Get the idea of internal dialogue? If you train yourself (through practice) to react to what you read, then you will be better able to build a solid sense of what you are reading, paragraph by paragraph.

If you adopt this active and multifaceted approach—*visualize, react, respond*—you will be far more likely to remember what you have read when it comes time to tackle the ten questions that follow each of the four reading selections.

ANSWER all ten questions on the reading selection to the best of your ability. Concentrate as you read the questions and train yourself to notice important key words in the questions themselves such as: *never, not, always, all, most, except, agrees, disagrees, undermines, underscores, initially, ultimately, contradicts, counters, verifies,* and *confirms.* There are other key words that are likely to appear in the questions. Be on the lookout for them, and underline these key words in the question itself.

Answer based on what the passage states or implies. No outside knowledge allowed! You have learned a great deal throughout your high school coursework, but be sure to not bring any of your outside knowledge to the question. You may love reading and you may like to forge personal connections to what you read, but do not answer reading passage questions based on your personal opinions or viewpoints. You are insightful and broadminded, the kind of person who can think outside the box and go beyond the text. Although this skill is valuable and welcome in literature discussion circles, "reading beyond the text" can get you in trouble on the ACT Reading Test. The bottom line: Answer questions based on what the text suggests or states; do not "read into" and beyond what the author has written.

CIRCLE ADJECTIVES to absorb the author's or narrator's perspective on the topic at hand. Follow the lead of effective test takers, and unwaveringly refer back to the passage. Do not rely solely on your memory. Although the ACT does not always provide specific line references, you will have a sense of where to revisit the passage and where to skim based on your initial reading of the passage. Return to the passage to read, with *greater and more precise focus* now, around the context of the referenced or pertinent lines. Using your Active Pencil, add an extra quick but effective step: circle the adjectives in those surrounding lines.

This pencil-to-paper technique is well suited for both visual and kinesthetic learners. Quick and easy, this active reading approach helps you to absorb the author's perspective on his or her topic—whether it be a place, theory, custom, or person. Your circles remind you to thoughtfully consider the precise adjectives the author or narrator has chosen to describe the topic at hand.

It may be helpful for you to know that for each reading selection, the set of ten questions appears in an ascending order of difficulty: easiest questions first, medium questions next, and hardest questions at the end. *Good news:* Even though the difficulty levels are in rising order, the point values earned for each correctly answered question remain the same.

No Sweat Points

No Points Lost For Wrong Answers—Hooray!
The ACT does not penalize you for answering questions incorrectly! Isn't this great! Life is fair, after all! The ACT test gives you a break. You don't even lose a fraction of a point—not even an iota—for a wrong answer! This means that it is *always* to your benefit to answer rather than to omit. Always, however, answer mindfully by using process of elimination and by making an educated guess. Yes, a win-win situation for you!

Notice how, unlike the SAT, the ACT questions do not go in consistent order of how the material and information is presented in the passage. For example, you may be asked a question based on lines 83–86, but then the very next question may ask you about a word used in context in line 12! If you are used to SAT Critical Reading, then this characteristic of the ACT Reading Test can seem strange. Although this random ordering of questions may seem uncomfortable at first, practice with reading passages and answering questions will soon make this jumbled ordering of questions seem like an old hat.

Main idea questions are fairly common and come in several varieties: *best title, author's purpose, overarching idea,* and *primary focus.* To solidify the main idea, review the introductory paragraph, paying close attention to the final lines in which the thesis usually appears. To reinforce the main idea, examine the concluding paragraph in its entirety. In this paragraph, the author will do one of several things: drive home his idea, take it a step or two further, or do a flip-flop and contradict himself! After all, every writer has the right to change his mind or concede to an alternate perspective. And you—as an astute reader—need to know how the writer ends off.

Not all answer choices are created equal:

- Wrong answers could be *true*.
- Wrong answers could be *reasonable and fair*.
- Wrong answers could be *factually correct*.
- Wrong answers could be statements that you find *agreeable*.
- Wrong answers could come across as *sounding intellectual, even erudite* (scholarly).
- Wrong answers could be supported by *what you have learned* in social studies, science, English, or art class.
- Wrong answers could even be supported by *facts and information that you have learned* on quality television, including the Discovery Channel, History Channel, or major network news broadcasts.
- Right answers are fully supported by what is written in the passage. This black-and-white support is called *textual evidence*.

Be a Page Flipper!

If you were a fly on the wall in an ACT testing center, you would notice two types of test takers. The first type calmly work on one page, then the next—one page right after the other—in consecutive order until the test booklet's end. They don't break a sweat or expend any more bodily energy than one does reading a magazine at home on Sunday morning. The pages of these test-takers' booklets are relatively still and quiet.

LICK AND FLIP!

Lick your fingertips, make some wind, and be a page flipper!

The second type of test takers are finger-lickers, with wind in their hair and movement in their bangs! Their test booklets become fans as their pages are in continual motion. These are the page flippers! These test takers *flip* back and forth, from page to page, eyes darting here and there within the test booklet, rereading a chunk of the passage, then quickly flipping back to the answer choices again. This type knows the great benefits of referring back to the text. Page flippers know not to rely on memory too heavily or too confidently. These test takers tend to be less distracted by false-positives, decoys, and partially correct answers among the choices. They go back to the passage to spot the evidence that supports one answer choice over all of the others.

FIVE LEVELS OF CONCENTRATION AND COMPREHENSION

Even very conscientious students mistakenly see a *big* difference between reading the passage and reading the questions. They fire up their full-blown concentration when reading the passage, but apply a casual degree of attention when reading the questions.

But to really rank on the ACT Reading Test, you should maintain a disciplined vigilance. In other words, sustain a steady, focused, and high-grade concentration throughout all of the following "five levels of concentration and comprehension":

- LEVEL ONE: Read the introductory material that precedes the passage and follows the genre name; for example, humanities, natural science, social science, prose fiction.

- LEVEL TWO: Read the passage carefully, giving the first third of the passage your greatest level of focus and concentration. Make brief marginal notations to help yourself build a sense of the passage.
- LEVEL THREE: Read the questions with elevated focus and attention; underline key words. Knowing specifically what the question asks is imperative to answering the question with accuracy.
- LEVEL FOUR: Reread pertinent and/or referenced parts of the passage with intense focus. Maintain your concentration. Make some wind: Be a page flipper!
- LEVEL FIVE: Read the four answer choices very carefully. Notice and underline key words in the answer choices that can change the nature of the choice such as *always*, *never*, *quickly*, and so on. Once you've narrowed the answer choices down to two possibilities, shift your concentration into high gear as you scrutinize the two answer choices, hone in on their differences, subtleties, and key words, and finally select the best choice.

READING SKILLS IN CLOSER FOCUS

Finding the Main Idea

Sifting through the insignificant pebbles, rubble, and excess. Narrowing in on a "just right" idea . . . this describes the process behind finding the main idea. Finding the main idea or best title is a high-frequency question type. So, every time you read an ACT reading selection, newspaper column, magazine article, or textbook chapter, practice narrowing in on the main idea.

> **MAIN IDEAS**
>
> should not be too broad (the whole pizza) or too narrow (just one slice); they should be just right.

Main ideas should not be too *broad*, encompassing more than that which is dealt with in the passage. Main ideas are *not* the entire pizza pie! By the same token, main ideas should not be too *narrow*, focusing in on just a small slice—like a supporting detail or example—of what is addressed in the passage. Main ideas should be "just right." Think of them, metaphorically, as "centerpiece" ideas that fit just perfectly, in size and scope, at the middle of the table.

The main idea of a passage is typically woven throughout, yet sharp readers know the three most reliable places to look for the overarching idea: introductory paragraph, concluding paragraph, and the last sentence or two of the introductory paragraph (typically where the thesis is found).

When are you best equipped to answer main idea questions? Regardless of the order in which the reading questions are listed, it is always best to answer main idea questions at the *very end* of your reading and question answering. This way, you will have absorbed the full gist of the passage.

Also, working through the full scope of the questions and answers (which most often requires that you refer back to the passage) often helps to clarify the overarching idea for you. In your test booklet, circle the main idea questions, boldly and sweepingly, so that you have a visual reminder to return to them later.

Locating and Interpreting Details

In architecture, the aesthetic beauty is in the details: ornamental scrolls, columns, keystones, carvings, decorative wood moldings, corbels, cross beams, and so on. In critical reading, the subtler meanings behind the text are detected through the details, which come in the form of words and phrases. Read and visualize the following vignettes (short, descriptive pieces of writing), paying close attention to the details and descriptions used by the author.

VIGNETTE #1

In the following mini-excerpt, what do the details tell you about the *atmosphere* within the concert hall?

> Filled with stiff bodies and upwardly stretched necks, the spectators looked on in demure reverence. Most wore sensible black or gray. After the first piece was played, the audience clapped tightly—hands no more than
> Line three inches apart, applause that was not too soft and not too loud. Although
> (5) the culminating compositions of the concert were more beautiful than any one of them had ever heard, no one offered a standing ovation at the end. They simply continued to clap, softly yet firmly, and added a steady nodding of the head coupled with a slight smile.

✎ Your response: Based on the details, the atmosphere within the concert hall can be described as _____ or _____.

VIGNETTE #2

In the following mini-excerpt, what do the details tell you about the *mental state* of the college professor?

> Making his way from the faculty room to the department chair's office, then returning back to his cubicle in the math and science department, Professor Chausky felt unhinged, as if his neck, trunk, and limbs were barely
> Line holding together. Lecturing to his less than interested freshmen, he would
> (5) sometimes feel unsteady on his feet, as if experiencing a faint and passing dizzy spell. A well-rounded lunch would sometimes make him feel glued together and buttoned up, but most of the time he just moved around the building in his typical, wobbly way.

✎ Your response: Based on the details, the mental state of the college professor can be described as _____ or _____.

VIGNETTE #3

In the following mini-excerpt, what do the details tell you about the *relationship* between the mother and daughter?

It's no wonder she named her Faith. Mother always strived for ease and good nature when interacting with the people in her world; she had faith that the relationship with her daughter would be no different. And it wasn't.
Line Mother and Faith would listen to each other's ideas, delight in each other's
(5) stories, and try their best to be as pleasant as possible when in the company of the other. This led to a good-natured rapport and easefulness that was apparent even to a newcomer who entered their midst.

Your response: Based on the details and descriptions, the relationship between the mother and daughter can be described as _____ or _____.

VIGNETTE #1 WITH DETAILS IN BOLD:

Filled with **stiff bodies and upwardly stretched necks**, the spectators looked on in **demure reverence**. Most wore sensible **black** or **gray**. After the first piece was played, the audience clapped **tightly**—hands no more
Line than three inches apart, applause that was **not too soft** and **not too loud**.
(5) Although the culminating compositions of the concert were more beautiful than any one of them had ever heard, **no one offered a standing ovation at the end**. They simply continued to clap, softly yet firmly, and added a **steady nodding of the head** coupled with a **slight smile**.

Possible Answer: The atmosphere is rather staid, austere, and reserved.

VIGNETTE #2 WITH DETAILS IN BOLD:

Making his way from the faculty room to the department chair's office, then returning back to his cubicle in the math and science department, Professor Chausky felt **unhinged**, as if his neck, trunk, and limbs were **barely**
Line **holding together**. Lecturing to his less than interested freshmen, he would
(5) sometimes feel **unsteady on his feet**, as if experiencing a **faint and passing dizzy spell**. A well-rounded lunch would sometimes make him feel **glued together and buttoned up** [*opposite of how he usually feels*], but most of the time he just moved around the building in his typical, **wobbly** way.

Possible Answer: Professor Chausky's mental state is most likely unstable, unsound, or shaky.

VIGNETTE #3 WITH DETAILS IN BOLD:

It's no wonder she named her Faith. Mother always strived for **ease** and **good nature** when interacting with the people in her world; she had faith that the relationship with her daughter would be no different. And it wasn't.

Line Mother and Faith would **listen to each other's ideas, delight in each**
(5) **other's stories, and try their best to be as pleasant as possible** when in the company of the other. This led to a **good-natured rapport** and **easefulness** that was apparent even to a newcomer who entered their midst.

Possible Answer: The relationship between the mother and daughter can be described as harmonious, agreeable, and peaceful.

The following is an example of a question that asks you to find the one detail that serves as the "best pragmatic tool." (Pragmatic means practical.) This question type is a bit time-consuming because it requires you to skim around each of those details to find the one that best fits the requirements posed by the question.

6. According to the author, which of the following is the best pragmatic tool that a salon can use to define its signature style for its current and prospective clients?
   (F) community (line 12)
   (G) celebrities (line 16)
   (H) look books (line 43)
   (J) e-mail (line 73)

Recognizing Events in Sequence

Now you will need to know which came first, the chicken or the egg? Just joking! The ACT is not a philosophy test, and that one question can take life scientists and great sages *ages* to ponder.

Back to recognizing events in sequence: To ace this category of questions, make it a habit to cultivate a *mental timeline* as you read through the selection. In your mind's eye, chart the events on your timeline so that you have a sense of the *order* in which the significant and pivotal incidents occur.

To cultivate your mental timeline, make it a habit to read with a bent for detecting the sequence of events. Make it a habit to differentiate between a scientist's *initial* objective in studying dolphin behavior and his *later* one. Keeping in mind the order and sequence of things, ask yourself, for example: Did General Jones galvanize General Smith's troops, or vice versa? Does this scientist examine the heavens several times a day because he has a dearth (undersupply) of observation data or because a plethora (abundance) of data has aroused in him greater enthusiasm? The sequence of events comes into play in many different ways.

> **SEQUENCE OF EVENTS**
>
> Chart the major events that occur in the reading selection in vivid color on your mental timeline. Visualizing in color will help illuminate your timeline in your mind's eye so that you can call upon it later when you need it.

The sample questions that follow give you a sense of how the sequence of events plays into questions based on a reading passage. Notice the words in italics:

- Did Politician A inspire Politician B, or did Politician B present her motivating platform *first?*
- Was the animal behaviorist interested in birds *initially*, or did bird enthusiasm follow his interest in monkeys?
- Did the charlatan (imposter, fraud) *at first* say he was from an upper-middle-class neighborhood in the suburbs of Boston, or did he *initially* say that he was from the South?

To a story line or an historical timeline, the sequence of events matters. To a vacation itinerary, the sequence of events matters. *And*, to answer a category of questions on the ACT Reading Test, the order of events matters.

Drawing Comparisons

Juxtapositions, in which characters/points of view/explanations are placed near each other for the sake of comparing and contrasting, sometimes come into play on the reading selections on the ACT. When juxtapositions present themselves, your job is to put on your detective's hat and pinpoint the various points of comparison and contrast.

To be prepared for questions that require you to draw comparisons, keep a *mental tally* of similarities and differences as you read. By the time you are done with the passage, you should be able to draw a conclusion about whether similarities between cultures (for example) outweigh their differences, or whether differences between two careers (for example) outweigh their similarities.

Based on the humanities passage ("Single-Breath Meditation") that appears in the Practice Test, the question that follows asks you to compare the functions of two interrogative statements that the author raises about breathing in terms of one's yoga practice:

27. As used in their respective contexts, the questions, "How can one breath . . . practice at all?" (lines 18 and 19) and "Who is breathing?" (line 33) function as follows:
    (A) The first is used as a topic sentence, and the second is intended as a question for the reader to ponder.
    (B) The first is used sarcastically; the second, somberly.
    (C) The first is a rhetorical question posed for the purpose of persuasion; the second is intended as an ironic, interrogative statement.
    (D) The first undermines the author's underlying assumptions; the second is an unrealistic stretch of the imagination.

To ace this question, you need to compare not only the purposes but also the tones of the respective questions.

Understanding Cause and Effect

Remember when you'd wind up your jack-in-the-box real tight? He'd pop straight up! Remember when you'd wind the string tight around a top? That top would spin out fast! And that time you didn't read the assigned history chapter? You failed the quiz! Everything you do causes a result (an effect). These are real-world examples of cause and effect.

On the ACT Reading Test, cause–effect questions can be posed on any of the four passage genres. With a natural science passage, for example, you may be asked what led to the scientist's findings; in other words, what <u>caused</u> her results, the <u>effect?</u> With a prose fiction piece, you may be asked the <u>effect</u> of one character's action (the <u>cause</u>) on his peers or on the larger community. Some effects are narrow and limited; others are vast and far-reaching. Sensitize yourself to cause–effect relationships as you read so that you'll be ready if this question type pops up in the mix.

The question below, which is posed in the ALL/EXCEPT format, is an example of a cause–effect question. This question is based on a humanities passage about yoga which appears later in this chapter.

24. Throughout the passage, the author suggests that "imbalances" (line 21) may result from ALL of the following EXCEPT:
    (A) eating overly processed foods.
    (B) living beyond one's fiscal means.
    (C) a misdirected stream of energy throughout the body.
    (D) a physical illness.

Grasping Meanings in Context

"Sand!" To a glassmaker, surfer, beach enthusiast, sand artist, and toddler in a sandbox, this word takes on several different meanings and values.

"Bridge!" To a card player, architect, yogi, and dental surgeon, this word also adopts particular meanings and images.

All words take on different meanings and nuances, depending upon the contexts in which they are used.

The vocabulary-in-context questions that follow appeared on the real ACT exam of June 2017. The questions are followed by the relevant part of the text that offers context clues into the meaning of the word.

19. As it is used in line 56, the phrase *stumbled across* most nearly means:
    (A) found by accident.
    (B) staggered toward.
    (C) unearthed.
    (D) tripped over.

(relevant excerpt from Social Science reading passage)
Recently, I **stumbled across** Abernethy House where Stevenson lived briefly in London when he was 23. It stands in a secluded corner of Hampstead, high up on a hill, and separated from foggy London by farms and heath.

35. As it is used in line 5, the word *greenery* most nearly refers to:
   (A) cultivated plants.
   (B) protected natural landscapes.
   (C) weeds.
   (D) crops.

(relevant excerpt from Natural Science reading passage)
The ecology of the city is defined not only by the cultivated plants that require maintenance and the protected remnants of natural landscapes, but also by the spontaneous vegetation that dominates the neglected interstices. **Greenery** fills the vacant spaces between our roads, homes, and businesses; lines ditches and chain-link fences; sprouts in sidewalk cracks and atop neglected rooftops. Some of those plants, such as box elder, quaking aspen, and riverside grape, are native species present before humans drastically altered the land.

The vocabulary-in-context questions that follow appeared on the real ACT exam of April 2017. The questions are followed by the relevant part of the text that offers context clues into the meaning of the word.

16. As it is used in lines 82–83, the phrase *named and nurtured* most nearly means:
   (F) nominated and encouraged.
   (G) identified and cultivated.
   (H) pointed to and groomed.
   (J) cited and fed.

(relevant excerpt from Natural Science reading passage)
And whittle away we have done. Here in North America, according to apple historian Dan Bussey, some 16,000 apple varieties have been **named and nurtured** over the last four centuries. By 1904, however, the identities and source of only 7,098 of those varieties could be discerned by the USDA scientist W. H. Ragan.

26. As it is used in line 35, the word *court* most nearly means to:
   (F) seek to attract.
   (G) romantically pursue.
   (H) dangerously provoke.
   (J) pass judgment upon.

(relevant excerpt from Humanities reading passage)
Oddly enough, Berry's geniality might help explain his failure to **court** history's favor; it wasn't in his nature to call attention to himself or his playing.

Grab your pencil and jot down the meaning of each of the words listed below. Do this quickly, without much thought. In other words, let the definition that you write down be your *initial* idea about or *feel* for the word. The first three words appeared in word-in-context questions on a real SAT exam; the last three are from actual ACT assessments.

Hail: _____

Crush: _____

Charged: _____

Silent Communion: _____

Projectile: _____

Circumscribed: _____

Your handwritten definitions might look something like this:

Hail: icy rain or to praise
Crush: orange soda or to flatten
Charged: made a purchase with a credit card
Silent Communion: religious ritual or being together without talking
Projectile: flying object
Circumscribed: a circle is drawn around

On reading comprehension passages, however, depending on the context in which the words and/or expressions (as in *silent communion*) are used, they could take on unexpected meanings:

Hail: to summon or call forth
Crush: a crowd of students; a throng
Charged: inspired
Silent Communion: an exchange of emotions
Projectile: an asteroid
Circumscribed: limited

In the question below, *vehicles* takes on a meaning other than what might first come to mind: trains, planes, and automobiles.

Define your salon through all possible avenues. Today, people hear about us on the Web, on television, through charity events, and in magazines and newspapers. A lot of these vehicles are free.

1. The word *vehicles* in the above refers to:
   (F) trendy cars.
   (G) public media.
   (H) free advertising sites.
   (J) publicity venues.

Once the word *vehicles* is plugged into its context, you understand that *vehicles* actually refers to publicity venues! If you do not go back to the text and if you rely on your memory or a personal hunch instead, you are likely to pick the wrong answer. If you think about it, when *vehicles* is considered in isolation, without its particular context, each answer choice can seem valid.

Formulating Generalizations

Let your mind be a sponge. For this type of question, you are asked to absorb and digest a great amount of information (several paragraphs or even the whole passage) and condense it into a *general statement* about what was stated or suggested. You should strive to "streamline" or simplify, to a reasonable extent, what is being said so that the general lines of reasoning stand out. In other words, you need to sift through the muck and the sand (extraneous details, tangential ideas, off-topic asides) to get to the pearl!

To answer this category of question correctly, you will need to select general statements that reflect the gist of a character, the author's overall point of view, or the prevailing mood or tone that flavors the reading selection in a holistic (complete) sense.

The following is an example of a question that would require you to engage your mind as an absorbent sponge: Soak up the author's philosophy, as expressed throughout the passage, and boil it down to match one of the four common sayings:

27. Based on the reading selection as a whole, which of the following adages* most closely mirrors this author's philosophy?
    (A) The early bird gets the worm.
    (B) We practice what we preach.
    (C) Waste not want not.
    (D) Do as I say, not as I do.

Vocabulary note: An *adage* is a proverb or old familiar saying, usually intended to impart a wise message.

Examining Author's Voice and Method

Have you ever participated in summer stage, a school play, or an improvisation troupe? If you have, then you are most likely familiar with the terms *voice* and *method* as they relate to those experiences. Indeed, voice and method are theater terms when considered in these particular contexts, but on the ACT Reading Test they mean something very specific. *Voice* is the author's point of view, style, or attitude. *Method* refers to the author's writing craft: the purpose of part of the passage as it relates to the whole and the author's overall purpose for writing.

The following question, based on the natural science passage on pages 161 to 162, asks you to *doubly* define the *author's style* by selecting the two adjectives that best describe the speaker's style as she delivers a speech on the dynamic cross cylinder:

To avoid careless errors or partially correct answers, address style questions at the very end. Typically, there is no one single sentence in which the author's style is revealed. Sometimes, style may surface within a particular paragraph, in which the author's voice (pessimistic, aloof, analytical, impulsive, for example) is very pronounced. Otherwise, it's most prudent to say that only once you have read the entire selection are you in a solid position to describe the author's style, which is a component of her overall voice.

39. The author's style is best described as:
    (A) cynical and wry.
    (B) direct and scholarly.
    (C) technical and persuasive.
    (D) jocular and belittling.

One part of the answer choice being correct doesn't quite cut it; partially correct answer choices do not earn you partial credit. For this type of question, both adjectives must effectively describe the author's style in order for the answer choice to be correct.

More No Sweat Points

Things You Don't Have to Worry About on the Reading Test

:) There's no need to make an effort to memorize key points and details as you read. In fact, this is inefficient. Instead, read carefully and at a time-savvy pace. (Practice with timing—about eight or nine minutes per passage—can help you to determine a pace that's not too speedy and not too sluggish.)

Memorization is not crucial because you have the reading passage available as a reference for you to refer back to as much as you would like. In fact, rereading (skimming, really) sections of the passage will help you to answer questions with the greatest accuracy.

:) There's no need to cram in order to do well on the Reading Test. You do not have to cram for the prose passage by trying to memorize the titles/authors/themes/settings/conflicts/symbols of the books and short stories you have read throughout your high school career. You do not have to know the major literary elements of the great canon of literature. Nor do you need to remember plot details from great classic novels. Likewise, to do well on the natural science passages, you do not need to cram by reading every article from *Scientific American* that you can get your hands on.

In a nutshell: You do not need to come to the test with specific background information about any particular book, author, genre, historical period, or body of writing, whether it pertains to natural science, social science, humanities, or prose fiction. Ahhh . . . another sigh of relief.

:) There's no need to identify the time period from which an excerpt was taken.

:) There's no need to study books and books of vocabulary words, and it's not necessary to master several sets of flash cards. Vocabulary does not play a starring role on the verbal portions of the ACT, as it arguably does on the critical reading sections of the SAT.

VOCABULARY

You do not need to cram vocabulary review into your study schedule; however, a strong and varied vocabulary *will* help you to make your way through and better understand the four passages that comprise the Reading Test. In addition to challenging words that may appear in the reading selections, there are likely to be word-in-context questions that specifically ask you about the precise meanings of words, based on how they are used in context. The bottom line is that a strong vocabulary will be an asset to you on test day. A healthy and broad vocabulary will allow you to avoid "big word" obstacles that could slow you down or confuse you and cause you to forgo precious points on test day.

✔ Self-check

How well do you know the vocabulary words that are listed below?
Ready for a reality check? All of the words listed below appeared on the Reading Test of an actual ACT assessment. Check the appropriate box along the continuum (*I know it.* → *Clueless*) to indicate your level of familiarity or comfort with each of the words listed below. Taken directly from the reading passages, these words were pulled as a sampling from among the four reading genres: prose fiction, natural science, social science, and humanities.

Check the appropriate box to indicate how well you know each word:

Threshold
☐ I know it.
☐ Fuzzy meaning
☐ Pretty certain I know it.
☐ Clueless

Console
☐ I know it.
☐ Fuzzy meaning
☐ Pretty certain I know it.
☐ Clueless

Latter
☐ I know it.
☐ Fuzzy meaning
☐ Pretty certain I know it.
☐ Clueless

Despairing
☐ I know it.
☐ Fuzzy meaning
☐ Pretty certain I know it.
☐ Clueless

Resigned
☐ I know it.
☐ Fuzzy meaning
☐ Pretty certain I know it.
☐ Clueless

Whim
☐ I know it.
☐ Fuzzy meaning
☐ Pretty certain I know it.
☐ Clueless

Rationality
☐ I know it.
☐ Fuzzy meaning
☐ Pretty certain I know it.
☐ Clueless

Mammoth
☐ I know it.
☐ Fuzzy meaning
☐ Pretty certain I know it.
☐ Clueless

Anomaly	☐ I know it. ☐ Fuzzy meaning	☐ Pretty certain I know it. ☐ Clueless
Scribes	☐ I know it. ☐ Fuzzy meaning	☐ Pretty certain I know it. ☐ Clueless
Bewildering	☐ I know it. ☐ Fuzzy meaning	☐ Pretty certain I know it. ☐ Clueless
Painstaking	☐ I know it. ☐ Fuzzy meaning	☐ Pretty certain I know it. ☐ Clueless
Intricate	☐ I know it. ☐ Fuzzy meaning	☐ Pretty certain I know it. ☐ Clueless
Dearth	☐ I know it. ☐ Fuzzy meaning	☐ Pretty certain I know it. ☐ Clueless
Ineptitude	☐ I know it. ☐ Fuzzy meaning	☐ Pretty certain I know it. ☐ Clueless
Causative	☐ I know it. ☐ Fuzzy meaning	☐ Pretty certain I know it. ☐ Clueless
Preoccupation	☐ I know it. ☐ Fuzzy meaning	☐ Pretty certain I know it. ☐ Clueless
Subsistence	☐ I know it. ☐ Fuzzy meaning	☐ Pretty certain I know it. ☐ Clueless
Virtuosic	☐ I know it. ☐ Fuzzy meaning	☐ Pretty certain I know it. ☐ Clueless
Sardonic	☐ I know it. ☐ Fuzzy meaning	☐ Pretty certain I know it. ☐ Clueless
Evangelical	☐ I know it. ☐ Fuzzy meaning	☐ Pretty certain I know it. ☐ Clueless
Successive	☐ I know it. ☐ Fuzzy meaning	☐ Pretty certain I know it. ☐ Clueless
Suffused	☐ I know it. ☐ Fuzzy meaning	☐ Pretty certain I know it. ☐ Clueless
Antidote	☐ I know it. ☐ Fuzzy meaning	☐ Pretty certain I know it. ☐ Clueless
Luminous	☐ I know it. ☐ Fuzzy meaning	☐ Pretty certain I know it. ☐ Clueless

Demeanor	☐ I know it. ☐ Fuzzy meaning	☐ Pretty certain I know it. ☐ Clueless
Awe	☐ I know it. ☐ Fuzzy meaning	☐ Pretty certain I know it. ☐ Clueless
Nostalgia	☐ I know it. ☐ Fuzzy meaning	☐ Pretty certain I know it. ☐ Clueless
Stagnation	☐ I know it. ☐ Fuzzy meaning	☐ Pretty certain I know it. ☐ Clueless
Elicited	☐ I know it. ☐ Fuzzy meaning	☐ Pretty certain I know it. ☐ Clueless
Placebo	☐ I know it. ☐ Fuzzy meaning	☐ Pretty certain I know it. ☐ Clueless
Impaired	☐ I know it. ☐ Fuzzy meaning	☐ Pretty certain I know it. ☐ Clueless

SELF-CHECK FINALE: HOW DO YOUR CHECK MARKS LOOK?

There is the evidence; now *you* be the judge. Do you think it's worthwhile to study a good amount of vocabulary words in order to reach your personal best score on the ACT? Do you realize that having facility with challenging types of words (like those featured in the previous list) can help you to succeed on the reading portions of the ACT?

Strive for Rapid Recall

To give yourself even more of a running start on test day, be at the top of your game by striving for "rapid recall." Rapid recall is the keen ability to recall the meanings of "college-bound" vocabulary with dispatch (speed). This ability is considerably beneficial because it allows you to work through the Reading and English Tests more quickly. Fortified with rapid recall, you will not get bogged down by spending too much time on any one question because of the hard vocabulary within that question. Keep in mind that the words on pages 145–147 were not selected randomly or pulled out of thin air—*all of these words appeared on just one very recent ACT Exam!*

Now is your chance to test your critical reading ability with a prose fiction passage. If dramatic prose is not your thing, don't worry because the ACT serves up a social science passage next!

Chapter Summary

You've sharpened your critical reading skills, and now you are ready for action on the Reading Test, one of the three verbal sections of the ACT. You know how to exercise an effective, four-step approach—**preview, focus, read, answer**—that will help you to tackle the four reading passages that comprise the Reading Test. You have also been informed about how imperative test-taking intangibles such as **focus, concentration,** and **discipline** are when it comes to performing your personal best. Without a doubt, you appreciate how important it is to block out distractions, white noise, and static. Embracing a testing frame of mind, you are ready to hunker down, square off your shoulders, and focus on the test material.

You now understand how to maintain **five levels of concentration and comprehension** as you work your way through the four reading passages and their respective question sets. You know that, to a considerable extent, knowing what the question is asking is as important as making distinctions among answer choices.

Five Levels of Concentration and Comprehension

Now roll up your sleeves, sharpen your pencils, and put your repertoire of critical reading skills into action by **practicing the four passage genres**: prose fiction, humanities, social science, and natural science. Leaving no stone unturned, peruse the answer explanations and make sense of the reasoning behind valid and invalid answer choices.

Practice Exercises

Prose Fiction (1)

Written in first-person narrative point of view, this prose passage was adapted from a free-verse poem, entitled "Driving Down Broadway," that was featured in *tabula rasa* (Latin for "blank slate"), a literary magazine written and published by students enrolled in the Teaching of English program within the Teaching of Literature, Language, and Social Studies department at Teachers College, Columbia University, New York. The original poem was inspired by student Linda Benzoni's commute from Long Island to Manhattan's Teachers College campus.

Leaning to the right, I pull down the passenger seat visor. So this is the countenance of stress, I say aloud to my strained forehead and weary eyes in the mirror. The
5   cab's nose is one inch from my right fender. Slow moving, it intrudes my lane like a sly panther. I try meeting the driver's eyes; he looks dead ahead, as if in a trance.

Driving down Broadway is like being
10   stuck on a conveyor belt with a mind of its own. When I attempt to change lanes, my direction signals blink in vain. The road has a sidetracking mind of its own. I've become adept at maneuvering, though; I
15   have learned to avoid unplanned turns. Side streets lead to who … knows … where? Seems a labyrinth of buildings and streets.

Now I'm the first in line at a traffic light. A jolly-looking panhandler is approaching
20   my window, smiling widely. I'm not. I catch myself in the rear view mirror: aggravation. The unfortunate man is hunched over, peering at me through the window. His breath collects on the glass and his out-
25   stretched hand, upturned, shows a stained

palm. Fluttering like a leaf, his hand caresses a few gold coins.

Honk! Beep! Hoooonkkk! Beeeeep!

Usual reflex: shoulders lift, tension. The
30   light's green and I've failed to move on quicksilver. Now I'm trailing a bicycle rider. I marvel at the lady on wheels darting in and out the lanes. Exaggerated hand signals and gestures afford her an upper-
35   body workout. My hands strangle the steering wheel. Frenetic and lean, rollerbladers show no humility as they skate by—bumper by bumper—flaunting their agility. "I can't hear you," say their headphones to honkers.

40   Wishing it were broad daylight, I drive down Broadway, blinded by red brake lights.

1. The overarching theme of this prose piece concerns the:
    (A) jocular reaction of those who are observing this driver.
    (B) striking contrasts one may witness on the streets of Manhattan.
    (C) challenges of commuting to and from work on a daily basis.
    (D) anxieties experienced by a driver who navigates a crowded urban avenue.

2. The effect of the word "strangle" in line 35 is best described as:
    (F) creating a sense of foreboding.
    (G) adding a note of humor to temper the cynicism.
    (H) emphasizing the driver's tension behind the wheel.
    (J) including an instance of dark imagery.

3. Which of the following does NOT
illustrate personification?
   (A) The cab's nose (lines 4–5)
   (B) Conveyor belt (line 10)
   (C) Hand signals and gestures (lines 33–34)
   (D) Headphones (line 39)

4. As used in lines 2–3, the word
"countenance" most nearly means:
   (F) face.
   (G) comedy.
   (H) façade.
   (J) nature.

5. As used in line 12, the effect of the
expression "in vain" is to:
   (A) characterize the conceited personality
   of the driver.
   (B) raise questions about inadequate traffic
   flow in metropolitan areas.
   (C) comment on an additional area in
   which the narrator lacks pragmatic
   skill.
   (D) express that the driver's attempt to
   move into a new lane was ineffective.

6. Which of the following questions is NOT
answered by information in the passage?
   (F) Is the driver traveling alone?
   (G) Are there potentially dangerous
   physical obstacles that the driver faces
   as she travels along Broadway?
   (H) What time of day is it?
   (J) Is the driver feeling tired?

Now that you have left the genre of prose
fiction, you can test your critical reading savvy
with a social science passage. If topics pertaining
to sociology, education, economics, or political
science hold your interest, terrific! If these disciplines are not your cup of tea, keep your chin up
because a humanities passage is coming up next!

Prose Fiction (2)

The following passage entitled "The Magician,"
is an excerpt from an unpublished fantasy adventure novel written by *New York Times* best-selling
author Michael Friedman. Friedman has written
sixty-five books for children and adults, most
of them science fiction or fantasy. Eleven of his
books, including an authorized biography of Hulk
Hogan, have appeared on the prestigious *New
York Times* best-seller lists. He has also written
for television, radio, and comic books. Friedman,
a high school English teacher on Long Island's
North Shore, is a graduate of the University of
Pennsylvania.

Edwyn Arwynsson studied the bustling
open-air market to make sure no one was
watching him. Fortunately, everyone's
attention was in the middle of the plaza,
5 where a gaily dressed stilt-walker—his red
pants billowing like sails, his bronze earrings
glistening in the sunlight—was swaggering
down the center aisle, his assistant following
afterward with a hat full of coins.

10 *Perfect*, Edwyn thought. In his business,
misdirection was everything.

As unobtrusively as he could, he emptied
a handkerchief full of flame-rocks unto the
pocket of his linen jacket. The rocks were
15 tiny and they looked like mere road-gravel,
but they would burst into flame when he
ground them together.

It was a more spectacular trick on a
cloudy day, when the appearance of a flame
20 could be startling. A day like this one, in
which the sun was exceedingly bright in the
azure depths of the sky, was less than perfect
in that regard. Still, as Edwyn's father had
instructed him time and again, it was all in
25 the presentation.

The boy had never worked his father's booth in the midsummer market all by himself. But then, he had never been compelled to do so. His father had always been there to draw in the curious, to give them a small display of his magical powers, and then to sell them some of his many charms—to ease their aches and pains, to secure them the promise of an ample harvest, or perhaps to turn the head of a fair maiden.

Edwyn laid the charms out side by side, each a small, leather pouch full of sticks and stones and dried flowers. The one thing they all had in common was that none of them worked. After all, magic had its limits. One could seem to make a coin disappear, or guess someone's name with the help of a secret accomplice, or reduce a strong man to tears with a pinch in the right place.

That was all feasible if the magician knew what he was doing, if he was quick enough and clever enough with his hands. But there was no real magic in the whole wide world from Tyronia in the north to Agapenthon in the south. And who knew that better than the son of a wily old mage?

Yet somehow not wily enough, Edwyn thought with a sigh.

Otherwise, Arwyn would never have gone on the duke's foolish quest into the steep vales of the western mountains, from which none of his party had yet returned. Edwyn still didn't understand what had lured his father into the duke's entourage. Not gold, or Arwyn would have given it to his wife for safekeeping, and not fame, for Arwyn didn't care a jot for prestige at court.

Whatever had drawn him away, he had departed with hardly a word of farewell, so it must have been tantalizing indeed. Truth be told, Edwyn had been excited about it too, if only at the outset. As people had remarked time and again, he was his father's son, and very much in tune with the old man's humors.

But that had been weeks ago. And with every passing day, the speculations of the aldermen in the square grew more dire. The duke's party had met with a landslide, said some. A pack of ravenous wolves, said others. No, whispered still others, it was a fierce and sudden storm that had washed the duke's men off the slopes and drowned them.

Edwyn did not lend credence to any of the stories. However, as the only man left in the house, he had to see to it that his family had enough to eat. Hence, the need for him to man his father's booth.

Once the stilt-walker came down for a rest, the people remembered why they had come to the market in the first place. Some headed for the butcher's stall or the baker's, seeking to stock their larders. Edwyn did not offer the staples of life, so no one came his way. But they would once the show began.

"Fire!" he cried out suddenly in his shrill boy's voice, drawing stares from here and there. "The breath of the gods!"

Knowing he had the people's attention, Edwyn reached into his pocket and grabbed a handful of flame-rocks. Then he held his fist to his forehead, inhaled and then exhaled a deep, theatrical breath, and opened his hand.

The grinding of the rocks, which were too small for the people to see, produced a flame in his palm. It was small and blue and not terribly impressive overall, but it
105 was a flame nonetheless. And it was already pulling people in closer to his booth.

He recited the words his father taught him, casting them like a long, strong fishing line. "Win your lady love! Bring down your
110 enemies! See the future!"

It worked. The people crowded around Edwyn, and believed in him despite his age, and bought his magicks. His pockets bulged with their coins.

115 *My father would be proud*, he could not help thinking.

Finally, there was but one customer left, a man with a mane of wild, gray hair and a patient look in his dark brown eyes. A
120 big man, it seemed to Edwyn, though the fellow's roomy, homespun robes made it difficult to know for sure.

"Would you like to see what the gods have in store for you?" the boy asked slyly.

125 The man's thick, gray brows lowered over the bridge of his aquiline nose, darkening his face as if a storm were rolling in. "You misunderstand, my young friend," he said in a deep, mellifluous voice. "It is I who has
130 come to reveal the future to *you*."

Note to Sharp Test Takers: Take a moment to notice and consider the varied vocabulary that appears in the prose fiction passage above. Here is a sampling of the potentially challenging words that appear in this engaging excerpt: billowing, swaggering, unobtrusively, azure, feasible, wily, mage, entourage, dire, credence, mane, mellifluous. The stronger your vocabulary, the easier the reading will be for you. Are you working to improve the scope, depth, and strength of your lexicon, your usable vocabulary?

7. It can be reasonably inferred from the first paragraph (lines 1–9) that Edwyn Arwynsson:
   (A) was mesmerized by the flamboyant stilt-walker.
   (B) covertly wished that he was as physically adept as the stilt-walker's assistant.
   (C) didn't want people watching him as he prepared his trick.
   (D) neglected to make himself the colorful—even eccentric—character that he was expected to be.

8. The passage is written from the point of view of:
   (F) Edwyn himself.
   (G) the stilt-walker's assistant.
   (H) an omniscient narrator.
   (J) Edwyn's long lost father.

9. Based on lines 54–62, which of the following could have been the impetus behind Edwyn's father's journey "into the steep vales of the western mountains"?
(A) his desire to gain a higher-ranking social stature
(B) his aspiration for increased renown among his fellow magicians
(C) his drive for monetary rewards
(D) his deep interest in the mysteries of nature

10. In context, as it is used in line 26, the action verb "worked" most nearly means
(F) begrudged
(G) streamlined
(H) managed
(J) toiled

11. It can be reasonably inferred that the magician boy most likely exclaimed "The breath of the gods!" (line 94) for which main purpose?
(A) to add to and underscore his prior, attention-seeking exclamation, "Fire!"
(B) to detract the crowd's attention from the stilt-walker
(C) to tout his wide reading by alluding to the fire-breathing gods of mythology
(D) to warn the townspeople of the dangers of the developing fire in the butcher shop that could threaten the entire marketplace

12. Based on lines 40–47, "After all … with his hands," the reader can infer that a skillful magician ought to possess all of the following EXCEPT:
(F) manual deftness.
(G) paternal intrigue.
(H) the ability to serve as an adept co-conspirator.
(J) celerity with his nimble hands.

13. It can be reasonably inferred that all of the following might comprise "the old man's humors" (lines 69–70) EXCEPT:
(A) his jocular ways.
(B) his financial assets.
(C) his decorum.
(D) his tendency to be festive.

14. Edwyn's exclamation, as expressed in lines 109–110, "Win your lady love! Bring down your enemies! See the future!" is intended to promise all of the following benefits EXCEPT:
(F) discover the precise whereabouts of your lost loved ones!
(G) gain the heart of the woman you adore!
(H) divine the future!
(J) undermine your adversaries!

15. In context, the phrase "the staples of life" (line 90) most closely stands for:
    (A) good-humored folly and entertainment.
    (B) savory meats and breads.
    (C) money to buy the necessities needed to sustain life.
    (D) mundane commercial dealings.

16. In the final paragraph, the author uses which of the following literary techniques as he elaborates upon his description of the "man with a mane of wild, gray hair" (line 118)?
    (F) hyperbole
    (G) metaphor
    (H) symbolism
    (J) simile

Social Science

This passage is written by Edythe K. Scro, LCSW, CASAC, who holds a Master of Social Work from Adelphi University in New York. A licensed clinical social worker in New York State, Ms. Scro has worked as a substance-abuse counselor at Long Island Jewish Hospital for more than fifteen years.

Mobilization for Youth started in 1958, as a collaborative effort between the leaders of the Henry Street Settlement and two Columbia University sociologists, Ohlin
5 and Cloward. The project was to design a large-scale neighborhood program to deal with the problems of juvenile delinquency. Their basic premise was that the many problems confronted by poor people—depriva-
10 tion, lack of opportunity, et cetera—were at the root of the juvenile delinquency problems. Thus, with funding provided by the National Institute for Mental Health and, later, the Ford Foundation, a comprehen-
15 sive program was developed.

The area studied was Manhattan's Lower East Side (the community surrounding the Henry Street Settlement), which had a population of 100,000 people, twenty
20 percent of whom were poor. The project was designed to help the residents and to serve as a demonstration. Its approach was scientific with problems defined, goals set, and performance checked. It was staffed
25 and governed by many kinds of experts and pulled together many different interests.

Mobilization for Youth was a delinquency control project that sought to get at the pervasive frustrations of poverty which were at
30 the root of delinquency. Deprived youth were ill-equipped to compete in society with the more advantaged upper class youths. The organization offered services to individual families, group work, and community
35 organization with special emphasis on education and job training.

President Kennedy was interested in Mobilization for Youth and formed a committee on juvenile delinquency. Subse-
40 quently, an Office of Juvenile Delinquency was established as part of the HEW; the Juvenile Delinquency and Youth Offenses Control Act was passed in 1961 which provided for other programs like Mobilization
45 for Youth. Finally, Mobilization for Youth was a keynote in the War on Poverty and the inspiration for the Economic Opportunity Act which set up programs such as Job Corps, Neighborhood Youth Corps, and
50 Work Study Programs.

17. Which of the following best describes the author's overall tone as expressed in this passage?
   (A) Humble
   (B) Ambivalent
   (C) Indifferent
   (D) Objective

18. In developing this selection, the author uses ALL of the following EXCEPT:
   (F) numbers and statistics.
   (G) defining terms and programs.
   (H) allusions to philosophical works about government's ethical role in helping its people.
   (J) references to scholars and influential people.

19. Based on the passage as a whole, you can infer that the author would most closely consider which of the following as "deprived youth" (line 30)?
   (A) Youngsters who are neglected by the "experts" who are referred to in line 25
   (B) Young people who forfeit opportunities in job training and education
   (C) Youngsters who live in New York City's Lower East Side
   (D) Young people who are financially challenged and who lack opportunities in education and job training

20. President Kennedy's role in terms of Mobilization for Youth can be best expressed as:
   (F) an advocate whose interest precipitated the passing of youth-supporting government acts and whose support led to additional programs for young citizens.
   (G) a detractor who slowed down the program of Mobilization for Youth by spreading his interest and support too thin.
   (H) a skeptic who veered away from the original goals and intentions put forth by Mobilization for Youth.
   (J) an avid supporter whose unfocused enthusiasm led, unintentionally, to the dissolving of Mobilization for Youth.

21. If the author were to continue this essay, what would she most likely discuss next?
   (A) President Kennedy's influence on other city programs
   (B) The young people's role in creating their own futures
   (C) How funds are raised to support the programs mentioned in the final paragraph
   (D) One of the programs mentioned in the last paragraph in more detail

Another reading "flavor" is coming up: humanities. Maybe you will find that the reading selections of this genre are most engaging for you! On the other hand, if essays pertaining to philosophy, art, dance, and music—among other topics—do not hold your interest, rest assured that a different flavor (natural science) is coming up around the bend.

Humanities (1)

This piece was written by Donna Rovegno, a Long Island-based yoga instructor, who holds certification through the National Yoga Alliance. Ms. Rovegno teaches inspiring classes, including Power Yoga, at several popular fitness clubs and has a devoted following of students of all ages.

It is important for me to teach about the Yamas and Niyamas. The Yamas and Niyamas serve as guidelines of care and conduct toward oneself and others. Teaching
5 awareness and application of these principles will keep my students in touch with their true and most fulfilling purposes during their journeys of existence. Commitment and internalization of these codes awaken
10 a higher discipline governed primarily by a sense of honor to self and others.

I believe that I need to have knowledge about and teach the chakras. The chakras harness and channel the flow of energy
15 throughout the body and mind systems throughout and within glands and nerve bundles. Since all elements of one's physical and mental self are connected, understanding the governing qualities of each
20 chakra will help me recognize deficiencies or superfluous imbalances that may impede someone in his or her body or emotion. I can tune in to redirect the flow of energy within the chakras to restore the balance
25 and function within these channels.

How we eat makes a difference, in yoga and in life. Food is our source of energy and sustenance. Living food, unlike processed or preserved, is optimal for digestion, absorp-
30 tion, and nutrition. Inappropriate or ill-prepared foods will clog the body and mind, zapping one's energy and acuity. "You are what you eat," and how an individual's body performs and functions are direct
35 results of how one eats!

Working part-time around the schedules of my two children, with a set week of group classes at local studios, suits me ideally. I also enjoy working privately with individu-
40 als who are striving to achieve specific goals, such as pain relief or relaxation. I focus my attention on their personal program at their convenience. I accept opportunities that come my way with optimistic faith, as I
45 feel I will gain the insight and direction to choose that which I am best suited for and fulfilled by.

22. "These codes," mentioned in line 9, most closely refer to:
    (F) behavioral rules of humane treatment toward fellow man and self.
    (G) business ethics in the health and fitness industry.
    (H) habits of personal conduct that mirror military training.
    (J) the life ambitions of individuals.

23. In context, the word "governed" (line 10) most closely means:
    (A) legislated.
    (B) mandated.
    (C) coerced.
    (D) directed.

24. Throughout the passage, the author suggests that "imbalances" (line 21) may result from ALL of the following EXCEPT:
    (F) eating overly processed foods.
    (G) living beyond one's fiscal means.
    (H) a misdirected stream of energy throughout the body.
    (J) a physical illness.

25. As expressed in lines 36–38, "Working part-time around the schedules of my two children, with a set week of group classes at local studios, suits me ideally," suggests that the author:

(A) harbors an unrealistic mindset about the workings of the health and fitness industry.

(B) possesses a methodical mindset that will edify her in the business world.

(C) does not fully embrace her role as yoga instructor.

(D) has pragmatic ideas about attaining a work program that supports her priorities and suits her lifestyle.

26. By saying, "I focus my attention on their [the clients'] personal program at their convenience" (lines 41–43) followed immediately by, "I accept opportunities that come my way . . . as I feel I will gain the insight and direction to choose that which I am best suited for and fulfilled by" (lines 43–47) suggests which of the following about the author?

(F) She cares about her well-being just as she cares about the well-being of her yoga students.

(G) She has tunnel vision when it comes to her career goals: Self-gain is the one thing worth seeking.

(H) She is self-sacrificing to a fault, as she revels in over-catering to her yoga clients.

(J) She feels a great urgency to satisfy the needs of all of her students at once, while putting her own satisfaction on the back burner.

Humanities (2)

This passage by Brooke Huminski, entitled "Loving the Questions," is taken from *We Are the Ones We've Been Waiting for*, a publication by the Capstone Class of 2007, Providence College, Rhode Island, and a compilation of reflections on life and service from the public and community service.

"Be patient towards all that is unsolved in your heart and try to love the questions. Do not now seek the answers, which cannot be given you because you would not be able to live them. Live the questions now. Perhaps you will then gradually, without noticing it, live along some distant day into the answer."
—Rainer Maria Rilke, "Letters to a Young Poet"

One does not enter college a blank slate. This is perhaps one of the most important premises with which the Public and Community Service major operates. Perhaps this
5　is one reason I was drawn to the study, (which uses reflection to tie volunteer experience in the community with study in the classroom); it afforded me the chance to look for some meaning in my experiences,
10　past and present.

Indeed first semester I was provided the opportunity to spend my Saturday mornings at Amos House, a local soup kitchen. Why would a young adult willingly give up
15　precious Saturday mornings? I started off desperately curious to learn about people *different* than me. I wanted to hear people's stories of homelessness and hunger, connect faces with the problems, ones which I had
20　never experienced. Ironically, looked at from a different angle, I can also see that I was longing to be with people *like* me. As a freshman, the question of suffering was fresh on my mind from personal experiences I had had

back in high school. What shocked me most that semester was not the differences between us but the similarities and connection I felt to the people who came to the Amos House, and the universality of suffering.

As I progressed in my years at Providence College, I changed settings in my volunteer placements, but the question was still the same: Why do people suffer? I wondered, "What is so universal about suffering, in its different forms and degrees?" While spending time at Hasbro Children's Hospital, I contemplated why innocent children suffer from terrible cancers and other illnesses. How do they smile through their pain and play board games with volunteers? How do children have such strength? I was moved and inspired by the spirits of these children. Yes, there were nights when I would break down to my roommate, at the shear irrationality of these living questions for which there were no answers.

Yet I moved onward, towards new service opportunities, until at the cusp of despair and burnout I found another important question, "How do I practice joy?" One Catholic Worker retreat provided a fine example of the need to pay attention to such a question. It was held in Worcester, Massachusetts, and attended by marvelously passionate people who made me painfully aware of the many problems our world is facing. Should not we go act now?! I had some to learn. At the dance party, I participated in the wild movement to ridiculous songs and felt immense joy. Movement announced an end to the day of contemplation, for what else is there to do when all leads to unanswerable questions?

During that dance party, I felt a strong calling to live a life with these untamed workers. Drawn to their explicit practice of the Catholic faith through peace issues, I wondered if my right livelihood would be to join the Catholic Workers upon graduation. Would that be where I would find my peace and purpose? Senior year Capstone gave me a time, place, and company with which to explore these questions of vocation. Together, guided by Keith, our wise and fearless leader, our class journeyed on a path lit by questions, immediate as well as those far-reaching into the future.

It was this year that I was introduced to the works of the sensitive observer, Rainer Maria Rilke. Upon first reading the passage cited above, I felt a soft but powerful wave of calmness wash over me. My hands unclenched a little. I could intuitively understand and agree with what Rilke was proposing; yet it was not until recently that I truly made time to process the meaning for my life. I suppose I had only half believed his words. With graduation approaching, I realized I was frustrated that I did not have answers for many of the questions that I have devoted considerable time and energy studying over the past four years. When pressed by a wise person close to me, I had no fine answer as to why I loved the questions, and how I practiced living them in my life.

This was incredibly bothersome to my core, not being able to explain and practice wisdom I felt was true. I knew that not living the questions led to much inner turmoil. There have been times when I really found myself stuck in questions to the point of paralysis. How have I moved through the questions through those times? It is evident from recalling experiences from the past four years that service has been one way to move, allowing me to process and learn while still living. This is where I am most grateful to have had the opportunity to be in this major and to my teachers and

110 mentors along the way. Few other depart-
ments value experiential learning and reflections so highly.

Another way I try to live the questions is
one slow in coming, but has been supported
115 and developed as well by this major, that is
trusting myself. Some of the questions frus-
trating me as I prepare to leave Providence
College are, "Have I made a difference?" and
"Will I be missed?" Also, "Will I be import-
120 ant in the future?" A shift in myself and sign
of growth come in the understanding that I
can only look inside myself for how to live
with such questions. A considerable amount
of trust needs to be afforded to that inner
125 voice we are all said to have, an idea which
scares me. It is not a spring I tend to tap
often. Yet, in doing so I learn to rest with
some of the unanswered questions and not
doubt my insights. Keith began Capstone
130 telling us that we all know what we want to
do; the struggle is voicing that true part of
ourselves, often for fear of judgment. It has
taken me until now to understand what he
means. This major and the mentors I have
135 had along the way really have helped me
strengthen that voice, accepting that we do
not enter college empty slates. Perhaps I am a
slow learner, but that is something that I am
only feeling awakened to now, five days from
140 graduation. It is undoubtedly an important
part of my living out the questions.

Rilke does not stop with advising his
young correspondent with living the unre-
solved questions, he pushes that one should
145 love the questions. Going beyond accepting
the questions, I believe am slowly seeing the
ways I also love the questions. For example,
exploring the questions has moved me to
service, opening doors to opportunities and
150 relationships I may have never encountered
otherwise. Not knowing the answers will
keep me moving, beyond graduation, to new
places and people as I travel across the globe.

155 Furthermore and rather simply, unanswered
questions keep life interesting. In this respect
I love not having the answer to my vocation
because then there would not be as much
excitement in the exploration.

Indeed it is with excitement and a healthy
160 amount of heartache that I move onward.
I have given and received more than I
could have imagined in my time here at
Providence. My mentors have been invaluable and precious to me. I am immensely
165 thankful for their open hearts and minds to
my young spirit, full of questions. Endings
bring new life and while my formal education as a public and community service
major are over, the challenges are not and
170 nor is my journey. Through the wild questions, I will keep trying to dance.

27. The image evoked by the words "My hands
    unclenched a little" (lines 82–83) most
    closely conveys a sense of:
    (A) the author's mitigating anxiety and
        tension.
    (B) Rainer Rilke's far-reaching wisdom.
    (C) Capstone leader Keith's effect on his
        colleagues.
    (D) a wise person's (line 93) physical
        manifestation of his mental state.

28. For the author, "turmoil" (line 100) and
    "paralysis" (line 102) primarily result from:
    (F) her inability to decide on a graduate
        program of study once she leaves
        Providence College.
    (G) her difficulties experienced when she
        would try to put her book learning and
        college coursework into action in the
        "real world."
    (H) her struggle, one based in self-explora-
        tion, to answer pressing inquiries with
        clarity and focus.
    (J) her lack of adequate resources required
        to put public welfare programs into
        action.

29. For this author, one can reasonably infer that the "spring" mentioned in line 126 is:
    (A) an allusion to the untapped resources, primarily financial and internship-related, afforded to her during her college years.
    (B) a metaphor for her inner wisdom and voice.
    (C) an image of the internal contradictions and enigmas that affect most thoughtful people.
    (D) an infinite source of wisdom one can achieve through studying the sagacious quotations and writings of others.

30. In Paragraph 8 (lines 113–141), the author most closely expresses a mixture of which of the following emotional dynamics?
    (F) Confusion and desolation
    (G) Despondency and vexation
    (H) Internal struggle and despair
    (J) Introspection and self-reliance

31. Based on the information presented in the passage as a whole, one can reasonably conclude that according to the author, she has witnessed or believes that ALL of the following groups of people suffer EXCEPT:
    (A) the convalescents at Hasbro Children's Hospital and her former high school peers.
    (B) Catholic Workers and hospital volunteers.
    (C) high school students.
    (D) the homeless and the hungry.

32. In which of the following settings does the author feel the greatest level of ease and bliss?
    (F) Hasbro Children's Hospital (line 36)
    (G) The dance party (line 58)
    (H) Amos House (line 13)
    (J) High school (line 25)

33. In the first two paragraphs, the author makes use of ALL of the following narrative techniques EXCEPT:
    (A) telling her story by dramatically shifting between the singular, third-person pronoun *one* and the first-person pronouns *I* and *me*.
    (B) using italics for the purposes of irony and emphasis.
    (C) including parenthetical comments.
    (D) raising a rhetorical question.

34. The closing sentence of this passage "Through the wild questions, I will keep trying to dance" brings about which of the following rhetorical effects?
    (F) It provides a framework effect between the opening and closing paragraphs.
    (G) It belies Rilke's quotation, which is featured at the top.
    (H) It contradicts the essay's title, "Loving the Questions."
    (J) It refers back to images and change-of-heart expressed in paragraphs 4 and 5.

35. In context, the word "progressed" (line 30) most closely means:
    (A) earned an advanced academic distinction.
    (B) matured and became braver in personal conviction and spirit.
    (C) continued along.
    (D) provided service to others who were less fortunate.

36. The word "cusp," as used in line 48, most nearly means:
    (F) point of no return.
    (G) pinnacle.
    (H) precipice.
    (J) pointed edge.

Natural Science

This is the oral text from a PowerPoint presentation co-authored by Mark Rosenfield, PhD, MCOptom, FAAO, and Jaclyn Anne Benzoni, BS, OD, MS. The passage below was presented at an annual meeting of the American Academy of Optometry in Denver, Colorado. It is about a clinical optometric test called the Dynamic Cross Cylinder. The speaker, Ms. Benzoni, recently traveled to Honduras with SVOSH (Student Volunteers for Optometric Service to Humanity, a national service organization dedicated to providing eye care to those in need) to implement and deliver a large-scale screening to the Honduran people.

Good morning ladies and gentlemen. The dynamic cross-cylinder test is a standard clinical procedure used to measure the accommodative response subjectively.
5 The patient views a pattern of intersecting horizontal and vertical lines while a ±0.50D cross cylinder is introduced to create mixed astigmatism, with the horizontal and vertical lines theoretically lying equidistant in
10 front of and behind the retina. The patient is asked to report whether the horizontal or vertical lines appear clearer, and spherical lenses are then added until the two sets of lines appear equal.

15 It is most appropriate that we are discussing this test here in Denver, since Edward Jackson, after whom the JCC (Jackson Cross Cylinder, also known as the Dynamic Cross Cyliner) is named, spent
20 the majority of his professional life in the Department of Ophthalmology at the University of Colorado, right here in the city of Denver. In 1887, Jackson noted that a cross-cylinder lens could be used to quan-
25 tify the amount of astigmatism, and later in 1907, he observed that it could also be used to measure the astigmatic axis, using techniques with which we are all so familiar today.

30 However, with all due respect to Edward Jackson, the use of a cross cylinder to quantify the accommodative response (the change in the crystalline lens associated with an increase in focusing power) in a young
35 patient does have significant problems. For example, the assumption is made that in a patient with an accurate accommodative response, that is where the response is equal to the accommodative stimulus, then the
40 patient will maintain the circle of least confusion on the retina, as is shown in this diagram, where the horizontal focal line and vertical focal line lie at an equal distance away from the retina. When viewing
45 the rectilinear target, this has the effect of making both sets of lines equally blurred. Frequently, patients prefer to alter their accommodative response so that one set of lines becomes clear, and it is not uncommon
50 for patients to be able to switch between having the horizontal and then vertical lines appear clear.

In addition, once the patient reports a preference for one set of lines, then spher-
55 ical lenses are introduced to make the two sets of lines appear equal. The *assumption* is the existing accommodative response will be maintained as the lenses are introduced. However, this seems unlikely, and
60 one could imagine that once plus lenses are introduced, the accommodative response would decline, since the need for accommodation is reduced. Further, it is traditional to perform the test under reduced illumina-
65 tion conditions, since this will maximize the patient's pupil diameter and thereby reduce the depth-of-focus of the eye. However, the accommodative response under these illumination levels may differ from that found
70 under more habitual and optimal viewing conditions.

Accordingly, the aim of the present study was to compare clinical measurements of the accommodation response obtained sub-
75 jectively with the dynamic cross-cylinder test with those found using an objective infra-red optometer, namely the Grand Seiko WAM 5500, while subjects viewed the same cross-cylinder target at a distance
80 of 40 cm. For both the objective and subjective findings, the target was viewed under binocular fused conditions, and the objective data was recorded from the right eye only. The experiment was carried out on
85 25 subjects having a mean age of 23.4 years, covering an age range between 20 and 30 years.

While there was a significant correlation between the two sets of findings, the slope
90 of the regression line, shown here in red was only 0.51, reflecting the lower objective findings. The difference between the two sets of findings is emphasized further here. The difference between the subjective and
95 objective data is represented on the Y-50 axis, while the X-axis shows the objective findings. The dashed horizontal line shows the mean difference, with the subjective findings being higher in all but two of the
100 twenty-five subjects.

Eight subjects showed a lag of accommodation subjectively, that is an accommodative response less than the accommodative stimulus level of 2.50D, and all of these
105 eight subjects also showed a lag of accommodation objectively. Once a lag of accommodation is reported by virtue of the subject indicating that the horizontal lines appear clearer on the rectilinear target, then con-
110 ventionally, plus spheres are added until the patient reports that the two sets of lines become equally clear. We used the objective infra-red optometer to measure the accommodative response through these

115 lenses, and it can clearly be observed that the accommodative response declined significantly when plus lenses were introduced. Thus the test methodology itself altered the parameter that the practitioner was trying
120 to measure.

In conclusion, the results of the present study indicate that the subjective dynamic cross cylinder does not provide veridical measures of the accommodative response
125 to a near target in young patients. The test tends to overestimate the number of individuals having a lead of accommodation, and there is poor agreement between the findings of this subjective test and objec-
130 tive measurements of the accommodative response obtained while viewing the same rectilinear target.
Thank you for your attention.

37. The authors do ALL of the following EXCEPT:
    (A) contradict one of their former studies.
    (B) define a scientific term.
    (C) refer to an authority.
    (D) provide a bit of historical background.

38. Based on the passage as a whole, it can be inferred from "as is shown in this diagram," (lines 41–42) and "the slope of the regression line, shown here in red" (lines 89–90) that the speaker:
    (F) frequently refers to textbook pages when she lectures.
    (G) is most likely accomplished as a graphic artist.
    (H) must rely on various visual aids to meet the learning styles of her audience.
    (J) is pointing to figures as illustrated in her PowerPoint presentation.

39. The author's style is best described as:
    (A) cynical and wry.
    (B) direct and scholarly.
    (C) technical and persuasive.
    (D) jocular and belittling.

40. The author italicizes the word *assumption* in lines 56–57 most likely to emphasize the:
    (F) tentative state of this experimental use of spherical lenses.
    (G) concern she has about the long-term detriments of using spherical lenses.
    (H) absurdity with which these lenses have been vehemently doubted by the scientific population.
    (J) confusion felt by those who advocate the widespread use of these spherical lenses.

41. In consideration of the phrases *astigmatic axis* (line 27), *veridical measures* (lines 123–124) and *rectilinear target* (line 109), the author's diction reveals which of the following about the passage as a whole?
    (A) The passage contains details that are doubtful as well as fallacious.
    (B) The passage contains terminology that is esoteric as well as technical.
    (C) The passage contains information that is hypocritical as well as abstruse.
    (D) The passage contains knowledge that is hypothetical as well as physiological.

42. By the statement in lines 30–31, *with all due respect to Edward Jackson,* the speaker most nearly means to express:
    (F) that Jackson should be acclaimed as having made the most noteworthy impact in the field of eye care.
    (G) her gratitude toward Jackson is profound and unwavering.
    (H) that while Jackson is renowned for his introduction of the DCC, there are inherent flaws within this clinical test.
    (J) sarcasm in an attempt to degrade Jackson's authority.

43. The passage indicates that the *Grand Seiko WAM 5500,* as mentioned in lines 77–78, is an instrument used to:
    (A) discriminate between varying hues of redness.
    (B) draw subjective conclusions about the physiological state of the subjects being tested.
    (C) keep track of time while testing patients.
    (D) quantify the accommodative response in the subjects tested.

44. It can be inferred that which of the following populations was NOT tested in this study using the Dynamic Cross Cylinder?
    (F) college-age students
    (G) young adults of both genders
    (H) elderly subjects
    (J) twenty-three-year-olds

45. According to the passage, the author believes that which of the following is a disadvantage of performing this test under "reduced illumination" (lines 64–65)?
    (A) In everyday life, people do not typically function in dimly lit circumstances.
    (B) The optometrist cannot clearly see what he is doing.
    (C) Reduced lighting maximizes the size of the subject's pupil.
    (D) Lower levels of illumination decrease the depth-of-focus of the subject's eye.

COMPARATIVE READING

The ACT typically contains one set of paired passages on the Reading Test. A graph may or may not accompany this passage set. The paired passages can reflect any one of the following reading themes: fiction, natural science, humanities, or social science. Unlike the SAT, the ACT breaks down the questions, indicating when you should answer questions based on Passage A only, Passage B only, or both passages. The exercise that follows provides practice in natural science reading.

Natural Science

Both Natural Science passages are excerpted from articles appearing on the National Science Foundation website, *www.nsf.gov*. Passage A is titled, "Cheetah's Inner Ear Is One-of-a Kind, Vital to High-Speed Hunting," published February 2, 2018. Passage B is titled, "Older Is Better for Hunting Dogs," published on January 17, 2012.

PASSAGE A

The world's fastest land animal, the cheetah, is a successful hunter not only because it is quick, but also because it can hold an incredibly still gaze while pursuing prey. For
5 the first time, researchers have investigated the cheetah's extraordinary sensory abilities by analyzing the speedy animal's inner ear, an organ that is essential for maintaining body balance and adapting head posture
10 during movement in most vertebrates. The study, led by researchers at the American Museum of Natural History, finds that the inner ear of modern cheetahs is unique and likely evolved relatively recently.

15 "If you watch a cheetah run in slow motion, you'll see incredible feats of movement: its legs, its back, its muscles all move with such coordinated power. But its head hardly moves at all," said lead author Camille
20 Grohé, who conducted this work during a National Science Foundation and Frick Postdoctoral Fellowship in the Museum's Division of Paleontology. "The inner ear facilitates the cheetah's remarkable ability to
25 maintain visual and postural stability while running and capturing prey at speeds of up to 65 miles per hour. Until now, no one has investigated the inner ear's role in this incredible hunting specialization."

30 In the inner ear of vertebrates, the balance system consists of three semicircular canals that contain fluid and sensory hair cells that detect movement of the head. Each of the semicircular canals is positioned at a
35 different angle and is especially sensitive to different movements: up and down, side-to-side, and tilting from one side to the other.

The researchers used high-resolution X-ray computed tomography (CT) at the
40 Museum's Microscopy and Imaging Facility, the National Museum of Natural History in Paris, and the Biomaterials Science Center of the University of Basel in Switzerland to scan the skulls of 21 felid specimens,
45 including seven modern cheetahs (*Acinonyx jubatus*) from distinct populations, a closely related extinct cheetah (*Acinonyx pardinensis*) that lived in the Pleistocene between about 2.6 million and 126,000 years ago,
50 and more than a dozen other living felid species. With those data, they created detailed 3-D virtual images of each species' inner ear shape and dimensions.

They found that the inner ears of liv-
55 ing cheetahs differ markedly from those of all other felids alive today, with a greater overall volume of the vestibular system and longer anterior and posterior semicircular canals.

60 "This distinctive inner ear anatomy reflects enhanced sensitivity and more rapid

responses to head motions, explaining the cheetah's extraordinary ability to maintain visual stability and to keep their gaze locked in on prey even during incredibly high-speed hunting," said coauthor John Flynn, the Frick Curator of Fossil Mammals in the Museum's Division of Paleontology.

These traits were not present in *Acinonyx pardinensis*, the extinct species examined by the researchers, emphasizing the recent evolution of the highly specialized inner ear of modern cheetah.

PASSAGE B

Older dogs and male dogs are better hunting companions than younger dogs and female dogs says the author of a new study on the hunting ability and nutritional status of domestic dogs in lowland Nicaragua. In addition, he says, dogs are more suited to wildlife sustainability than other hunting options.

"I was a little surprised to find that male dogs are harvesting more than females because few anthropologists have commented on sex-related variation in hunting ability," said University of Cincinnati (UC) anthropologist and lead investigator Jeremy Koster. "In fact, when anthropologists have reported anything along these lines, it's usually to report informants' claims that there are no differences between males and females."

Koster and anthropologist Kenneth Tankersley, also with the UC in Ohio, recently examined key demographic variables such as age and sex on the amount of harvested game that dogs contribute from subsistence hunting in an indigenous community, which has a long and important role in community survival. The research is one of few projects to study these differences in hunting dogs.

"Dr. Koster's and Dr. Tankersley's research findings make a crucial contribution to understanding human subsistence strategies in tropical rainforest environments," said Deborah Winslow, a program director for NSF's Cultural Anthropology Program. "Such knowledge is essential for preserving these environments while still allowing sustainable economic exploitation. On a larger scale, the research also helps us to understand our evolutionary past, including the reasons that dogs may have been domesticated in the first place."

Koster and Tankersley found that as both male and female dogs reach three years of age, they tend to increase their hunting success and produce greater harvests. Older, male and female dogs in the study population returned more game to their owners than did younger dogs. "The increase in hunting success with age could reflect learning via experience," said Koster, director of graduate studies in anthropology at UC. "On the other hand, the apparent age-related increase in ability might indicate that only talented hunting dogs reach advanced ages, perhaps because unskilled hunting dogs receive poorer care and die relatively young."

"We expect that hunting ability would eventually decline as dogs get older, but the reality is that few dogs reach eight or nine years old because even well-treated dogs often succumb to snakebites or jaguar attacks."

There also seems to be a trend that bigger dogs are able to track and corral bigger prey, said Koster, which increases the hunting return rates of their owners, and in general, male dogs are bigger than females. Even so, more work needs to be done to determine if males are better hunting companions at

other locations in which locals use dogs to
145 harvest prey, he said.

Koster and Tankersley conducted the study in Nicaragua's Bosawas Biosphere Reserve, which is part of the largest unbroken tract of neotropical rainforest in Central
150 America, north of the Amazon Rainforest. The researchers based the study on the hunting activities of the Mayangna and the Miskito, two indigenous ethnic groups who live along a tributary of the Coco River,
155 not far from the border with Honduras. Community members in the region capture about 85 percent of harvested mammals with the aid of dogs, according to the report.

"Conservation biologists are justifiably
160 concerned about the impact of subsistence hunting on wildlife populations," said Koster, "but if sustainable hunting is the goal, then hunting with dogs might be a better option than the alternatives."

165 Koster argues that hunters with firearms tend to disproportionately hunt prey that lives in trees, including slow-breeding primates that are easy to over-hunt, whereas hunters with dogs tend to harvest relatively
170 fast-breeding animals such as agoutis, pacas and armadillos. He says these populations are harder to deplete, partly because they adapt well to the heavily-used forests near human settlements.

175 "Overall, then, if you have a choice of hunting with guns or hunting with dogs, the latter will more likely result in long-term sustainability in many settings," said Koster, who promotes Amazon Cares, a non-profit
180 organization devoted to the welfare of dogs in rural Latin America. Most dogs in the study were mutts observed one of Koster's colleagues at the Saint Louis Zoo. Koster personally observed that there didn't seem

185 to be much managed breeding of dogs, if at all, among the study population.

The finding leaves open the question which type of dog makes the best hunter, although hunters in the region talk about
190 the different breeds that one encounters in the reserve. Meanwhile, dogs that are not good hunters are almost never taken on excursions. Instead, they are allowed to lounge around the house and "patio."

Questions 46–48 are about Passage A.

46. Based on lines 27–29, "Until now, no one has investigated the inner ear's role in this incredible hunting specialization," the narrator of Passage A most strongly suggests that most people attribute the cheetah's exceptional hunting ability to all of the following EXCEPT its:
    (A) steadfast gaze.
    (B) muscular physique.
    (C) hardy diet.
    (D) inner ear sensitivity.

47. Based on the information in the passage, for a cheetah to have extraordinary hunting prowess, which of the following is a relatively new discovery in terms of the cheetah's anatomy?
    (F) Burly leg and lower back muscles
    (G) Certain inner ear dimensions and shape
    (H) Sturdy yet flexible skeleton
    (J) Eyesight that is penetrating and nearly perfect

48. As the term is used in line 55, "markedly" most closely means:
   (A) surprisingly.
   (B) haphazardly.
   (C) distinctly.
   (D) indistinctly.

Questions 49–52 are about Passage B.

49. The author of Passage B believes that most people consider which of the following types of dogs to be the best hunters?
   (F) Younger male dogs
   (G) Younger female dogs
   (H) Older female dogs
   (J) All of the above

50. Based on Passage B, all of the following can contribute to a hunting dog's decline or demise EXCEPT:
   (A) snakebites.
   (B) bad genes.
   (C) poor care.
   (D) lack of hunting skill.

51. As used in line 96, the phrase "harvested game" most nearly refers to:
   (F) competition among human hunters.
   (G) competition among hunting dogs.
   (H) biogenetically altered prey.
   (J) prey gathered by hunting dogs.

52. As used in Paragraph 6 of Passage B, "We expect that . . . dogs often *succumb to* snakebites or jaguar attacks," the phrase *succumb to* most closely means:
   (A) resist.
   (B) attack against.
   (C) contend with.
   (D) perish due to.

Questions 53–55 are about both Passages A and B.

53. Both passages make use of which of the following?
   (F) Quotations from experts
   (G) Humorous hyperbole
   (H) Rhetorical questions
   (J) Specialized scientific terminology

54. Unlike Passage B, Passage A focuses on which aspect of the animal's hunting competency?
   (A) Anatomy
   (B) Gender
   (C) Upbringing
   (D) Age

55. In discussing cheetahs and dogs, respectively, both passages focus most closely on which quality of these animals?
   (F) Family dynamics
   (G) Group behavior
   (H) Hunting ability
   (J) Dietary needs

Answer Key

PROSE FICTION (1)

1. **D**	3. **C**	5. **D**
2. **H**	4. **F**	6. **F**

PROSE FICTION (2)

7. **C**	9. **D**	11. **B**	13. **B**	15. **B**
8. **H**	10. **H**	12. **G**	14. **F**	16. **J**

SOCIAL SCIENCE

17. **D**	18. **H**	19. **D**	20. **F**	21. **D**

HUMANITIES (1)

22. **F**	23. **D**	24. **G**	25. **D**	26. **F**

HUMANITIES (2)

27. **A**	29. **B**	31. **B**	33. **A**	35. **C**
28. **H**	30. **J**	32. **G**	34. **J**	36. **G**

NATURAL SCIENCE

37. **A**	39. **C**	41. **B**	43. **D**	45. **A**
38. **J**	40. **F**	42. **H**	44. **H**	

COMPARATIVE READING: NATURAL SCIENCE

46. **D**	48. **C**	50. **B**	52. **D**	54. **A**
47. **G**	49. **F**	51. **J**	53. **F**	55. **H**

Answers Explained

PROSE FICTION (1)

1. **(D) Sharp readers read with an intent to absorb the passage's overall theme, main idea, or message.** By doing this habitually, you will be ready when this type of question appears. Choice A is way off; no mention is made of those who are actively observing the driver, whether in a jocular (joking around, merry) fashion or otherwise. While Choice B may seem valid—striking contrasts can certainly be witnessed on the streets of Manhattan—depicting contrasts is not the overarching theme of the passage. Choice C is tempting, but the reader cannot know both parts of this answer choice for certain. Is the narrator definitely commuting to *work*? Is the narrator taking this drive on a *daily basis*? **The correct answer is Choice D**, *anxieties experienced by a driver who navigates a crowded urban avenue.*

2. **(H) Sensible critical readers return to the passage and concentrate on the effect of the word within its larger context:**
   Honk! Beep! Hoooonkkk! Beeeeep!
   *Usual reflex: <u>shoulders lift, tension.</u> The light's green and <u>I've failed to move on quicksilver</u>. Now I'm trailing a bicycle rider. I marvel at the lady on wheels <u>darting in and out the lanes</u>. Exaggerated hand signals and gestures afford her an upper-body workout. My hands **strangle** the steering wheel.*
   The underlined parts (above) accentuate the stress and tension that follow the car honks and beeps! Even though Choice F (*to create a sense of foreboding*) is appropriately negative, it is not quite right. No part of the text necessarily points to something bad that is about to happen; likewise, no specific incident or event happens that is misfortunate.
   Choice G is incorrect; the driver's strangling (holding very tightly) the steering wheel is not meant to be humorous, so there is no support for tempering (lessening, moderating) the cynicism that may be detected. Choice J doesn't work; this is not a "dark" passage (one that is gloomy, even morbid or sinister), so the author most likely does not intend to add a note of dark imagery. Together, process of elimination (an old reliable test-taking technique) and context clues reveal that **the best answer is Choice H**, *to emphasize the driver's tension behind the wheel.*

3. **(C) To prepare yourself to be a skillful critical reader, brush up on literary terms; you never know when a question will refer to simile, metaphor, hyperbole, or pathos, among other literary devices.** One definition of personification is the assigning or expression of human-like traits to nonliving things. Because some degree of subjectivity and interpretation may be involved, finding instances of personification is more of an art than a science. Three of the four answer choices, however, can be perceived as description tinged with personification. Choice A (*The cab's nose*, lines 4–5) evokes personification because the inanimate (nonliving) cab is described as

having a *nose*, a body part just like you and I have! Choice B (conveyor belt, line 10) also uses personification because the conveyor belt is described as having a *mind of its own*. We know people who similarly have stubborn heads! Choice D (headphones, line 39) also utilizes personification; the headphones are actually talking! *"I can't hear you," say their headphones to honkers.* **The correct answer is Choice C** because the hand signals and gestures (lines 33–34) are performed by a bicycle rider, who *is* a human being. This is NOT an example of personification and, therefore, the correct answer.

4. **(F) An astute reader has the discipline to return to the passage to consider the meaning of a word in context and *not* to rely on memory alone.** A quick peek reveals that the opening lines say:
Leaning to the right, I pull down the passenger seat visor. So this is the countenance of stress, I say aloud to my strained forehead and weary eyes in the mirror.
Since the narrator is looking at her *strained forehead and weary eyes*, she must be looking at her *face* in the visor. Choices G (comedy), H (façade), and J (nature) cannot be substantiated by the passage evidence excerpted above. Neither of these three choices fits or flows in context. A *façade* is a false exterior. **The correct answer is Choice F**, face. Another challenging word that you may encounter for "face" is *visage*.

5. **(D) Be a page flipper! Lick your fingertips, flip back to the passage, and generously nestle this phrase in its context as you consider its main effect:**
Driving down Broadway is like being stuck on a conveyor belt with a mind of its own. When I attempt to change lanes, my direction signals blink in vain. The road has a sidetracking mind of its own.
Yes, a vain individual is conceited and arrogant, but this idiomatic usage (*in vain*) does not describe a personality trait of the narrator; cross off Choice A. While it is likely that there is *inadequate traffic flow in metropolitan areas*, the purpose of this expression (in vain) is not to inquire about the specifics of this problem or its solution; Choice B is out. The intent of this passage and expression is not to deride (ridicule) the narrator, so Choice C is incorrect. This is not about mocking the narrator's lack of pragmatic (practical) skill. **The best answer is Choice D.** The sentences before and after the sentence in which this expression appears both hint to the fact that the driver is struggling to control her driving path. So, it is most likely that *in vain* expresses that the driver's attempt to change lanes was ineffective.

6. **(F) Recall details to determine which of the four questions is NOT answered by the information that is stated or implied in the passage.**
Choice G is answered by several details that can be reasonably perceived as potentially dangerous . . . obstacles: rollerbladers, bicycle riders, panhandlers, among others. The closing line intimates that it is twilight, dusk, or downright dark outside: *Wishing it were broad daylight, I drive down*

Broadway, blinded by red brake lights. Therefore, the question posed in Choice H (<u>What time of day is it?</u>) is addressed. Choice J (<u>Is the driver feeling tired?</u>) is answered by lines 3–4: *I say aloud to my ... weary eyes in the mirror. Weary* means tired. **The correct answer is Choice F** because readers cannot unequivocally determine whether the driver is traveling alone.

PROSE FICTION (2)

7. **(C) Inference questions require the reader to read "between the lines," to pick up on subtleties between and beneath the text.** Paying particular attention to the underscored parts, review the first paragraph to detect something about Arwynsson: *Edwyn Arwynsson studied the bustling open-air market <u>to make sure no one was watching him</u>. <u>Fortunately, everyone's attention was in the middle of the plaza, where a gaily dressed stilt-walker</u>—his red pants billowing like sails, his bronze earrings glistening in the sunlight—<u>was swaggering down the center aisle</u>, his assistant following afterward with a hat full of coins.* Choice A, Arwynsson *was mesmerized by the flamboyant stilt-walker,* is invalid because the paragraph doesn't imply that Edwyn can't take *his* eyes off of the street entertainer.

Choice B is also unsupported; there is nothing to hint at Edwyn's covert (secret) wish to be as physically adept (skilled) as the stilt-walker's *assistant.* The word *assistant* makes this choice way off! After all, the assistant is not the one on stilts. Pay attention to each and every word that makes up an answer choice. Just because the stilt-walker is dressed in red and bronze, doesn't mean that Edwyn is expected to be a colorful and unusual character. Cross off Choice D.

As the underlined parts strongly suggest, **the correct answer is Choice C:** Edwyn *didn't want people watching him as he prepared his trick.* More specifically and practically speaking, Edwyn didn't want anyone watching him as he transferred his flame rocks into his jacket pocket.

8. **(H) To identify point of view, determine from whose perspective the story is told.** The first-person pronouns *I* and *me* do not appear in the narrative, so this tale is not told from Edwyn's point of view. Cross off Choice F. *The stilt-walker's assistant* is such a minor character; cross off Choice G.

Choice J is off the mark; *Edwyn's long lost father* is not the narrator, for he does not have a "voice" in the telling of these events.

The correct answer is Choice H. It makes sense that *an omniscient* (all-knowing) *narrator* is telling this story, for he reveals the main character's innermost thoughts and feelings; for example, *<u>My father would be proud</u>, he could not help thinking* (lines 115–116).

9. **(D) Return to the prose fiction passage and review the lines on which this question is based. Do not rely on your memory, particularly under test-taking conditions; this leaves too much room for error.** Which of the

following could likely have been the impetus (the driving force, the reason) behind Edwyn's father's journey "into the steep vales of the western mountains"? *Otherwise, Arwyn would never have gone on the duke's foolish quest into the steep vales of the western mountains, from which none of his party had yet returned. Edwyn still didn't understand what had lured his father into the duke's entourage. Not gold, or Arwyn would have given it to his wife for safekeeping, and not fame, for Arwyn didn't care a jot for prestige at court.* Choice A, *his desire to gain a higher-ranking social stature,* must be invalid because the last lines indicates, *Arwyn didn't care a jot* (an iota, a trifling amount) *for prestige at court.*

B is unfounded; these lines do not allude to Arwyn having *aspiration for increased renown* (fame) *among his fellow magicians.*

C, *his drive for monetary rewards,* is incorrect; after all, the text directly states, *Not gold.* By process of elimination, the only likely choice is **D**, **which is the best answer**: *his deep interest in the mysteries of nature.*

10. **(H) Words-in-context questions require you to methodically plug in each and every answer choice and to decide which term flows and fits the best.** Return to the passage and review the context in which the word *worked* appears:

The boy had never worked his father's booth in the midsummer market all by himself. But then, he had never been compelled to do so. His father had always been there to draw in the curious, to give them a small display of his magical powers, and then to sell them some of his many charms.

Choice F, *begrudged,* makes no sense. To *begrude* is to give or allow in a reluctant, uncertain manner. There's nothing to suggest that Edwyn straightened and uncluttered his father's magic booth, so G, *streamlined,* is also out.

Choice J is close, but *toiled* (worked hard; labored) does not flow in the given phrasing as well as Choice H.

The correct answer is H, *managed,* which is a more comprehensive term that implies taking care of the multifarious aspects of the booth, including attracting an audience, showing them some magic items, and selling them.

11. **(B) To gain insight into the purpose of a particular phrase, return to the passage and read the parts leading up to and following "The breath of the gods!" (line 94) to determine the meaning of these words within their larger context:**

Once the stilt-walker came down for a rest, the people remembered why they had come to the market in the first place. Some headed for the butcher's stall or the baker's, seeking to stock their larders. Edwyn did not offer the staples of life, so no one came his way. But they would once the show began.

"Fire!" he cried out suddenly in his shrill boy's voice, drawing stares from here and there. "The breath of the gods!"

Knowing he had the people's attention, Edwyn reached into his pocket and grabbed a handful of flame-rocks.

Notice the effect of Edwyn's exclamation: before he cried out, "no one came his way," but after he cries out, … "he had the people's attention." Indeed, this exclamation adds to his prior exclamation, "Fire!" (line 92), but his main purpose is not simply to emphasize this prior word. Cross off Choice A.

The readers do not know if Edwyn has, in fact, read widely, particularly in the genre of mythology, so Choice C cannot be verified.

Choice D is invalid; there is no passage evidence to support the idea that there is a fire developing in the butcher shop!

The correct answer is B, for in order to draw attention to himself and his show, Edwyn must first "*detract the crowd's attention from the stilt-walker,*" who is described in the paragraph just preceding Edwyn's exclamatory phrase.

12. **(G) To ace this ALL/EXCEPT question, return to the referenced lines and find proof for three of the four answer choices. The choice that lacks passage support is the correct answer.**

After all, magic had its limits. One could seem to make a coin seem to disappear, or guess someone's name with the help of a secret accomplice, or reduce a strong man to tears with a pinch in the right place.

That was all feasible if the magician knew what he was doing, if he was quick enough and clever enough with his hands.

Choices F (*manual deftness*) and J (*celerity with his nimble hands*) are supported by the underlined part above. Notice how vocabulary plays a key role in answering this question correctly. *Celerity* means quickness, and *nimble* means agile.

Choice H (*the ability to serve as an adept co-conspirator*) is also supported by a magician being able to *guess someone's name with the help of a secret accomplice*. More vocabulary! An *accomplice* is a co-collaborator or a partner-in-crime.

The correct answer is G because *paternal intrigue* lacks substantiation. The meaning of this answer choice is heady; *paternal* refers to fatherly or father figure, and *intrigue* refers to planning and scheming. Put those together and you do not have something that works in relation to this part of the passage.

13. **(B) Use contextual evidence to determine the meaning of this phrase: "the old man's humors."**

Lines 67–70 indicate, *As people had remarked time and again, he was his father's son, and very much in tune with the old man's humors.*

Choice A (*his jocular ways*), Choice C (*his decorum*), and Choice D (*his tendency to be festive*) could all contribute to Edwyn being "his father's son" because these choices reflect qualities of character and personality that make a person who he is. Vocabulary review: *jocular* means playful, jovial, fun-loving; *decorum* means properness of conduct; *festive* means liking to be around people, merry.

The correct answer is B because *his financial assets* do not contribute to the intangible qualities of a man's nature.

14. **(F)** **Carefully consider what promises are suggested by Edwyn's three exclamations: "Win your lady love! Bring down your enemies! See the future!"**

Choice G (*Gain the heart of the woman you adore!*) is related by the first exclamation.

Choice H (*Divine the future!*) is expressed by the last exclamation, and Choice J (*Undermine your adversaries!*) is promised by Edwyn's second cry. Sharpen your vocabulary: *undermine* means to weaken, as if to sap the energy of one's rivals. *Divine* (which appears in Choice H) means to predict the future.

The correct answer is F because even though finding his father is a desire that rests at the core of Edwyn's heart, his expletives (exclamations) do not communicate that his audience will be able to *Discover the precise whereabouts of [their] lost loved ones!*

15. **(B)** **Do not be hasty when answering reading comprehension questions. Traps and false-positives lurk amid the answer choices. Be a page flipper! In other words, be disciplined about returning to the passage in order to refresh your memory about what, precisely, was said in the passage:**

…the people remembered why they had come to the market in the first place. Some headed for the butcher's stall or the baker's, seeking to stock their larders. Edwyn did not offer the staples of life, so no one came his way.

Choice A is out; *good-humored folly and entertainment* is what Edwyn hopes to offer his spectators once they come his way.

No shopkeepers are offering to give out money, so Choice C is out.

Choice D, *mundane commercial dealings*, is too vague; commercial dealing could mean a lot more than just buying bread and meat for dinner.

Using process of elimination and passage proof, **the best answer is B** (*savory meats and breads*) because the people were going to the butcher's and the baker's to buy things they need as sustenance (nourishment).

16. **(J)** **Review the final paragraph to determine which literary technique the author uses when he elaborates on his description of the "man with a mane of wild, gray hair"** (lines 126–130). The underscored parts are relevant to the man's description:

The man's <u>thick, gray brows</u> lowered over the bridge of his <u>aquiline nose, darkening his face as if a storm were rolling in</u>. "You misunderstand, my young friend," he said in a deep, mellifluous voice. "It is I who has come to reveal the future to you."

Choice F is incorrect; in describing the man, the author is not using *hyperbole* (exaggeration.)

Choice G, *metaphor*, is also out because no direct comparisons are made. *Symbolism* is not used to describe the man, so Choice H is invalid. **The correct answer is J** because the second underlined part functions as a *simile*. A *simile* is an indirect comparison, usually one that uses *like* or *as*. Vocabulary check: *aquiline* means "like, or resembling, an eagle."

SOCIAL SCIENCE

17. **(D) To ace tone questions, familiarize yourself with the vocabulary of tone and mood (see Chapter 3).** Choice A does not work, for the author is not noticeably coming across as *humble* (modest, self-effacing). The author is by no means *ambivalent* (uncertain, equivocal) about the Mobilization for Youth project; in fact, she seems to be in favor of it, so Choice B is out. Choice C is also out since *indifferent* describes an author who is uninterested in or apathetic about the topic. Why, then, would she be writing about programs to remedy juvenile delinquency? **The best answer is Choice D**, *objective*, because the author is reporting the facts and circumstances as they occurred without regularly interjecting her bias or opinion.

18. **(H) While you can rely on your reader's memory to an extent, skimming around to find proof for four of the five elements listed is the best way to nail this question.** Choice F stays in since *numbers and statistics* appear in lines 19 and 20. Choice G stays, too, since the author defines the *problems confronted by poor people* in lines 8–9. The author refers to Columbia University sociologists, Ohlin and Cloward, and President Kennedy, so Choice J stays. Choice H is unsupported and therefore **the best answer is Choice H**: *allusions (references) to philosophical works (books, articles, etc.) about government's ethical role in helping its people* simply do not exist in this passage.

19. **(D) The word "infer" means that the answer is not directly stated but requires you to draw a logical conclusion.** Reread the sentence in which this phrase appears. Choice A is unsupported; nowhere in the reading selection does it say that the "experts" in line 25 neglect the youngsters living within the Lower East Side—just the opposite, the experts are pooling together to help them! Answer Choice B is way off the mark: Nowhere in the passage does it even allude to young men and women who turn up their noses at work and educational opportunities. Choice C doesn't hold any water, either. Remember, there are no sweepingly general statements that attest to *all* youngsters living on the Lower East Side being deprived (somehow disadvantaged). **The best answer is Choice D.** Combining the passage evidence from lines 8–10—*problems confronted by poor people— deprivation, lack of opportunity*—and the evidence from lines 35 and 36, which tells us that the program put a *special emphasis on education and job training*, logically leads to **Choice D as the best answer.** "Deprived youth"

refs to *Young people who are <u>financially challenged</u> and who <u>lack opportunities in education</u> and <u>job training</u>*.

20. **(F) No line reference is given, so skim for *President Kennedy* (proper nouns stand out because they're capitalized) to review his role in Mobilization for Youth.** Answer Choice G is out since Kennedy (as the last paragraph illustrates) was not a *detractor* but a supporter of youth programs. There's also no proof that Kennedy was a *skeptic* (doubter), so cross off Choice H. Choice J is only partially correct and, therefore, out. Yes, he was an *avid* (enthusiastic and passionate) *supporter*, but the passage does not substantiate an *unfocused* zeal that contributed to the dissolving (demise) of Mobilization for Youth. **The best answer is Choice F.** Reviewing the last paragraph shows that Kennedy was indeed <u>an advocate (supporter) whose interest precipitated the passing of youth-supporting government acts and whose support led to additional programs for young citizens.</u>

21. **(D) Skim the closing paragraph to get a sense of where the author left off and, therefore, where she's likely to go next.** As an immediate projection, Choice A is too broad. Answer Choice B reflects ambition and truth: *young people's role in creating their own futures,* but this topic wouldn't flow from this point. Choice C is out since funding and fiscal topics (*fiscal* pertains to financial matters, even specific ones like debt and taxation) are not central to the passage. **Choice D is the best answer:** At this juncture, elaborating on <u>one of the programs mentioned in the last paragraph</u> is a logical next move.

HUMANITIES (1)

22. **(F) Reread the sentence in which the indicated phrase appears— *Commitment and internalization of <u>these codes</u> awaken a higher discipline governed by a sense of honor to self and others*—then *backtrack* to figure out, like a detective, what "these codes" refers to.** Choice G, *business ethics in the health and fitness industry,* sounds lofty, but ethics (morals, codes of conduct) are not stressed here. Answer Choice H, *habits of personal conduct that mirror military training,* is also not supported in and around this vicinity of the passage. Choice J, *the life ambitions of individuals,* is not what is expressed by "these codes." Using process of elimination and seeking passage support, **Choice F is correct.** You will find that the reference of *behavioral rules of humane treatment toward fellow man and self* clearly paraphrases "guidelines of care and conduct toward oneself and others" in lines 3–4.

23. **(D) In order to absorb this word's meaning in context, reread the sentence in which the action verb "governed" appears: *Commitment and internalization of these codes awaken a higher discipline <u>governed</u> primarily by a sense of honor to self and others.*** One by one, plug in each

answer choice and try to get a sense of which one flows and fits best. Choice A, *legislated,* and Choice B, *mandated,* are similar in that these terms remind us of government. To *legislate* is to make laws; to *mandate* is to command or order—as by law. As you can see, in this context neither legalese term applies. Choice C does not fit either because *coerced* means ruled by force. **The best answer is Choice D**, *directed.*

24. **(G) ALL/EXCEPT questions can be rather time-consuming because they require you to find textual evidence to support three of the four answers.** The unsupported point is the correct answer. In lines 30–32, the author states, *Inappropriate or ill-prepared foods will clog the body and mind, zapping one's energy and acuity,* so Choice F (*eating overly processed foods*) is supported by textual proof. Choice H (*misdirected stream of energy*) and Choice J (*a physical illness*) are both justified (you may need to read between the lines, for evidence is not always directly stated) as causes of imbalance in the second paragraph. **Choice G is the best answer** since *living beyond one's fiscal (financial) means* is not even hinted at as a determining factor of imbalance.

25. **(D) Reread up from, down from, and around this sentence to absorb its full sense as it applies to the context of the passage. Do not add to or detract from what the statement actually says:** *Working part-time around the schedules of my two children, with a set week of group classes at local studios, suits me ideally.* Choice A is rather extreme, given the basic and practical ideas behind this statement. By no means does this quote explicitly say or insinuate (suggest) that the author *harbors (holds, embraces) an unrealistic mindset about the workings of the health and fitness industry.* For all we as readers know, the author may be the savviest of businesswomen! Choice B is not too much of a stretch, but this statement alone does not testify to the author's "methodical mindset." Answer Choice C is way off the mark; this statement by no means implies that the author does not fully embrace her role as yoga instructor. Yoga may be one of her single most passions! She is simply striving, at the same time, to organize a work schedule that allows her to fulfill her familial responsibilities. **The best answer is Choice D** because the author has pragmatic (practical) ideas about formulating a work schedule that supports her role as mother (an evident priority).

26. **(F) Reread the end of the closing paragraph in which these quotes appear. Think carefully about the author's intentions.** Choice G is way off the mark; in consideration of the first quote in particular, there is no way one can say that the author believes that "self-gain is the one thing worth seeking." Choice H is also out because, to reiterate, this author has a healthy and balanced mindset and certainly cannot be considered "self-sacrificing to a fault" even though she does cater to her clients. Choice J doesn't work either; while the author may feel passionate ("great urgency") about helping her students, there is no evidence that says she is "putting her own

satisfaction on the back burner" (position of lowest priority). **The best answer is Choice F**, *She cares about her well-being just as she cares about the well-being of her yoga students*, for the author's intentions come across as both healthy and balanced.

HUMANITIES (2)

27. **(A) Carefully reread the context surrounding the sentence: "*My hands unclenched a little*" (lines 82–83) to gain a sense of its meaning.** While Rainer Rilke's wisdom is far-reaching, this image does not directly apply to Rilke, so Choice B is out. Choice C is also incorrect because although the Capstone leader, Keith, has a positive effect on the students whom he mentors, we are never made aware of his effect on his *colleagues* (his contemporaries and coworkers). While Choice D is a provocative answer choice, *a wise person's physical manifestation of his mental state*, the wise person is not connected to this image. **The correct answer is Choice A**, *the author's mitigating (lessening, subsiding) anxiety and tension.*

28. **(H) Since two terms are being questioned, you have to read around both of them to get a sense of where these emotions or physical manifestations come from.** Focus in on what the author writes: *This was incredibly bothersome to my core, not being able to explain and practice wisdom I felt was true. I knew that not living the questions led to much inner turmoil. There have been times when I really found myself stuck in questions to the point of paralysis.* Choice F is not substantiated by these lines, for the author's vacillating about her potential graduate program is not mentioned or even alluded to neve. Choice G, *difficulties experienced when . . . try to put her book learning . . . into action in the "real world,"* is a reasonable and likely outcome when a young adult graduates from college; however, these lines do not support the author experiencing hardship in this regard. Choice J is out since it lacks textual support; in fact, the author never mentions *her lack of adequate resources* (money? time? connections?) that are needed to implement public welfare programs. **The correct answer is Choice H**, for the text does confirm the author's *struggle* as she finds herself mired in *inquiries* (passage evidence: *stuck in questions to the point of paralysis*) for which she is seeking some measure of *clarity and focus.*

29. **(B) Concentrate as you reread lines 120–129 (an adequate context) to get a sense of what the "spring" stands for:** *sign of growth come in the understanding that I can only look inside myself for how to live with such questions. A considerable amount of trust needs to be afforded to that inner voice we are all said to have, an idea which scares me. It is not a* spring *I tend to tap often. Yet, in doing so I learn to rest with some of the unanswered questions and not doubt my insights.* Choice A is unsupported because finances and internships are not mentioned outright or even suggested. (This answer might be chosen, however, after a good dose of "reading into" the passage.) While it's

true that *internal contradictions and enigmas* (mysteries, puzzling situations) might *affect most thoughtful people* and while it's true that the mention of a spring might bring an *image* to the reader's mind, Choice C is too far off the mark because, like Choice A, it is fueled by "reading beyond" the text. Choice D, *an infinite source of wisdom one can achieve through studying the sagacious (discerning, wise) quotations and writings of others*, is a lofty answer! While you may believe, and reasonably so, that infinite wisdom can be derived from studying the perceptive ideas of others, nowhere in the vicinity of the word "spring" does the author mention great sages, wise monks, or quotable authors. Remember, stick to the passage evidence. **The correct answer is Choice B**, *a metaphor for her inner wisdom and voice*. A spring is a tangible object (hot water spring or natural geyser) that the author is directly comparing (as a metaphor) to her *inner voice* (lines 124–125).

30. **(J)** **Gear up your emotional compass, and skim Paragraph 8 with a heightened sensitivity to the sentiments expressed by the author.** Two emotions are mentioned in each answer choice, so both have to be supported by the paragraph in order for that answer choice to be valid. Choice F is partially correct, but partially correct doesn't cut it. Arguably, *confusion* can be supported by the author's words, *It has taken me until now to understand what he means* and even, *Perhaps I am a slow learner,* but *desolation* (anguish, misery) is too strong of an emotion to be supported by this paragraph. Choice G is off the emotional mark as well, for *despondency* (hopelessness, dejection) *and vexation* (annoyance, anger) are overly intense levels of emotion, which are not evident here. Choice H is too extreme, for while the author may be relating a degree of *internal struggle*, she is not relating it to an extreme of *despair* (hopelessness.) **The correct answer is Choice J**, *introspection* (looking inward) *and self-reliance* (autonomy). After all, the author talks about *trusting myself* (line 116) and her personal growth in building *the understanding that [she] can only look inside [herself] for how to live with such questions*. As you can see, plenty of passage evidence (the words and phrases written by the author) supports both *introspection and self-reliance*.

31. **(B)** **This is a time-consuming ALL/EXCEPT question that requires you to hunt around the passage for references to these eight groups of people and decide whether, according to the author's view, they "suffer."** Choice A stays in: It is clear that the author is deeply affected by how much the convalescents (the patients, those who are attempting to recover and heal) at Hasbro Children's Hospital suffer; also, if the author confesses that she endured a sort of emotional suffering during high school, then it logically follows that her peers did as well. Choice C stays in because the author gives herself as an example of a high school student who endured some level of suffering. Choice D also remains, but is not the correct answer, because the author feels for the homeless and hungry, who undoubtedly suffer. **The correct answer is Choice B.** First, the Catholic Workers is a group of people who the author aspires potentially to join;

second, the hospital volunteers engage with children-patients in a manner that makes the children *smile*: *How do they* [the children-patients] *smile through their pain and play board games with volunteers?* (lines 39–40)

32. **(G) This is another time-consuming question that requires you to read around four separate sections of the passage with your emotional compass geared to detect "ease and bliss" on the part of the author.** Choice F is incorrect because at Hasbro Children's Hospital (line 36) the author asks herself a string of heart-wrenching questions like, *Why innocent children suffer from terrible cancers?* and *How do they smile through their pain and play board games?* At Amos House (line 13), the author feels primarily *curious to learn about people . . .* (line 16), so Choice H should be eliminated. Choice J should be eliminated also because lines 22 to 25 suggest that the author experienced some degree of suffering during her high school years. **The best answer is Choice G** because at the dance party (line 58) the author feels "immense joy" and comments that (on the dance floor) *Movement announced an end to the day of contemplation,* which suggests a level of "ease."

33. **(A) Reread the first two paragraphs with your eyes peeled for these narrative techniques.** ALL/EXCEPT questions require you to find evidence for three of the techniques listed; the one *not* found is the correct answer. Choice B is supported because the author chooses to italicize the words *different* (line 17) and *like* (line 22) for the purposes of irony and/or emphasis. Choice C is also supported since parenthetical comments appear in the first paragraph: *(which uses reflection to tie volunteer experience in the community with study in the classroom).* Choice D is valid because a rhetorical question (one raised not to be literally answered, but to provoke thought or have an effect on the reader) is raised in the second sentence of Paragraph 2: *Why would a young adult willingly give up precious Saturday mornings?* **The correct answer is Choice A,** *telling her story by dramatically shifting between the singular, third-person pronoun ONE and the first-person pronouns I and ME.*

34. **(J) Focus on the main components of the closing sentence—*wild questions* and *dance*—then determine which rhetorical effect is achieved.** Choice F does not work because the opening paragraph does *not* reference those main components, so a narrative "framework" is not formed between the opening and closing paragraphs. Choice G is out because the closing sentence does not *belie* (contradict, debunk) Rilke's quotation, as the quotation advocates embracing the questions and patiently living with them. Choice H is also unfounded because this final sentence certainly does not contradict the title, "Loving the Questions," which, if anything, confirms the essence of the title. **The correct answer is Choice J** because images of both dance and embracing questions, like those following, appear in

Paragraphs 4 and 5: *At the dance party, I participated in the wild movement to ridiculous songs and felt immense joy* (Paragraph 4) and *Capstone gave me a time, place, and company with which to explore these questions of vocation . . . our class journeyed on a path lit by questions . . .* (Paragraph 5).

35. **(C) Concentrate on the meaning and usage of this word as you reread the sentence in which it appears.** Choice A is unsupported. Even though this passage has an academic context (reflecting on her major while at Providence College), still no mention is made of the author's earning an *advanced academic distinction*, which is a nebulous (vague) expression anyway. Choice B, *matured and became braver in personal conviction and spirit,* is a lofty choice and, therefore, it may be appealing; however, that sense of *progress* is not supported in this vicinity of the passage. While the author did *provide service to others who were less fortunate* during her volunteer time at the soup kitchen, for example, this notion of providing service does not fit into this context. **The best answer is Choice C**, simply, *As I progressed (continued along) in my years at Providence College, I changed settings in my volunteer placements, but the question was still the same . . .*

36. **(G) Word-in-context questions require that you focus in on the word's particular usage in a particular sentence:** *Yet I moved onward, towards new service opportunities, until at the cusp of despair and burnout I found another important question, "How do I practice joy?"* (lines 47–50). Out of this context, *cusp* takes on myriad and peculiar definitions including a border between signs of the zodiac, a ridge on a molar tooth, a pointed end, and a feature of Gothic architecture! But, the contextual definition, as used in the passage, must make logical sense and flow. While F, the *point of no return,* may be dramatic, it is not the most fitting choice. The sentence is not saying—thank goodness—that once the author hit *despair* (hopelessness), she never recovered or returned from it! Choice H, *precipice,* is more fitting as an earth science term, meaning a rocky cliff or drop. While Choice J, *pointed edge,* relates to the pointed tip of a molar, this meaning does not fit smoothly. **The best answer is Choice G**, *pinnacle*, because it makes sense that after much service work, she reached a *pinnacle,* or peak (high point, apex, acme!) of despair, until she finally had to ask about the antithesis: *How do I practice joy?* It's as if, only at the climax of despair, does she contemplate its polar opposite, joy.

NATURAL SCIENCE

37. **(A) Find evidence for three of the four answer choices, and use process of elimination to narrow in on the one choice that is *not* substantiated by the passage.** Cross off Choice B since the author defines "dynamic cross-cylinder test" in line 1. The author refers to an authority, Edward Jackson, in Paragraph 2 and provides a bit of historical chronology at the

end of this same paragraph, so Choices C and D are out. **The best answer is Choice A.**

38. **(J) Recall information from the introductory italicized material and consider the passage as a whole.** Textbooks and other publications are never mentioned, so Choice F is out. There's no evidence that the presenter created the "diagram" herself, so Choice G is not verified. Yes, the cited phrases do refer to *visual aids*, but no mention is made regarding the audience as having a predominantly visual learning style. Choice H is out. **Choice J is the best answer** because the passage introduction at the beginning mentions that the speaker is using a PowerPoint presentation, so that is most likely where the illustrations appear.

39. **(C) Read every passage on the test with yours eyes and ears tuned to picking up the author's style, since this question type is predictable.** Choice A is out since *cynical and wry* (bitterly ironic, devious in purpose; ironically humorous) are inappropriate and too strong for this passage. Choice B is close, but a *scholarly* style would rely more on referring to great scientific works and studies, well-known scholars, academic studies, and the like. Choice D, *jocular and belittling*, does not fit this passage; there's no joking around and no one is being belittled. **The best answer is Choice C,** *technical and persuasive*. The author ultimately persuades her audience that the DCC test has inherent drawbacks.

40. **(F) Return to the text and carefully reread the sentence (at minimum) in which the italicized word appears with the intention of understanding the purpose of the italicization:** . . . *once the patient reports a preference for one set of lines, then spherical lenses are introduced to make the two sets of lines appear equal. The assumption is the existing accommodative response will be maintained as the lenses are introduced. However, this seems unlikely, and one could imagine that once plus lenses are introduced, the accommodative response would decline, since the need for accommodation is reduced.* Choice G is not substantiated by passage evidence because nowhere in this vicinity (or anywhere else in the passage) does the author express concern *about the long-term detriments of using spherical lenses.* Choice H is invalid as well; nowhere does the author discuss how the spherical lenses *have been vehemently (fervently, passionately) doubted by the scientific population,* so the italics could not be used for this intent. Perhaps there are myriad *advocates* who tout (praise, publicize) *the widespread use of these lenses,* but Choice J is out because this notion is not clearly expressed here or elsewhere. **The correct answer is Choice F;** it is very likely that the italics emphasize the *tentative (hesitant, not fully worked out) state of this experimental use of spherical lenses,* especially given the fact that the latter sentence (as reproduced above) mentions their "unlikely" effect.

41. **(B)** **Draw a reasonble conclusion about what is revealed about the passage, based on the author's diction (word choice):** *astigmatic axis* (line 27), *veridical measures* (lines 123–124) and *rectilinear target* (line 109). Choice A is groundless; there is nothing in the passage to suggest that the details expressed by these three terms are *doubtful* or *fallacious* (misleading, false). Choice C is also unfounded. Even though readers might find these terms *abstruse* (abstract, hard to undersand), there's nothing to support the passage being written in a *hypocritical* (false, insincere) mode. While this lofty natural science passage contains knowledge that is *physiological* (it pertains to the functional processes of living systems and their organs, as related to changes of accomodation in the crystalline lens within they eye), *hypothetical*, by no means can the knowledge expressed by these terms be construed as *physiological*, so cross off Choice D. Using passage proof and process of elimination, it boils down to this: **The correct answer is Choice B**, *the passage contains terminology that is esoteric* (understood by a select few, typically those who have been trained in a specialized field) as well as *technical* (in this case, terminology that is particular to optometry).

42. **(H)** **Determine the meaning of this idiomatic phrase by embedding it within context. Pay particular attention to the underscored parts:** <u>However</u>, *with all due respect to Edward Jackson, the use of a cross cylinder to quantify the accommodative response . . . in a young patient <u>does have significant problems</u>* (lines 30–35). Since the phrase *with all due respect to Edward Jackson* appears within a sentence that introduces the idea of Jackson's test having problems, Choice F is out because it unabashedly praises Jackson as one who *should be acclaimed as having made the most noteworthy impact in the field of eye care*. By the same token, Choice G is out because the adjectives (*profound* and *unwavering*) used to describe the gratitude towards Jackson unconditionally extol the man: *her gratitude toward Jackson is profound (deep) and unwavering (steady, resolute)*. Choice J is rather extreme and is also incongruous with the tone of the passage as a whole; the purpose of this phrase is not harsh or caustic, so the purpose is *not* to express *sarcasm in an attempt to degrade Jackson's authority*. **The best answer is Choice H**, the more tempered choice, which says *that while Jackson is renowned for his introduction of the DCC, there are inherent flaws within this clinical test*. This choice is both fitting and on-the-mark.

43. **(D)** **Use information that is explicitly stated in the passage to determine the use and purpose of the Grand Seiko WAM 5500. Pay particular attention to the underlined portions:** *Accordingly, the aim of the present study was <u>to compare clinical measurements of the accommodation response</u> obtained subjectively with the dynamic cross-cylinder test with those found using an <u>objective</u> infra-red optometer, namely the <u>Grand Seiko WAM 5500</u>, while subjects viewed the same cross-cylinder target at a distance of 40 cm. For both the objective and subjective findings, the target was viewed under binocular*

fused conditions, and the objective data was recorded (written down) from the right eye only. Even though the WAM 5500 is called an *infra-red optometer,* there is no proof to support that this tool can *discriminate between varying hues of redness;* so cross off Choice A. Choice B, *draw subjective conclusions about the physiological state of the subjects being tested,* is not substantiated by any information stated or implied in that passage. The WAM 5500 does not play doctor or psychologist. Arguably, while it is both handy and pragmatic for a health care practitioner to have a device that can *keep track of time while testing patients,* Choice C is invalid because the passage neither states nor implies that the WAM 5500 can serve as a clock, stopwatch, or hourglass! According to the passage evidence excerpted and reproduced above, **the correct answer is Choice D;** the WAM 5500 is used to *quantify (measure) the accommodative response in the subjects tested.*

44. **(H) Find details within the passage in order to answer this relatively easy question with accuracy:** *The experiment was carried out on 25 subjects having a mean age of 23.4 years, covering an age range between 20 and 30 years* (lines 84–87). The key piece of objective information is that the *mean age* (average age) was 23.4 years. Use process of elimination to narrow in on the population that was NOT tested. Be sure to notice the key word NOT; otherwise, you can get this question wrong due to a careless and/or hasty reading of the question. Choices F (*college-age students*), Choice G (*young adults of both genders*), and Choice J (*twenty-three-year-olds*) comprise populations that were tested. Therefore, **the correct answer is Choice H** (*elderly subjects*).

45. **(A) Return to the passage and read around the concept of "reduced illumination" (lines 64–65) in order to determine a *dis*advantage (Notice this key word!) of performing the DCC test under dim lighting conditions.** Choice B (*The optometrist cannot clearly see what he is doing*), while it may be true, is not the correct answer because this choice lacks passage support and does not express a key disadvantage of the test in terms of its impact on its subjects. While Choice C (*Reduced lighting maximizes the size of the subject's pupil*) and Choice D (*Lower levels of illumination decrease the depth-of-focus of the subject's eye*) are true, they do *not* indicate disadvantages of performing this clinical test with reduced lighting. **The correct answer is Choice A** because it is true that *In everyday life, people do not typically function in dimly-lit circumstances;* so, a drawback of this testing scenario is that it does not consider the subject's performance in "real-life" conditions.

COMPARATIVE READING: NATURAL SCIENCE

46. **(D) This is an ALL/EXCEPT question.** Find evidence for three of the four answer choices, and use process of elimination to narrow in on the one choice that is not substantiated by the passage. The question asks you to determine what the narrator of Passage A does *not* attribute the cheetah's

exceptional hunting ability to. Cross off Choice A, *steadfast gaze* because the author mentions this in line 4. Cross off Choice B, *muscular physique*, because this is referenced in Paragraph 2. The opening line mentions the cheetah's speed so cross off Choice C, *celerity*. **The best answer is Choice D**, *inner ear sensitivity*.

47. **(G) Find details within the passage in order to answer this question.** The question asks about the hunting prowess of the cheetah and its relation to a *relatively new discovery in terms of the cheetah's anatomy*. In lines 4–5, the passage says that researchers investigated "For the first time . . . ." This means that the study focused on a *new discovery*. Then lines 6–7 say that the study was on "the cheetah's extraordinary sensory abilities by analyzing the speedy animal's inner ear." The passage goes on to describe the cheetah's inner ear. For example, see lines 23–29 ("The inner ear facilitates . . . incredible hunting specialization") as additional passage evidence. For these reasons, **the best answer is Choice G**, *certain inner ear dimensions and shape*. The other answer choices are distractors.

48. **(C) Word-in-context questions require that you focus in on the word's usage in a particular sentence.** The word's meaning has to fit and flow as seamlessly as possible in this context: "They found that the inner ears of living cheetahs differ *markedly* from those of all other felids alive today . . ." Cross off B because *haphazardly* means randomly or arbitrarily, so this choice doesn't make sense in this usage. Also cross off Choices A and D, as *surprisingly* and *indistinctly* are not good fits. **The best answer is Choice C**, *distinctly*. In terms of diction, this word fits and flows nicely because distinctly means separate unto itself.

49. **(F) This question is holistic and an inference question as it is largely based on what is implied or stated in the passage in its entirety.** Consider Paragraph 6 as evidence of the best hunting dogs. Koster says, "We expect that hunting ability would eventually decline as dogs get older, but the reality is that few dogs reach eight or nine years old because even well-treated dogs often succumb to snakebites or jaguar attacks." Eliminate Choice H, *older female dogs*, as the evidence suggests most would consider older dogs to be less adept at hunting. It logically follows then, to eliminate Choice J, *all of the above*. In terms of gender, consider this evidence that appears in lines 137–141: "There also seems to be a trend that bigger dogs are able to track and corral bigger prey, said Koster, which increases the hunting return rates of their owners, and in general, male dogs are bigger than females." Eliminate Choice G, *younger female dogs*, and **the best answer is Choice F**, *younger male dogs*.

50. **(B) This is an ALL/EXCEPT question.** Find evidence for three of the four answer choices, and use process of elimination to narrow in on the one choice that is not substantiated by the passage. The question asks you to

select the answer that does NOT contribute to a hunting dog's decline or demise. Recall that evidence in Paragraph 6 says, "few dogs reach eight or nine years old because even well-treated dogs often succumb to snakebites or jaguar attacks," so eliminate Choices A, *snakebites*. Factor in this evidence as it appears in Paragraph 5—"unskilled hunting dogs receive poorer care and die relatively young"—and cross off Choices C, *poor care* and D, *lack of hunting skill.* **The best answer, therefore, is Choice B**, *bad genes.*

51. **(J) This is a *phrase used in context* question.** Reread the full sentence in which the phrase appears to glean its meaning from context. The question asks what the phrase in line 96, *harvested game*, most refers to. In Paragraph 3 of Passage B, the text states: "Koster and anthropologist Kenneth Tankersley ... recently examined key demographic variables such as age and sex on the amount of *harvested game* that dogs contribute from subsistence hunting in an indigenous community, which has a long and important role in community survival." Choice F, *competition among human hunters*, is incorrect because the passage does not deal with humans competing against each other with regard to their hunting skills. Also, Choice G, *competition among hunting dogs*, is invalid because this meaning does not fit and flow seamlessly in the sentence referenced above. Likewise, Choice H, *biogenetically altered prey* is incorrect because the text does not state or imply aspects of the biogenetic altering of prey. **The best answer is Choice J**, *prey gathered by hunting dogs.*

52. **(D) This is a phrase (an action verb phrase, in this case) used in a context question.** Reread the entire sentence in which the vocabulary word appears (lines 131–136). Focus on the underscored clues of the fuller context: "We expect that hunting ability would eventually decline as dogs get older, but <u>the reality is that few dogs reach eight or nine years old because</u> even well-treated <u>dogs often *succumb to* snakebites or jaguar attacks.</u>" Eliminate Choice A, *resist*, as logically the dogs would not have difficulty reaching eight or nine if they were able to resist the snakes and jaguars. Cross off Choice B, *attack against* for the same reason. Likewise, Choice C, *contend with* is invalid. **The best answer is Choice D**, *perish due to*; plug in this phrase and hear how it fits and flows most seamlessly.

53. **(F) This question is holistic and based on both natural sciences passages. The best answer is Choice F** because both passages use *quotations from experts*. Koster is quoted in Passage B and Grohé is quoted in Passage A. Neither passage author uses *humorous hyperbole*, exaggeration, so eliminate Choice G. Choice H can also be eliminated because *rhetorical questions* are not posed. While specialized scientific terminology is used in Passage A (*Acinonyx jubatus* and *Acinonyx pardinensis*, for example), it does not appear in Passage B.

54. **(A) Comparing how the content of each passage differs is key to answering this question accurately.** The question asks about the specific focus in Passage A of the animal's hunting competency. Both passages address the gender of the animals, so Choice B is out. While upbringing is discussed in Passage B, it is not a topic in Passage A; therefore, cross off Choice C, *upbringing*. Choice D, *age*, is incorrect because age is only addressed in Passage B; for example, the opening line says, "Older dogs and male dogs are better hunting companions than younger dogs . . . ." **The best answer is Choice A** because only Passage A discusses anatomy.

55. **(H) This is an overarching question type, in that it asks the reader about the focus that the two passages share.** While *family dynamics* is addressed minimally, it is neither the main focus of Passage A or Passage B. Cross off Choice F. Likewise, cross off Choice G, *group behavior*, because the passages do not delve into various circumstances and situations in which group behavior is analyzed or examined. While dietary needs of animals is an important topic, it is not the primary discussion in these passages, so eliminate Choice J. **The best answer is Choice H**, as *hunting ability* is the primary topic in these comparative passages.

Writing Test

5

- How to Be a Class ACT on Test Day
- Writing Skills in Closer Focus
  - Prewriting, Freewriting, Revising/Editing
  - Flexible Timing Plans
- Writing Prompts, Sample Responses, Evaluations
- Guidelines for Evaluation

ptional—This delightful word is associated with the ACT Writing Test only. If you elect to take the ACT, you *must* take the tests in Reading, English, Science, and Math. Only if you elect to register to take ACT Plus Writing will you take the Writing Test, which you will work on after you have finished the four multiple-choice tests in Reading, English, Science, and Math.

One Test, Two Scores! You earn two separate scores on the Writing Test:

ELA Score (Combined English/Reading/Writing)	Based on a Scale of 1 to 36
Writing Subscore	Based on a Scale of 2 to 12 Your essay will be scored holistically (based on overall effect and impressions rather than on separate elements). You will not earn separate scores for *mechanics* and *content*, as you may or may not be accustomed to earning at school. Your essay will be read and evaluated by two trained readers. Each reader will rate you somewhere between a 1 (lowest score) to a 6 (highest score). If your essay evaluators disagree about their ratings by more than one point, a third reader will be brought in to evaluate your essay. Together, these three readers will discuss your work, reach a meeting of the minds, and settle the inconsistency between your two original ratings.
Some Specific and Constructive Comments on Your Essay	Your high school and/or college may see your essay that you have written on the test day that you report.

ACT Essay Rubric

IDEAS AND ANALYSIS: Considers multiple perspectives. Produces a clear and sophisticated thesis. Provides a useful context for analyzing the issue. Analyzes the implications, complexities, and underlying assumptions of different viewpoints.						
6: Excellent	5: Skillful	4: Adequate	3: Fair	2: Weak	1: Poor	_____ /6

DEVELOPMENT AND SUPPORT: Provides an insightful and well-supported argument, placing the issue in a broad context. Uses reasoning and illustration to express the significance of the issue. Demonstrates an understanding of the complexity of the topic.						
6: Excellent	5: Skillful	4: Adequate	3: Fair	2: Weak	1: Poor	_____ /6

ORGANIZATION: Shows a skillful overall organizational approach. Has a clear, sustained position, accompanied by a logical sequence of ideas that builds the writer's argument. Uses clear and logical transitions between sentences and paragraphs.						
6: Excellent	5: Skillful	4: Adequate	3: Fair	2: Weak	1: Poor	_____ /6

LANGUAGE USE: Uses language that is well-suited to the argument. Uses a vocabulary that is precise and appropriate. Provides clear and varied sentence structure. Establishes an effective tone, voice, and style. Minimizes grammar, usage, and mechanics issues so as not to interfere with the reader's understanding.						
6: Excellent	5: Skillful	4: Adequate	3: Fair	2: Weak	1: Poor	_____ /6

ESSAY RAW SCORE:	_____ /24
Divide your Essay Raw Score by 2 to get your estimated ACT Essay Score between 2 and 12: Essay Raw Score: _____ ÷ 2 = _____ out of 12 possible points.	
ACT WRITING SCALED SCORE:	_____ /12

HOW TO BE A CLASS ACT ON TEST DAY

You wouldn't blindly take a three-hour drive to a secluded beach cove situated along some little traveled coastline along the southernmost corridor of Cabo San Lucas, Mexico, would you? Right? Most likely, you'd ask for solid directions first, plug the location into your navigation system, or get a good printout from MapQuest. Likewise, you wouldn't venture on this drive without a few solid landmarks to watch out for, right? Similarly, you wouldn't want to save the testing "directions" for the day of the ACT!

To be a class ACT on test day, it is always a good idea to know the essay directions thoroughly before you arrive at the testing center. Knowing the ins-and-outs of how to approach the essay, the directions, the timing, and the expectations ahead of time will save you precious minutes.

Review the list below *now* so that you won't have to read the approximately two-hundred-word explanation, which appears on the test booklet cover, *on the day of the test!*

WRITING SKILLS IN CLOSER FOCUS

The ACT Essay

Here is a bulleted summary of key instructions to keep in mind about writing your essay:

- You have 40 minutes to write your essay in pencil without skipping lines. Do not use mechanical pencils. Your essay must be written in English. (Either print or script is fine. Choose whichever style allows you to write most legibly.)

- First, read the writing prompt, which typically pertains to a reflection on how the world and its people are changing. (Don't worry much about the topic. Chances are, you're not going to be asked about the eating habits of arboreal monkeys or about precisely how a pearl forms within a mollusk!)

- You are evaluated on how clearly you take a position and support your argument with appropriate and specific examples. You couldn't ask for anything more straightforward than that!

- As you write, use logical reasoning, stay focused on the topic, and do your best to use language that is grammatically sound, clear, and concise.

Good news: The information and quick drills in Chapter 3 (English Test) will strengthen your foundation in sound grammar; this knowledge, in turn, will organically translate into your writing. Use effective transitional words and phrases between your sentences and paragraphs. Transitions aid and accentuate the logic and flow of your writing.

✏️ Put down your pencil when the proctor says time is up! Play by the rules; do not go back—even for a few seconds—to check your work or change an answer that you've already bubbled in. Time is up means time is up!

Writing Your Essay Is a Three-Stage Process

- **Stage One:** Brainstorming and Planning
- **Stage Two:** Getting It Down on Paper
- **Stage Three:** Polishing and Buffing

To think of this process in another way, consider the bold terms that represent the three stages listed above:

Stage One: **Prewriting**	➡	Stage Two: **Freewriting**	➡	Stage Three: **Revising/Editing**

Note: Although each stage is treated separately, realize that there is a very workable, recursive, and free-flowing relationship among them. These stages are not strictly linear. In other words, as you're rolling and getting a wealth of ideas down on paper (freewriting), you might take a moment to jot down a few key words that indicate examples you want to discuss in the next paragraph (prewriting). Similarly, as you are midway through your freewriting, you might change a word, cross off a redundant phrase, or insert a comma (editing).

STAGE ONE: BRAINSTORMING AND PLANNING

PREWRITING Think of prewriting as a brainstorming session that gets your ideas flowing. The good news is that your brainstorming can be like an unruly, winding river. There are no dams to hold you back or geographical borders to restrict you. Write down, jot down—even scrawl, if you'd like—your brainstorming notes on the unlined pages that are provided in your test booklet. Neatness does not count at this stage. Use a free-form brainstorming style, like one of the following: a list of bullet notes, a rough concept map of ideas (also called a "spider web"), a casual outline, or a bunch of interrelated phrases—with or without those Roman numerals is fine.

After you have listed some basic notes, use numbers (1, 2, 3 . . .), letters (a, b, c . . .), or arrows (→ ↓ ↑) to indicate your organizational plan. Consideration of an organizational "plan" is important at this stage so that your final essay has an organizational structure that flows and makes sense. There are no hard and fast rules—but to play it safe, plan to write a substantial piece that includes three or four well-supported body paragraphs.

STAGE TWO: GETTING IT DOWN ON PAPER

FREEWRITING Now start writing—*neatly*—in either print or script. The choice is yours. Write in the style in which you write most neatly. It is important that your writing is legible so that you don't give the essay evaluators a hard time working their way through sloppy penmanship. Do *not* use a felt-tip pen, a ballpoint pen, or ink in any color. Only a soft, lead #2 pencil will do!

You are given four lined pages on which to write. Relax—it is not imperative that you fill all four pages. Just do your best to develop your ideas as clearly and as thoroughly as you can within the time given. Give this test your best shot: Fill as much of the four pages as you can with quality, pertinent examples, and a key ingredient—insight. Insight is an intangible quality that comes through in some essays and not in others. Your essay score does not ride solely on insight, but sentences that express depth of thought or even a sense of thinking outside the box are likely to impress the evaluators.

Any Ol' Word Will Do? Not True!

Try to select effective words that really stand for what you want to say. Appropriate diction (word choice) is an important writing skill. To develop more effective diction, make it a habit to consult a thesaurus when you write by hand, or regularly check for synonyms when you use the word-processing program on your personal computer.

Quick Drill: Choosing the Best Word

In each of the groupings below, circle the word or phrase in each line that you think is most effective. Most effective can be considered in terms of clarity, specificity, and conciseness of expression. Most effective can also be in terms of appropriately using upper-level vocabulary in your essay to illustrate your expository strength to the essay readers. Remember to avoid colloquialisms, slang, off-color, controversial, and overly casual expressions in your ACT essay. Note that there are no "right" answers.

Nouns	lady	seamstress	worker	person
Verbs	moved	ran	scurried	went
Adverbs	boisterously	loudly	noisily	at full volume
Nouns, Pronouns	there	place	Robert Moses State Park	recreational area
Adjectives	spine-tingling	interesting	scary	frightening
Verbs	eat	devour	gulp down	gobble up
Nouns	this kid	Jack McKenna	a guy I know	dude

ANSWERS*

Nouns	lady	(seamstress)	worker	person
Verbs	moved	ran	(scurried)	went
Adverbs	(boisterously)	loudly	noisily	at full volume
Nouns, Pronouns	there	place	(Robert Moses State Park)	recreational area
Adjectives	(spine-tingling)	interesting	scary	frightening
Verbs	eat	(devour)	gulp down	gobble up
Nouns	this kid	(Jack McKenna)	a guy I know	dude

*These are suggested answers.

Develop paragraphs using specific and concrete examples. Examples should be carefully selected, vivid, and clearly defined. "A period in American history" is not as good as "the Great Depression." Likewise, "in a modern short story" is not as good as "in Ray Bradbury's short science fiction story, 'All Summer in a Day'." Again, "a political rebellion" is not as poignant as "the Bolshevik Revolution."

Write Juicy-Burger Body Paragraphs

At some time or other, you've heard that the body paragraphs are the "meat" of your essay. Right? Or, you've seen the drawing of a burger—the seeded buns are the opening and closing paragraphs; the sirloin layers in the middle are your body paragraphs that explain your supporting details.

Choose fortified over flimsy: A paragraph with two or three sentences comes across as wimpy or flimsy; strive for well-developed paragraphs fortified with five or more sentences instead. Yes, I am telling you that length *does* matter, to an extent, in this case.

Variety Is the Spice of Good Sentence Writing

Imagine every iTune song starting off with, more or less, the same line or beat (boring). Imagine every song having the same basic lyrics in its chorus (blah!) Imagine every magazine article starting off basically the same way (yawn). Imagine every text message beginning with *wazup* and ending with *gtg* (ho-hum).

To avoid the doldrums, keep in mind sentence variety and expressive "spice" as you write your essay. Don't start the majority of your sentences in the same way—boring! Instead, give each sentence its own "start-off flair."

- (Starts in traditional, subject–verb order) *The school lunch program (subject) has revised (verb phrase)* its menu to include more nutritious entrees and snacks.
- (Starts with a prepositional phrase) *In spite of a strict dress code,* the students at Maritime High School are able to express their individuality in a variety of ways.
- (Starts with a transitional phrase) *On the other hand,* too much individuality of expression can lead to a divisive student body.
- (Starts with a subordinate clause) *Whereas students conform to most school policies,* they sometimes defy others.

STAGE THREE: POLISHING AND BUFFING

REVISING/EDITING Even if you have the *perfect* shoes to go with your prom dress, or the perfect shoes to go with your dress suit, you wouldn't wear them scratched and dull. You would polish them, buff them up so that they shine for the occasion.

The same goes for your writing: Polish your prose! Now is your chance, so budget some time at the end (about two or three minutes is adequate) for reading through your essay and making any changes you would like. You will not have time for substantial and sweeping revisions, but you will have enough time to do smaller things like the ones listed below. One small revision does not a large impact make, but several revisions can make the difference between an essay that shows a firm handle of sound English, usage, and mechanics and one that does not. For this essay, your writing skills should reflect those exercised in high school English class and in beginning-level, college composition courses.

Insert (using a caret mark) a few additional words or adjectives that you would just love to add; additions inserted at the editing stage are often the icing on the cake! Do not, however, insert any new words or material in the margins. Writing that appears in the margin will not contribute to your score.

Substitute a few wimpy words with stronger, more fitting words. Use neat cross-offs to do this, and simply write the new word above. Cross-offs should be neat, using a single line. No scribble-scrabble or zig zag cross-outs. This stage is not meant to make your essay look messy. To an extent, neatness does count. You do not want your essay to strain the essay reader's eyes.

Add punctuation marks that you might have overlooked, such as: apostrophes, commas, end marks, and quotation marks.

Draw an asterisk (*) to add a sentence or two that you think can significantly substantiate your argument. Insert sentences (supporting details, for example) sparingly; otherwise, your final essay can come across as scatterbrained and messy.

Use standard proofreading symbols to clearly revise and edit your text:

∧ The caret mark, for adding a letter, word, phrase, juicy adjective, or a forgotten verb

* The asterisk, to show where long phrases, sentences, or an insightful comment should be added

∽ The transpose symbol, to indicate that letters should be reversed or that words or phrases should be reversed in order

◡ The close-up symbol, to indicate that two words that you have written separately should actually be joined as a compound word

— The clean, single-line cross-out, to replace a word with a more effective word

¶ The paragraph symbol, to show where you want to indent

At this stage of the writing process, you can insert effective transitional words or phrases that you have left out. Use a caret symbol. Using neat, single-line cross-outs, fix mechanical mistakes in spelling, word usage, punctuation, and grammar.

Flexible Timing Plans

Timing plans are flexible. Still, the chart below illustrates one way you can approach your forty-minute writing task. Notice how the full forty minutes is not given to the Getting-It-Down-On-Paper Stage. Prewriting and Polishing are important stages in the essay-writing process. Giving time to these "bookend stages" is important and will make a real difference in your essay in the end. Experiment with various time breakdowns. After several practice essay-writing sessions, you'll find a timing plan that is customized for you and works best!

Prewriting	The Planning Stage	2–3 Minutes
Freewriting	The Getting-It-Down-On-Paper Stage	35 Minutes
Revising/ Editing	The Polishing Stage	2–3 Minutes

GUIDELINES FOR EVALUATION

Each essay is scored on a scale of 6 to 1.

Performance Categories	Score
Outstanding	6
Very Good	5
Good	4
Fair	3
Poor	2
Very Poor	1

Essays scored 4, 5, and 6 are considered average or above and attest to a level of writing skill appropriate for first-year college students. Essays rated 1, 2, or 3 are below average and suggest the writer's need for remediation.

Each essay is evaluated by two readers. If their evaluations differ by more than a point, the essay is given to a third reader. No list of criteria can cover everything that readers take into account, but the descriptions below include many of the standards that ACT readers use in determining essay scores. No essay is likely to contain all the characteristics below. Readers make every effort to be objective, but being human they must ultimately rely on their judgment. Consequently, an essay that receives a low 5 may not be noticeably better than an essay that earns a high 4. The rating difference is likely to be based on intangibles that cause readers to assign the grade that in their view is most appropriate.

6 **Outstanding**. An *outstanding* essay is a well-conceived, orderly, and insightful treatment of the assigned task. The writer has fashioned a convincing thesis amply supported by appropriate and specific details. Its point of view, syntax, imagery, and diction demonstrate the writer's ability to control a wide range of elements of composition. Any errors that occur are inconsequential. Overall, the work is a model of clarity and sophistication.

5 **Very Good**. A *very good* essay contains a sound thesis and demonstrates the writer's grasp of the task. It develops the main idea with purpose and conviction, but it may be somewhat less thorough and insightful than the best essays. It also may fall short of the mastery, sophistication, and control of composition exemplified by the best essays. Nevertheless, its organization is sensible, its language and usage are appropriate, and its overall intent is clear and consistent.

4 **Good.** A *good* essay deals with the topic competently. It uses conventional language and sentence structure and provides some appropriate specific examples to support a thesis. It gives evidence of the writer's acquaintance with essay organization, coherence, and paragraph development. Some errors in word choice and awkward expression may exist, but no error seriously interferes with meaning.

3   **Fair.** *A fair* essay suggests mediocrity in writing. It may adequately respond to the prompt but gives evidence of an inconsistent control of the elements of composition. Although the essay has a recognizable structure, the organization may be confusing or not fully realized. Inaccuracies or lapses in logic may weaken the essay's overall effect. Occasional mechanical errors may detract from the essay's meaning.

2   **Poor.** A *poor* essay demonstrates a superficial or limited understanding of the prompt. The essay's development is meager and its treatment of the subject imprecise and unconvincing. The point of the essay may be perceptible, but the presentation of ideas is characterized by faulty diction, weak syntax, and incoherent or confused organization.

1   **Very Poor.** A *very poor* essay reveals the writer's inability to make sense of the prompt. It may wander off the topic or substitute an irrelevant or simplistic task. It may also be unacceptably brief or undeveloped. The prose may lack organization, coherence, and meaning. The writer shows little evidence of control of English syntax or the rules of usage and grammar.

Chapter Summary

Take a deep breath and relax: Writing a unified and **well-supported essay** is a skill, not rocket science. Trust in your ability to **plan your approach**, to select your examples, and to write down your ideas. You are equipped with a wealth of experience. Chances are, you have been writing essays since middle school, if not before.

You can learn to be a **more effective writer** by reading good books, newspapers, and informative periodicals. Finally, good essay writers do not underestimate the final **polishing stage**, which invokes your editing and revising talents. When you write essays for practice, give yourself an added preparation benefit by allowing yourself the full thirty minutes (and no more) allotted for this task. Make **timing** a regular part of your test prep routine; on the day of the exam, you will feel less pressure to perform under a time constraint.

Practice Exercises

Practice Writing Prompt 1

Chromebooks in the Classroom

More and more elementary school students are being supplied with Chromebooks. These devices are used for classwork as well as homework. While technology in the classroom has its advantages, both educators and parents should question whether the benefits outweigh the drawbacks. Are Chromebooks, in fact, effective teaching tools or merely a distraction to similar or even improved learning that could take place without them?

Read and carefully evaluate the following perspectives. Each demonstrates a specific way of thinking about using Chromebooks in the classroom.

Perspective One	Perspective Two	Perspective Three
Chromebooks are an unnecessary add-on to the school supplies needed for classroom learning and homework. Composition notebooks, workbooks, and homework sheets more than suffice. In fact, the last thing young students need is another screen to look at— on top of their smartphones, laptops, and televisions.	As technology is an indelible feature of the future for young minds, an added technology such as the Chromebook is a wise addition to their educational preparation. Students can learn to navigate and contribute to interactive learning tools such as Google classroom and peer review.	The addition of Chromebooks to the elementary school learning scope is a double-edged sword. While they enhance a student's facility with typing on a keyboard, inputting key commands, and organizing their files of work, the Chromebook can detract from verbal communication between students and their classmates and teachers. If used, they should be used cautiously and with frequent monitoring.

ESSAY ASSIGNMENT

Compose a cohesive essay in which you consider multiple viewpoints on using Chromebooks in the classroom. In your response, be sure to

- clearly state your point of view on the issue and analyze the relationship between your perspective and a minimum of one other perspective
- develop and support your ideas with specific examples and sound reasoning
- organize your ideas clearly and logically
- express your thoughts effectively in standard written English

You may completely agree with any of the perspectives given, partially agree, or have a completely different perspective.

Prewriting and Planning Page

Plan your essay on this page. You will not earn credit or be given a score for any of your work that appears on this page.

Please continue on the reverse side of this sheet if you need more space for your prewriting notes.

This page is also for planning. Your work and notes here will not be scored or earn you credit.

Sample Response—Score Level Range 10–12

Demonstrating effective and competent skills

The digital age is progressing rapidly and inexorably. Increasingly, elementary school students are being supplied with Chromebooks, which they will use throughout middle school and, perhaps, high school. While technology in education has undeniable benefits, educators and parents should certainly question whether the benefits outweigh the drawbacks. Indeed, Chromebooks are effective teaching tools; however, these screens create disconnects among students as well as distractions in the classroom setting.

I do not fully embrace Perspective One, as it emphatically opposes the integration of these screen-based devices in the classroom, calling them "unnecessary" and raising concerns about screen overload. Avoiding technology is back-stepping, as technology is inextricably tied to the future of learning, the workforce, and global culture at large. Regarding Perspective Two, I agree with two of its points: practice with Chromebooks enables students to learn to adeptly navigate sites and make contributions to interactive learning tools, such as peer review, sharing documents, and other Google classroom engagements. As with most technology, there are positives and negatives to consider.

On the whole, my perspective aligns most closely with that of the third viewpoint provided. This perspective is balanced and reasonable: it recognizes the benefits and detriments of the technology, calling the use of Chromebooks "a double-edged sword." Even though fine motor and keyboarding skills as well as file management can be improved, these devices can erode verbal communication among students, teachers, and support staff. In other words, students can find themselves alienated or isolated—excessively absorbed in the screen and features therein. Perspective Three also recommends mindful use and frequent monitoring with regard to this screen technology in the classroom. This caveat is imperative: without monitoring, students can easily become distracted and absorbed in the world of non-educational apps and social media. Schools should maintain blocks on sites and apps that are negative influences on students or that can sidetrack them from their learning.

While these perspectives inspire a thorough conversation regarding the use of Chromebooks in the classroom, there remain myriad questions to consider. For instance, if students are glued to their screens, what happens to verbal exchange accompanied by eye contact and facial expression? If the Chromebooks provide a world within themselves, what will be the future of reading aloud in front of *peers from a handwritten essay? What will be the future of working in cooperative groups in which dialoging and conversing are key to problem solving? These queries reinforce how vital it is to have frequent monitoring of the use of Chromebooks to determine what is weakening and what is edifying on behalf of student's social, emotional, and intellectual growth. Finally, monitoring and evaluation should be ongoing. Educators need to ask themselves and each other, what aspects of Chromebooks are beneficial or disadvantageous to students in terms of educational inquiry, absorbing the material, and collaborating with one's peer group.*

Explanation of Score

The ACT Essay is evaluated based on four domains: 1. Ideas and Analysis; 2. Development and Support; 3. Organization; and 4. Language Use and Conventions. Within each domain, the score range is 2–12. Domain scores are determined by adding together the individual domain scores, using a 1–6 scale, from each of two essay evaluators.

The score analysis that follows explains the reasoning that determined strong scores (5–6 range) within each of the four domains for this sample essay.

Ideas and Analysis

Score Range 5–6

This essay addresses the multiple viewpoints provided in the prompt. This in itself is an analytical strength, for it evidences the author's consideration of the varied sides of the issue. Furthermore, in the opening paragraph the author reveals analytical aptitude, as indicated by the balance of ideas (*benefits, drawbacks*) articulated in this statement: *While technology in education has undeniable benefits, educators and parents should certainly question whether the benefits outweigh the drawbacks.*

The reasoning and ideas presented in the body paragraphs firmly substantiate the interplay between the two sides (pros/cons of Chromebooks) as articulated in the thesis, in that benefits and drawbacks are clarified through illustrative examples: *Even though fine motor and keyboarding skills as well as file management can be improved, these devices can erode verbal communication among students, teachers, and support staff. In other words, students can find themselves alienated or isolated— excessively absorbed in the screen and features therein* (Paragraph 3).

Development and Support

Score Range 5–6

Throughout the argument, the writer focuses on the purpose at hand. The writer does not contradict the thesis or present an ambiguous stance. Toward the end of the opening paragraph, the author clearly articulates the argument's thesis statement: *Indeed, Chromebooks are effective teaching tools; however, these screens create disconnects among students as well as distractions in the classroom setting.*

Within each body paragraph, the author presents concrete reasons to support the viewpoint that Chromebooks invite a conversation that addresses both the benefits and detriments of the addition of this screen-based technology to the educational setting. For example, to stress the potential detriments of this screen technology, the author explicitly recommends: *Schools should maintain blocks on sites and apps that are negative influences on students or that can sidetrack them from their learning* (Paragraph 3).

Organization

Score Range 5–6
The organizational structure of the essay is logical, contributing to a clear presentation and flow of ideas. A unified sense of the argument to follow is clearly laid out in the introduction, and paragraphing is clearly indicated by indentation and by the cohesion of ideas within paragraphs.

Demonstrating an imperative writing skill, the argument employs transitional words and phrases in a manner that allows the train of thought to flow smoothly. Examples used in this essay include: *indeed, on the whole, for instance, in other words, even though,* and *finally.*

The conclusion restates the author's point of view, then proceeds to broaden the discussion to emphasize the importance and consideration the issue at hand merits. The author effectively accomplishes this by raising a series of thoughtful rhetorical questions: *if students are glued to their screens, what happens to verbal exchanges accompanied by eye contact and facial expression? If the Chromebooks provide a world within themselves, what will be the future of reading aloud in front of peers from a handwritten essay? What will be the future of working in cooperative groups in which dialoging and conversing are key to problem solving?*

Language Use

Score Range 5–6
This essay demonstrates numerous indicators of advanced diction and usage. Both word choice (for instance: *inexorably, adeptly, integration, inextricably, myriad, queries, caveat, edifying, embraces*) and sentence patterns are effective and varied (simple sentences, compound sentences, complex sentences, compound-complex sentences, interrogatives). This command of vocabulary and sentence structure contributes to an effective, skillful style of prose writing.

In addition, the author uses sound idiomatic phrasing (*on behalf of*), correct prepositions, and a skillful blend of language conciseness and precision. Last but not least, the author demonstrates a high level of proficiency with regard to the use of standard conventions of punctuation such as the comma, colon, semicolon, apostrophes, end marks, and quotation marks.

Practice Writing Prompt 2

Externships in College

Many colleges and universities today offer externships to their students to fulfill credit hours. Externships provide real life, hands on experience related to students' field of study. However, externship credits should not replace classroom learning, as the latter includes lecture, discussion, and question and answer sessions. Schools are not the workplace, so undergraduate programs should restrict the number of credit hours awarded for externships, should they be offered in the first place.

Read and carefully evaluate the following perspectives. Each demonstrates a specific way of thinking about colleges offering externships to students.

Perspective One	Perspective Two	Perspective Three
Summers offer ample opportunity for students to acquire workplace learning. College curriculum hours, therefore, should not be replaced with externship programs. The curricula required to earn a BA or BS, for example, is robustly and holistically defined, and externships can dilute the material and topics required for the degree program. In lieu of formal externships, students can volunteer discretionary hours at a work setting of his or her interest.	Externships provide invaluable learning experiences that the lecture hall or discussion group at a college or university cannot fulfill. In fact, colleges should require students to take a certain number of credit hours based on an externship's relevance to their undergraduate degree. Moreover, externships can help students decide if a particular career path is suited to him or her before pursuing the final requirement for the bachelor's degree.	While externships provide valuable learning experiences, they cannot be compared to learning content and reasoning that is provided by traditional lecture hall settings and the more intimate discussion sections. A professor has concentrated knowledge of his or her subject that is often research-based and stems from his or her long line of learning and studying. This content knowledge will be considerably depleted if students spend too many hours outside the lecture setting and in a work or clinic type setting instead.

ESSAY ASSIGNMENT

Compose a cohesive essay in which you consider multiple viewpoints on colleges offering externships to students. In your response, be sure to

- clearly state your point of view on the issue and analyze the relationship between your perspective and a minimum of one other perspective
- develop and support your ideas with specific examples and sound reasoning
- organize your ideas clearly and logically
- express your thoughts effectively in standard written English

You may completely agree with any of the perspectives given, partially agree, or have a completely different perspective.

Prewriting and Planning Page

Plan your essay on this page. You will not earn credit or be given a score for any of your work that appears on this page.

Please continue on the reverse side of this sheet if you need more space for your prewriting notes.

This page is also for planning. Your work and notes here will not be scored or earn you credit.

Now, write your essay. Ask a teacher to score it.

PRACTICE TESTS

ANSWER SHEET
Practice Tests

English Test

1. Ⓐ Ⓑ Ⓒ Ⓓ	20. Ⓕ Ⓖ Ⓗ Ⓙ	39. Ⓐ Ⓑ Ⓒ Ⓓ	58. Ⓕ Ⓖ Ⓗ Ⓙ
2. Ⓕ Ⓖ Ⓗ Ⓙ	21. Ⓐ Ⓑ Ⓒ Ⓓ	40. Ⓕ Ⓖ Ⓗ Ⓙ	59. Ⓐ Ⓑ Ⓒ Ⓓ
3. Ⓐ Ⓑ Ⓒ Ⓓ	22. Ⓕ Ⓖ Ⓗ Ⓙ	41. Ⓐ Ⓑ Ⓒ Ⓓ	60. Ⓕ Ⓖ Ⓗ Ⓙ
4. Ⓕ Ⓖ Ⓗ Ⓙ	23. Ⓐ Ⓑ Ⓒ Ⓓ	42. Ⓕ Ⓖ Ⓗ Ⓙ	61. Ⓐ Ⓑ Ⓒ Ⓓ
5. Ⓐ Ⓑ Ⓒ Ⓓ	24. Ⓕ Ⓖ Ⓗ Ⓙ	43. Ⓐ Ⓑ Ⓒ Ⓓ	62. Ⓕ Ⓖ Ⓗ Ⓙ
6. Ⓕ Ⓖ Ⓗ Ⓙ	25 Ⓐ Ⓑ Ⓒ Ⓓ	44. Ⓕ Ⓖ Ⓗ Ⓙ	63. Ⓐ Ⓑ Ⓒ Ⓓ
7. Ⓐ Ⓑ Ⓒ Ⓓ	26. Ⓕ Ⓖ Ⓗ Ⓙ	45. Ⓐ Ⓑ Ⓒ Ⓓ	64. Ⓕ Ⓖ Ⓗ Ⓙ
8. Ⓕ Ⓖ Ⓗ Ⓙ	27. Ⓐ Ⓑ Ⓒ Ⓓ	46. Ⓕ Ⓖ Ⓗ Ⓙ	65. Ⓐ Ⓑ Ⓒ Ⓓ
9. Ⓐ Ⓑ Ⓒ Ⓓ	28. Ⓕ Ⓖ Ⓗ Ⓙ	47. Ⓐ Ⓑ Ⓒ Ⓓ	66. Ⓕ Ⓖ Ⓗ Ⓙ
10. Ⓕ Ⓖ Ⓗ Ⓙ	29. Ⓐ Ⓑ Ⓒ Ⓓ	48. Ⓕ Ⓖ Ⓗ Ⓙ	67. Ⓐ Ⓑ Ⓒ Ⓓ
11. Ⓐ Ⓑ Ⓒ Ⓓ	30. Ⓕ Ⓖ Ⓗ Ⓙ	49. Ⓐ Ⓑ Ⓒ Ⓓ	68. Ⓕ Ⓖ Ⓗ Ⓙ
12. Ⓕ Ⓖ Ⓗ Ⓙ	31. Ⓐ Ⓑ Ⓒ Ⓓ	50. Ⓕ Ⓖ Ⓗ Ⓙ	69. Ⓐ Ⓑ Ⓒ Ⓓ
13. Ⓐ Ⓑ Ⓒ Ⓓ	32. Ⓕ Ⓖ Ⓗ Ⓙ	51. Ⓐ Ⓑ Ⓒ Ⓓ	70. Ⓕ Ⓖ Ⓗ Ⓙ
14. Ⓕ Ⓖ Ⓗ Ⓙ	33. Ⓐ Ⓑ Ⓒ Ⓓ	52. Ⓕ Ⓖ Ⓗ Ⓙ	71. Ⓐ Ⓑ Ⓒ Ⓓ
15. Ⓐ Ⓑ Ⓒ Ⓓ	34. Ⓕ Ⓖ Ⓗ Ⓙ	53. Ⓐ Ⓑ Ⓒ Ⓓ	72. Ⓕ Ⓖ Ⓗ Ⓙ
16. Ⓕ Ⓖ Ⓗ Ⓙ	35. Ⓐ Ⓑ Ⓒ Ⓓ	54. Ⓕ Ⓖ Ⓗ Ⓙ	73. Ⓐ Ⓑ Ⓒ Ⓓ
17. Ⓐ Ⓑ Ⓒ Ⓓ	36. Ⓕ Ⓖ Ⓗ Ⓙ	55. Ⓐ Ⓑ Ⓒ Ⓓ	74. Ⓕ Ⓖ Ⓗ Ⓙ
18. Ⓕ Ⓖ Ⓗ Ⓙ	37. Ⓐ Ⓑ Ⓒ Ⓓ	56. Ⓕ Ⓖ Ⓗ Ⓙ	75. Ⓐ Ⓑ Ⓒ Ⓓ
19. Ⓐ Ⓑ Ⓒ Ⓓ	38. Ⓕ Ⓖ Ⓗ Ⓙ	57. Ⓐ Ⓑ Ⓒ Ⓓ	

Reading Test

1. Ⓐ Ⓑ Ⓒ Ⓓ	11. Ⓐ Ⓑ Ⓒ Ⓓ	21. Ⓐ Ⓑ Ⓒ Ⓓ	31. Ⓐ Ⓑ Ⓒ Ⓓ
2. Ⓕ Ⓖ Ⓗ Ⓙ	12. Ⓕ Ⓖ Ⓗ Ⓙ	22. Ⓕ Ⓖ Ⓗ Ⓙ	32. Ⓕ Ⓖ Ⓗ Ⓙ
3. Ⓐ Ⓑ Ⓒ Ⓓ	13. Ⓐ Ⓑ Ⓒ Ⓓ	23. Ⓐ Ⓑ Ⓒ Ⓓ	33. Ⓐ Ⓑ Ⓒ Ⓓ
4. Ⓕ Ⓖ Ⓗ Ⓙ	14. Ⓕ Ⓖ Ⓗ Ⓙ	24. Ⓕ Ⓖ Ⓗ Ⓙ	34. Ⓕ Ⓖ Ⓗ Ⓙ
5. Ⓐ Ⓑ Ⓒ Ⓓ	15. Ⓐ Ⓑ Ⓒ Ⓓ	25 Ⓐ Ⓑ Ⓒ Ⓓ	35. Ⓐ Ⓑ Ⓒ Ⓓ
6. Ⓕ Ⓖ Ⓗ Ⓙ	16. Ⓕ Ⓖ Ⓗ Ⓙ	26. Ⓕ Ⓖ Ⓗ Ⓙ	36. Ⓕ Ⓖ Ⓗ Ⓙ
7. Ⓐ Ⓑ Ⓒ Ⓓ	17. Ⓐ Ⓑ Ⓒ Ⓓ	27. Ⓐ Ⓑ Ⓒ Ⓓ	37. Ⓐ Ⓑ Ⓒ Ⓓ
8. Ⓕ Ⓖ Ⓗ Ⓙ	18. Ⓕ Ⓖ Ⓗ Ⓙ	28. Ⓕ Ⓖ Ⓗ Ⓙ	38. Ⓕ Ⓖ Ⓗ Ⓙ
9. Ⓐ Ⓑ Ⓒ Ⓓ	19. Ⓐ Ⓑ Ⓒ Ⓓ	29. Ⓐ Ⓑ Ⓒ Ⓓ	39. Ⓐ Ⓑ Ⓒ Ⓓ
10. Ⓕ Ⓖ Ⓗ Ⓙ	20. Ⓕ Ⓖ Ⓗ Ⓙ	30. Ⓕ Ⓖ Ⓗ Ⓙ	40. Ⓕ Ⓖ Ⓗ Ⓙ

ENGLISH TEST

45 MINUTES—75 QUESTIONS

Directions: Selected words and phrases are underlined and numbered in the five passages that follow. You will find suggested versions for the underlined portions in the right-hand column. For most questions, you are asked to select the version that best expresses the ideas, makes the language appropriate for standard, written English, and is worded most consistently with the tone and writing style of the entire passage. If you think the original wording works best, select "NO CHANGE." Sometimes a question from the right-hand column will ask you something specific about the underlined part. Choose the best answer to that question.

Questions about a particular section of the passage—or based on the whole passage—may also be posed. These questions do not reference an underscored part of the reading selection, but rather are indicated by a number or numbers that are boxed.

For each question on the ACT English test, select the version that you consider to be the best, and darken in the corresponding oval on your answer sheet. Before you begin to answer the related questions, read each passage through once. For many questions, you must read a few sentences beyond the question to figure out the best answer. Before deciding on the best alternative in terms of language and phrasing, make sure that you have read far enough ahead in the passage.

Passage I

Baci

We gave her an endearing name even before

we had the occasion to meet her. Our Labradoodle puppy,
₁

Baci, arrived in Long Island, New York after an eight-hour

drive from Virginia during a snowstorm that was occurring
₂

in the month of January. We named her Baci, which means
₂

"kisses" in Italian, because we knew we would love her, and

we gave her this sweet name because she's chocolate brown,

like the color of Perugina *Baci* chocolates originating in

Perugia, which is the name of a town found in central Italy.
₃

1. (A) NO CHANGE
   (B) we had ever the occasion of meeting.
   (C) we met her on this occasion.
   (D) we had met her.

2. (F) NO CHANGE
   (G) snowstorm in January that had been occurring.
   (H) snowstorm occurring during January.
   (J) January snowstorm.

3. (A) NO CHANGE
   (B) central Italy.
   (C) a town in central Italy.
   (D) which is the name of a town, found in central Italy.

GO ON TO THE NEXT PAGE

Two years later, she's a bundle of warmth, fun, and fleecy fur. Part Labrador retriever, part poodle, Baci is a high-energy delightful mix. She will retrieve anything <u>you throw:</u>

                                               4
a rawhide bone, a knotted rope, a rubber ball. She's non-shedding, attributable to her hypoallergenic poodle part, and can jump as high as any circus dog we've seen!

    <u>Baci is athletic and dexterous, as well, in other ways, too.</u>

                           5
She can open all the lever-handled doors in the house; she even lets herself in after she's been let outside to "do her business." When it comes to steps, she can outstrip anybody up or down in record speed. When the family plays ping-pong, she <u>does nonstopping laps</u> around

                                      6

the table. I wonder if she thinks <u>she's, as well, somehow playing, too?</u>

                                   7

4. (F) NO CHANGE
   (G) that is thrown to her
   (H) you have thrown to her; including
   (J) you go ahead and throw:

5. (A) NO CHANGE
   (B) Baci is athletic and dexterous in other ways, too.
   (C) Baci is athletic and dexterous, as well, in other ways.
   (D) Baci, as well, is athletic and dexterous in several additional ways.

6. (F) NO CHANGE
   (G) does laps nonstop
   (H) runs nonstop laps
   (J) does laps, ceaselessly and nonstop,

7. (A) NO CHANGE
   (B) that, in addition to us, she's playing as well?
   (C) she's, as well, somehow playing, along with us?
   (D) she's somehow playing, too?

GO ON TO THE NEXT PAGE

Treats and <u>food is</u> Baci's delights. Her favorite
8

made-for-doggies dinner is dry kibble. Lamb and rice

is her favorite flavor <u>combination, with beef being</u> a close
9

second. Among her favorite <u>treats are</u> baby carrots, apple
10

chunks, and hot dog slices.

She even loves ice cubes, making herself a fixture at the

freezer door whenever it is being opened. ⬚11

The only food or beverage she finds revolting is coffee,

espresso especially; she'll bark if you put a cup of the

aromatic brew under her nose <u>and walk away in an offended</u>
12

<u>mannerism.</u>
12

8. (F) NO CHANGE
   (G) food, so enjoyable to her, is
   (H) food are
   (J) foods being

9. (A) NO CHANGE
   (B) combination, with beef snacks being
   (C) combination; beef and vegetables is
   (D) combination, while beef combined with
         vegetables, regarding flavor combinations, is

10. (F) NO CHANGE
    (G) treats are;
    (H) treats, them being;
    (J) treats would be the following:

11. If the author deleted the sentence below, what would
    the essay lose?
        She even loves ice cubes, making herself a fixture
        at the freezer door whenever it is being opened.
    (A) Nothing
    (B) An irrelevant detail that is superfluous when
          the essay is considered as a whole
    (C) A relevant and serious detail that detracts from
          the tone of the essay
    (D) An additional, fitting detail that adds a touch
          of humor as well as a cute image

12. (F) NO CHANGE
    (G) and walk away, offended.
    (H) and walk away in an offense.
    (J) but walk offendedly away.

GO ON TO THE NEXT PAGE

Baci enjoys many activities and outings. One of her

latest pastimes is going to the dog run at a local park.

First of all, she loves the car ride there. Second, she
13

loves seeing all of the other dogs and people.

Baci, who weighs forty-five pounds, plays with both the
14

smaller and the larger dogs, but she prefers the smaller ones.

Her continuously wagging tail is the evidence! ☐15

13. (A) NO CHANGE
    (B) Firstly,
    (C) First of all:
    (D) First,

14. (F) NO CHANGE
    (G) Baci who is weighing forty-five pounds,
    (H) Baci, with a weight of forty-five pounds;
    (J) Baci, forty-five pounds of weight,

15. If the author were to add something else to the last paragraph, which of the following would be most appropriate?
    (A) Tell about how Baci sometimes sleeps in her crate at night
    (B) Tell about how Baci is a great watchdog
    (C) Tell about how Baci loves playing basketball with her brothers, and how she's good at getting the rebounds
    (D) Tell about how Baci gets uptight at the groomer's, especially when the groomer trims around her face

Passage II

Cabo San Lucas

Situated due south of California, the Baja Sur Peninsula

stretches downward in reaching the naturally beautiful
16

city of Cabo San Lucas, a tropical desert paradise.

Among and between the Pacific Ocean and the Sea of
17

Cortez, this town offers breathtaking water views and

miles upon miles of palm tree and cactus-lined coastlines.
18

16. (F) NO CHANGE
    (G) in reach for
    (H) to reach
    (J) as it is reaching

17. (A) NO CHANGE
    (B) Among
    (C) Between
    (D) Nestled between

18. (F) NO CHANGE
    (G) miles after miles
    (H) miles
    (J) with miles

GO ON TO THE NEXT PAGE

If your family <u>is enthusiastic about</u> water sports,
                    19
Cabo has a great deal to offer. Get ready for snorkeling

or <u>a ride on</u> a wave runner! Taking a tour to Lover's Beach
      20
(Playa da Amore) in a glass-bottom boat is a fun

excursion—you will spot many colorful fish and coral

formations below.

For the more adventurous <u>beset</u>, Medano Beach offers
                                21
somewhat daring or, at least, faster-velocity water sports.

Here you can rent a kayak or experience the scenic aerial

views provided by parasailing, either individually or in

tandem. You and your friends can even test out your

balancing skills on a slippery and speedy banana-boat

ride! 22

At sunrise, midday, or dusk, you and your family can go

horseback riding—as part of a guided excursion—along one

of the many picturesque <u>and scenic</u> Cabo beaches. Imagine
                              23
how peaceful it would be to ride first thing in the morning,

feeling the rejuvenating spritz of water from the coastline.

Or, picture riding at sunset as the hot-cantaloupe sun <u>dips</u>
                                                        24
below the horizon. What a beautiful preview to a fine

dinner out!

19. (A) NO CHANGE
    (B) has enthusiasm with regard to
    (C) being enthusiastic about
    (D) is enthusiastic for

20. (F) NO CHANGE
    (G) get ready for going for a ride on
    (H) taking a ride with
    (J) riding

21. (A) NO CHANGE
    (B) sect
    (C) being so set
    (D) set

22. If the writer were to delete the preceding sentence,
    the essay would primarily lose:
    (F) a piece of information that is not pertinent to
        this paragraph.
    (G) an example that further supports the focus of
        this paragraph.
    (H) information about how people use water sports
        as a means of working out.
    (J) an irrelevant, though lighthearted, digression.

23. (A) NO CHANGE
    (B) while scenic
    (C) as they are scenic
    (D) Delete the underlined portion.

24. (F) NO CHANGE
    (G) is dipping
    (H) is seen as it dips
    (J) dip

GO ON TO THE NEXT PAGE

Speaking of dinner, many restaurants in Cabo San
<u>Cabo San</u>
25

<u>Lucas, many of which can be found in Cabo's splendorous</u>
25

<u>resorts,</u> offer excellent and extremely fresh-tasting seafood
25

dishes. Some are prepared in something of a southern

Californian style; others have a Mexican influence.

Great sushi, sashimi, and vegetable tempura <u>can be</u>
26

<u>found</u> at several Asian-style or "fusion" restaurants which
26

are located at the downtown marina. The marina restau-

rants offer great people-watching, as patrons enjoy a harbor

side stroll before or after dinner. Street vendors also walk up

and down the marina, selling everything from pashminas to

jewelry to bathing suit wraps. Also, most marina restaurants

offer outdoor seating, allowing you to watch the cruise

ships and fishing boats come and go.

27 You can shop 'til you drop while in Cabo.

Downtown there is a super-sized, multi-level mall. There

you can shop for anything under the sun, from shoes to

fashion wear to Mexican souvenirs.

<u>By</u> the downtown flea markets, you can find handicrafts
28

made by local artisans, hand-painted pottery, baskets of

silver jewelry, and colorful, beaded figurines.

25. (A) NO CHANGE
    (B) Cabo San Lucas, many being they are found in Cabo's splendorous resorts,
    (C) Cabo San Lucas—many of which can be found in Cabo's splendorous resorts,
    (D) Cabo San Lucas, many of which can be found in Cabo's splendorful resorts,

26. Which of the following alternatives to the underlined part of the sentence would NOT be acceptable?
    (F) NO CHANGE
    (G) are found
    (H) being found
    (J) are served

27. Which choice would least effectively open this paragraph and least convey excitement about something else to do while vacationing in Cabo San Lucas?
    (A) NO CHANGE
    (B) There are abundant prospects for the born-to-shop while in Cabo.
    (C) Water sports aside, there's the shopping.
    (D) Shopping enthusiasts will feel like kids in a candy shop while in Cabo.

28. (F) NO CHANGE
    (G) Out and about
    (H) Among
    (J) At

GO ON TO THE NEXT PAGE

Believe it or not, there are even several large

discount shopping chain stores just outside of
29

town center.

29. (A) NO CHANGE
    (B) Delete the underlined portion.
    (C) wholesale shopping
    (D) moderately-priced

> Question 30 asks about the preceding passage as a whole.

30. Suppose the writer's goal had been to write an essay about the advantages and drawbacks of vacationing in Cabo. Would this piece of writing fulfill this goal?
    (F) Yes, because the essay details the pros and cons of visiting Cabo.
    (G) Yes, because the essay presents a balanced exposition that encourages readers to be aware of the benefits and drawbacks of a Cabo vacation.
    (H) No, because this essay is objective; it neither persuades nor dissuades readers from considering this vacation destination.
    (J) No, because this essay mainly focuses on the positive aspects of a Cabo vacation.

Passage III

"The Hero's Journey"

Did you know that the steps Luke Skywalker

takes to defeat the Death Star in George Lucas's
31

epic film, *Star Wars*, are not just a series of
32

advancements—but, actually the progression of a
33

psychological voyage? In the movie, Luke's family and

home are destroyed by enemy storm troopers.

31. (A) NO CHANGE
    (B) Lucas'
    (C) Lucas'es
    (D) Lucas

32. (F) NO CHANGE
    (G) was
    (H) have been
    (J) is

33. (A) NO CHANGE
    (B) advancements, but actually,
    (C) advancements, but, actually,
    (D) advancements but actually

GO ON TO THE NEXT PAGE

He is distraught and alone, and determined on fighting
back. Luke goes with Obi-Wan (Ben Kanobi) to free
Princess Leia when it is discovered that she has been
captured by the Dark Side. During the journey, Luke
transforms and changes into a Jedi and the Force is with
him. He finalizes the mission by crushing the Empire
and conquering all, winning respect and hearts. Within
the duration of the movie, Luke learns and matures as he
follows the steps of Joseph Campbell's hero's journey.

Throughout the first stage of the hero's journey,
being called separation, Luke learns the power of the Force
and gains experience of leaving a safe haven. His first
obstacle is the call to adventure, which is when Obi-Wan
asks Luke to come with him to Alderon and learn about
the Force. From this, Luke gains a purpose and receives the

opportunity to become a Jedi. Campbell explains, "It asks,
are you going to be a person of heart and humanity—
because that's what life is, from the heart—or are you going
to do whatever is required of you by what might be called
'intentional power'?" He believes that the call to adventure
is about doing what is morally correct versus to do what is
expected.

34. (F) NO CHANGE
    (G) distraught, and alone, and determined to
        fight back
    (H) distraught, alone, and determined to fight back
    (J) distraughtly alone, with the determination for
        fighting back

35. Which is the best way to handle the underlined
    phrase?
    (A) NO CHANGE
    (B) Delete it.
    (C) and is changed
    (D) in changing

36. (F) NO CHANGE
    (G) called separation
    (H) the stage known as "separation"
    (J) separation

37. ALL of the following are acceptable replacements
    for *come with* EXCEPT:
    (A) join in the journey with
    (B) accompany
    (C) accommodate
    (D) travel with

38. (F) NO CHANGE
    (G) explains…"It
    (H) explains: It
    (J) explains; "It

39. (A) NO CHANGE
    (B) the doing of
    (C) about to do
    (D) doing

GO ON TO THE NEXT PAGE

Discovering the supernatural aid is the next step of separation. This [40] is represented by Obi Wan, Luke's guru, and the Force. Obi-Wan takes Luke under his wing and guides him along the path, while the Force helps him defeat his enemies. From this, Luke learns the Force has the power of manipulating people mentally as well as physically.

Next, the threshold point of adventure must be crossed. Young Luke accomplishes this step by leaving his home planet and traveling into the unknown, giving him experience of adventure, the new world, and helping him gain exposure. Luke also learns not to trust everyone, because there are new creatures that could be out to get him. Campbell states, "...the hero leaves the realm of the familiar over which he has some control and comes to a threshold, where a monster of abyss comes to get him." This remark means that when the home is left, one is vulnerable to danger. For example, when Luke leaves his farm to go with Obi-Wan, the 'monster' in the bar represents the dragon of the unfamiliar because he is a strange creature taunting Luke. Finally, Luke gains companions, including Princess Leia, R2-D2, C-3PO, and Obi-Wan. Han Solo is also one of Luke's companions, however, the two do not start off on the right foot. Ultimately, this teaches Luke to deal with others who he does not particularly like.

40. If the author wished to insert a word or phrase here, which of the following would be most appropriate?
(F) ability
(G) symbol
(H) character
(J) feature

41. (A) NO CHANGE
(B) in manipulating
(C) manipulating
(D) to manipulate

42. If the author eliminates this underlined portion, the effect would most likely be:
(F) to streamline the prose by eliminating an impertinent detail.
(G) to deemphasize Luke's growing sense of paranoia.
(H) to lose a specific aspect of Luke's personal growth.
(J) to improve the essay by eliminating a stereotype.

43. (A) NO CHANGE
(B) companions; however, the two
(C) companions, however being them two
(D) companions: However, the two of them

GO ON TO THE NEXT PAGE

After completing the separation state, Luke must complete the next phase: initiation, where he gains confidence in himself and learns how to rely on instinct as well as feeling. This begins with the road of trails, where each accomplishment proves ability. As Obi-Wan shows Luke methods of the light saber, he is able to pick up the skill and gain distinction, as only a Jedi can. Campbell clarifies, "The conscience personality here has to come in touch with a change of unconscious energy." This quote portrays how a Jedi must be able to subconsciously use Force. Luke completes this skill, obtaining higher levels of belief, feeling, and instinct. Secondly comes the dragon battle, depicted when Luke's mentor, Obi-Wan, dies. Luke is forced to work alone, which teaches him independence and brings his childish immaturity to that of an adult. Luke is proud of himself and revels in confidence of a true hero.

44. (F) NO CHANGE
    (G) next phase; initiation, where he gains
    (H) next phase: being initiation, where he will gain
    (J) next phase: initiation, in which he gains

45. Which of the choices below provides information that is most relevant to the main focus of this paragraph?
    (A) NO CHANGE
    (B) lose self-doubt
    (C) learn about the intricacies of electricity
    (D) gain instinctive impulses and sensations

GO ON TO THE NEXT PAGE

Passage IV

"Miguel Hidalgo"

¡Hola! I am the father of Mexican Independence,

Miguel Hidalgo. Throughout my lifetime, I have
    46

accomplished numerous feats, which have shown
                          47

me to be an effective leader and a strong man.
                        47

Resulting from these attributes, I should be the
    48

revolutionary Olympic champion.

    I have always strived to be the strongest leader

who I can be. From introducing pottery works to forming
    49

vineyards, my efforts have made my community a more

successful and content environment. In 1803, I was

appointed curate, a priest in charge of a parish, of the

church. This was a great honor, and it helped me

connect with my people through religion. I was also an

educator pushing myself to assist my followers in every
        50

plausible way. To help our society expand, I devoted much

46. (F) NO CHANGE
    (G) being Miguel Hidalgo
    (H) called Miguel Hidalgo
    (J) known as Miguel Hidalgo

47. Which of the following versions of the underlined part would NOT be acceptable?
    (A) feats, which having proving myself to be an effective leader and a strong man.
    (B) feats, which proved me to be a leader, effectively, and a strong man.
    (C) feats, proving me to be an effective leader and a strong man.
    (D) feats that prove me to be an effective leader and a man of strength.

48. (F) NO CHANGE
    (G) As a result and from
    (H) Being that I possess
    (J) Because of

49. (A) NO CHANGE
    (B) I can be.
    (C) that I can be.
    (D) which I can be.

50. (F) NO CHANGE
    (G) educator, pushing myself to assist
    (H) educator who, pushing myself, to assist
    (J) educator pushing myself in assisting

GO ON TO THE NEXT PAGE

time to industrial development. I clearly cared about my

public and wanted the best for them.
51

My greatest triumph was leading the first Mexican rebel-

lion against Spain in 1810. Though my troops and I did

not win this battle, it was a tremendously essential point in
52

Mexico's revolution. The revolt brought about a drastic

change, to inspire the Mexican populace to stand up for
53

their rights and to fight for their freedom. The people were

determined to obtain Mexico's independence, and were

able to fight with courage, due to my brave leadership years

before. I am proud to say that on September 21, 1821, my

fellow Mexicans reached our goal of obtaining our country's

long deserved independence. To this day, Mexico continues

to be a free and respectful country, proving that my
54

uprising had a lasting impact. This event also shows that I

was an effective leader, supported by the fact that I met the

needs of my people by protecting them from harm's way.
55

51. (A) NO CHANGE
    (B) public, and wanted,
    (C) public and wanted,
    (D) public while I was wanting

52. (F) NO CHANGE
    (G) a tremendous while being essential
    (H) a tremendous, essentially,
    (J) a tremendous as well as essential

53. (A) NO CHANGE
    (B) in inspiring
    (C) regarding the inspiration of
    (D) inspiring

54. (F) NO CHANGE
    (G) respective
    (H) respected
    (J) retrospective

55. (A) NO CHANGE
    (B) from being harmed in any way
    (C) from harm
    (D) from the way of harm

GO ON TO THE NEXT PAGE

As we marched on our way to battle, it occurred to me that not only would our untrained and weak army be outnumbered, but we would also not have as many supplies as our enemies. I decided it would be in our best interest to turn around and reach safety before war. This decision underscored my devotion and loyalty to my countrymen, my lasting leadership verified. I truly wanted my public to be satisfied with their lifestyles, and to have no desire to rebel against me. [57]

Due to this dream, I gathered all different sorts of people to be in my army; including Creoles, Indians, Mulattos, and Mestizzos. I believed in a society without social ranking, I stood for ethnic equality; I figured that joining everyone together would help extinguish the problem.

56. The writer is considering deleting the underlined part (placing a period after the word *outnumbered*): but we would also not have as many supplies as our enemies.
Should the writer make this deletion?
(F) Yes, because the information results in the paragraph losing its focus.
(G) Yes, because the information weakens Hidalgo's decision to turn back.
(H) No, because the information adds an important allusion to a former battle fought by the countrymen.
(J) No, because the information provides another reason why it is prudent for the men to retreat.

57. At this point, the writer is considering adding the following sentence:
I believed, however, that it would be unlikely for a great blend of ethnic groups to cooperate fully.
Should the writer make this addition here? Why or why not?
(A) Yes, because this sentence maintains the cynical attitude the author has put forth previously.
(B) Yes, because this author's pessimistic attitude is reflected in this statement.
(C) No, because this conjecture does not reflect the author's positive mindset.
(D) No, because this sentence would undermine the author's perspective of global unity.

GO ON TO THE NEXT PAGE

While I was alive, I made a clear fundamental change <u>in</u>
58

Mexico's status and <u>it's peoples'</u> determination. My actions
59

proved I cared about my people and my homeland. For

these reasons, I believe that I was an outstanding leader

who hands down deserves to be an Olympic Champion.

Thank you for your time; vote wisely.

58. (F) NO CHANGE
    (G) with
    (H) regarding
    (J) on

59. (A) NO CHANGE
    (B) they're
    (C) their
    (D) its

Question 60 asks about the preceding passage as a whole.

---

60. If the author intended to write an essay about a person who regrets many of his actions, would this essay fulfill the writer's goal?
    (F) No, because Hidalgo tends to neither reflect much on his past nor revel in his merits.
    (G) No, because Hidalgo seems proud of all that he has accomplished.
    (H) Yes, because Hidalgo sincerely wishes that he would have led his people differently.
    (J) Yes, because Hidalgo made many enemies because of his boastful personality and his arrogant leadership style.

Passage V

"How to Make Cinnamon-Nut Squares"

[1]

[1] This is an old family recipe that came from my great

Uncle Emil's sister, <u>"Aunt Louisa from Texas" we'd call her.</u>
61

[2] Over the years, my family and I relished many tins of

savory nut cookies whenever Aunt Louisa would visit.

[3] The recipe for those crunchy cinnamon-nut squares was

kept a secret for many years. [4] She had a slow and soft

way of talking, and she was as sweet as the powdered

61. (A) NO CHANGE
    (B) calling her "Aunt Louisa," the one from Texas.
    (C) as we were calling her "Aunt Louisa from Texas."
    (D) "Aunt Louisa from Texas," as we called her.

GO ON TO THE NEXT PAGE

sugar she'd sprinkle on her nut squares. [5] After much
                                                    62
prodding and frequent reminders, she finally brought
                                          62
the hand-written recipe with her to Long Island,
                    62
New York during one of her visits with her niece, Brandy,
                                                    62
in 1978. [63]
62

[2]

From then on, her one-and-only sister-in-law Helen
                                   64
would make the cookies herself and share them with her

immediate and extended family. Her niece Anne liked these

special cookies and so did her family. In fact, they liked the

Texan recipe so much that Anne started making them

regularly, and the recipe caught on throughout her family.

[3]

Always make a double recipe of these tasty nut

cookies for they go fast. This recipe fills one standard-size
65

62. (F) NO CHANGE
    (G) Begin a new paragraph with this sentence.
    (H) Delete the underlined portion.
    (J) Move this sentence to the very beginning of
        the passage.

63. For the sake of logic and coherence in the opening
    paragraph (Paragraph 1), the sequence of sentence
    numbers that makes the structure of the paragraph
    most logical is:
    (A) NO CHANGE
    (B) 4, 3, 2, 1, 5
    (C) 4, 5, 3, 2, 1
    (D) 1, 2, 4, 3, 5

64. (F) NO CHANGE
    (G) sister in law called Helen,
    (H) sister in-law, who was named Helen,
    (J) sister-in-law, Helen,

65. (A) NO CHANGE
    (B) cookies, for
    (C) cookies—for,
    (D) cookies; for

GO ON TO THE NEXT PAGE

cookie sheet. To serve, the cookies can be cut into squares
66

or rectangular-shaped bars. They also freeze beautifully, so
66

you can bake them well ahead of time.

[4]

Also, to whip up these timeless and delicious cookies,
67

you will need two sticks of margarine, one cup of sugar,

one large egg (split), one teaspoon of vanilla extract,

three teaspoons, heaping, of cinnamon, two and a half cups
68

of unsifted flour, about a cup of pecans or walnuts

(chopped), and sprinkle powdered confectioner's sugar,
69

which is white and soft in texture.
70

[5]

First, cream together the margarine and the sugar.

Next, add the creamed egg yolk, cinnamon, and vanilla.

Combine all of these ingredients together. Using a power

mixer is recommended so that all of the ingredients blend

fully. Add the flour, a little at a time, while you continue

66. The writer is considering deleting this sentence.
Should this sentence be kept or deleted?
(F) Kept, because it clarifies for readers the
particular benefits of using a cookie sheet
instead of a baking pan.
(G) Kept, because it elaborates upon the process of
making, baking, and serving these cookies.
(H) Deleted, because it should be moved to
Paragraph 4.
(J) Deleted, because it confuses the readers about
just how much cookie dough they should
make.

67. (A) NO CHANGE
(B) So,
(C) Though,
(D) Lastly,

68. (F) NO CHANGE
(G) three teaspoons of cinnamon-heaping-
(H) threefold teaspoonsful of heaping cinnamon
(J) three heaping teaspoons of cinnamon,

69. (A) NO CHANGE
(B) a sprinkle of
(C) you should then sprinkle
(D) to sprinkle

70. (F) NO CHANGE
(G) being
(H) as it is
(J) for it is

GO ON TO THE NEXT PAGE

mixing. Once all of the ingredients are fully incorporated and the dough is formed, shape into two balls. Next, press the balls of dough about one-quarter inch flat onto an ungreased cookie sheet, <u>using your hands.</u>
₇₁

[6]

Smooth out the surface of the dough with a lightly-floured rolling pin <u>that is either wooden or stainless steel.</u>
₇₂
With a nylon brush, coat the batter lightly with the egg white, slightly beaten.

Using your fingers, press the coarsely-chopped walnuts or the pecans into the batter. Feel free to modify the recipe according to your individual <u>preferences, you</u> may use, for
₇₃
instance, a mixture of *both* chopped pecans and walnuts. Furthermore, you may choose to skip the egg-white glaze altogether.

71. If the author were to move this phrase, the best placement for it would be:
   (A) where it is now.
   (B) before the word *Once.*
   (C) after the word *incorporated.*
   (D) after the word *Next.*

72. The writer is considering deleting this subordinate clause from the sentence. Should this adjective clause be kept or deleted?
   (F) Kept, because it provides a vivid description.
   (G) Kept, because it aids the reader in more fully understanding the specifics of the baking process.
   (H) Deleted, because it provides information that is irrelevant to the actual baking of these cookies.
   (J) Deleted, because it might dissuade readers who own plastic rolling pins from continuing with this recipe.

73. (A) NO CHANGE
   (B) preferences; You
   (C) preferences you
   (D) preferences; you

GO ON TO THE NEXT PAGE

[7]

Preset the oven to 350 degrees. Cook the flattened
——————————————————
74

dough for thirty to thirty-five minutes, or until golden

brown. When cooked, or a golden brown, and cooled, dust

with a light sprinkling of white powdered sugar. The sugar

will sink in and disappear so do not keep shaking on the

powdered sugar or the cookies will end up too sweet.

[8]

Once the batter is cool, cut into squares or bars;

completely cool on a stainless steel rack. These cookies are

scrumptious with either a cup of tea, coffee, or a glass of

milk. They freeze beautifully and store nicely in tins.

Serving them alongside squares of dark or bittersweet

chocolate makes a delectable dessert combination.

Enjoy. [75]

74. For the sake of the logic of the passage as a whole, this sentence should be moved to somewhere within:
(F) Paragraph 1.
(G) Paragraph 2.
(H) Paragraph 3.
(J) Paragraph 4.

75. Choose the sequence of paragraph numbers in the latter half of this essay (Paragraphs 5–8) that makes the structure and organization of the passage most logical.
(A) NO CHANGE
(B) 6, 5, 7, 8
(C) 5, 8, 7, 6
(D) 8, 7, 6, 5

STOP

READING TEST

35 MINUTES—40 QUESTIONS

Directions: The reading test consists of four passages. Ten questions follow each reading selection. After reading each passage, choose the best answer for each question and fill in the answer bubble on your answer sheet. You may refer to the reading selections as often as you like.

Passage I

PROSE FICTION: Passage A is excerpted from Richard Connell's "The Most Dangerous Game," 1924. iBooks. Passage B is excerpted from William Golding's *The Lord of the Flies.*

PASSAGE A

"You've done well, Rainsford," the voice of the general called. "Your Burmese tiger pit has claimed one of my best dogs. Again you score. I think, Mr. Rainsford, I'll see what you can do against my whole
5   pack. I'm going home for a rest now. Thank you for a most amusing evening."

At daybreak Rainsford, lying near the swamp, was awakened by a sound that made him know that he had new things to learn about fear. It was a distant
10 sound, faint and wavering, but he knew it. It was the baying of a pack of hounds.

Rainsford knew he could do one of two things. He could stay where he was and wait. That was suicide. He could flee. That was postponing the
15 inevitable. For a moment he stood there, thinking. An idea that held a wild chance came to him, and, tightening his belt, he headed away from the swamp.

The baying of the hounds drew nearer, then still nearer, nearer, ever nearer. On a ridge Rainsford
20 climbed a tree. Down a watercourse, not a quarter of a mile away, he could see the bush moving. Straining his eyes, he saw the lean figure of General Zaroff; just ahead of him Rainsford made out another figure whose wide shoulders surged through the tall jungle
25 weeds; it was the giant Ivan, and he seemed pulled forward by some unseen force; Rainsford knew that Ivan must be holding the pack in leash.

They would be on him any minute now. His mind worked frantically. He thought of a native
30 trick he had learned in Uganda. He slid down the

tree. He caught hold of a springy young sapling and to it he fastened his hunting knife, with the blade pointing down the trail; with a bit of wild grapevine he tied back the sapling. Then he ran for his life. The
35 hounds raised their voices as they hit the fresh scent. Rainsford knew now how an animal at bay feels. He had to stop to get his breath. The baying of the hounds stopped abruptly, and Rainsford's heart stopped too.

PASSAGE B

40 Ralph lay in a covert, wondering about his wounds. The bruised flesh was inches in diameter over his right ribs, with a swollen and bloody scar where the spear had hit him. His hair was full of dirt and tapped like the tendrils of a creeper. All over he
45 was scratched and bruised from his flight through the forest. By the time his breathing was normal again, he had worked out that bathing these injuries would have to wait. How could you listen for naked feet if you were splashing in water? How could you
50 be safe by the little stream or on the open beach?

Ralph listened. He was not really far from the Castle Rock, and during the first panic he had thought he heard sounds of pursuit. But the hunters had only sneaked into the fringes of the greenery,
55 retrieving spears perhaps, and then had rushed back to the sunny rock as if terrified of the darkness under the leaves. He had even glimpsed one of them, striped brown, black, and red, and had judged that it was Bill. But really, thought Ralph, this was not
60 Bill. This was a savage whose image refused to blend with that ancient picture of a boy in shorts and shirt.

The afternoon died away; the circular spots of sunlight moved steadily over green fronds and brown

GO ON TO THE NEXT PAGE

fiber but no sound came from behind the rock. At
65 last Ralph wormed out of the ferns and sneaked
forward to the edge of that impenetrable thicket that
fronted the neck of land. He peered with elaborate
caution between branches at the edge and could see
Robert sitting on guard at the top of the cliff. He
70 held a spear in his left hand and was tossing up a
pebble and catching it again with the right. Behind
him a column of smoke rose thickly, so that Ralph's
nostrils flared and his mouth dribbled. He wiped
his nose and mouth with the back of his hand and
75 for the first time since the morning felt hungry. The
tribe must be sitting round the gutted pig, watching
the fat ooze and burn among the ashes. They would
be intent.

Another figure, an unrecognizable one, appeared
80 by Robert and gave him something, then turned and
went back behind the rock. Robert laid his spear
on the rock beside him and began to gnaw between
his raised hands. So the feast was beginning and the
watchman had been given his portion.

85   Ralph saw that for the time being he was safe. He
limped away through the fruit trees, drawn by the
thought of the poor food yet bitter when he remembered the feast. Feast today, and then tomorrow . . .

He argued unconvincingly that they would let
90 him alone, perhaps even make an outlaw of him.
But then the fatal unreasoning knowledge came to
him again. The breaking of the conch and the deaths
of Piggy and Simon lay over the island like a vapor.
These painted savages would go further and further.
95 Then there was that indefinable connection between
himself and Jack; who therefore would never let him
alone; never.

Questions 1–4 are about Passage A.

1. The narrative effect of this fiction excerpt most
    closely brings about which of the following emotions
    in the reader?
    (A) Affection and compassion
    (B) Anticipation and suspense
    (C) Reverence and trepidation
    (D) Envy and mistrust

2. It can be most reasonably inferred from lines 1–6
    that General Zaroff regards Rainsford with an air of:
    (F) contentedness.
    (G) contention.
    (H) contrition.
    (J) condescension.

3. In lines 8–9, the phrase "he had new things to learn
    about fear" most closely means:
    (A) Rainsford lives an insulated life.
    (B) Rainsford is a daredevil who seeks risky
         situations.
    (C) Rainsford has difficulty dealing with his
         emotions.
    (D) Rainsford experiences a level of trepidation that
         he had not encountered until this moment.

4. As it is used in context, the expression "an animal
    at bay" (line 36) has the effect of characterizing
    Rainsford as which of the following?
    (F) An intruder who has an aggressive stance
    (G) A beast at heart who feels close to animal life
    (H) A fugitive who can no longer flee from danger
    (J) A nature-lover who communes with the spirit
         world

GO ON TO THE NEXT PAGE

Questions 5–7 are about Passage B.

5. In this excerpt, Ralph experiences all of the following aspects of discomfort EXCEPT:
   (A) excessive heat.
   (B) hunger.
   (C) physical pain.
   (D) fear.

6. As it is used in line 65, the term *wormed* most closely means:
   (F) wallowed.
   (G) wheedled.
   (H) wiggled.
   (J) wobbled.

7. In the final paragraph, the sentence "The breaking of the conch and the deaths of Piggy and Simon lay over the island like a vapor" serves:
   (A) as hyperbole to illustrate how Ralph obsesses about his circumstances unreasonably.
   (B) as imagery to lend a poetic tone to the narrative.
   (C) as a comparison to illustrate Ralph's overactive, pessimistic perspective.
   (D) as a simile that emphasizes Ralph's grim and foreboding mental outlook.

Questions 8–10 are about both passages.

8. With consideration of both passages, which characters share experiences that are most similar?
   (F) Ralph and Rainsford
   (G) Bill and General Zaroff
   (H) Ivan and Piggy
   (J) Simon and Ralph

9. Considered holistically, both passages can reasonably be interpreted to convey which of the following themes or maxims?
   (A) Nothing ventured, nothing gained.
   (B) The early bird gets the worm.
   (C) Better to be the hunter than the hunted.
   (D) Give them an inch, and they take a mile.

10. In both passages, the effect of "He had to stop to get his breath" (line 37) and "By the time his breathing was normal again" (lines 46–47) can best be described as showing how Rainsford and Ralph are characters who:
    (F) possess superhuman stamina and fortitude.
    (G) have endured physical stress and anxiety.
    (H) are physically out of shape.
    (J) neglect their health in the pursuit of beating their opponent.

GO ON TO THE NEXT PAGE

SOCIAL SCIENCE: This passage on child development examines Jean Piaget's theory on infant developmental stages in relation to their play with toys. Piaget was a Swiss philosopher and developmental psychologist, especially well known for his work studying children and his theory of cognitive development.

During infant play, Jean Piaget's cognitive-developmental stages are exercised, to some degree, by the use of toys with developmental play value. Infants'
toys, in particular, ideally activate characteristics of
5 the sub-stages of the Sensorimotor Period (Birth–2 years), whereby the baby understands his or her world in terms of what he or she can do with objects and their involvement with sensory processes.

During this major Piagetian stage, there are
10 several key features. The infant's response to the world is almost entirely sensory and motor. The infant functions in the immediate present, responding to whatever stimuli present themselves. The infant does not plan or intend. The infant has no
15 internal representation of objects—no mental pictures or words that stand for objects and that can be manipulated mentally. As this stage ends, the child gradually moves from reflexive to voluntary action.

For this study, I chose to examine the cog-
20 nitive-motor play values of three interactive and vibrantly colored toys produced by the Discovery Toys Company: Shake, Rattle and Roll, which is recommended for newborns, birth to five months; Up, Up and Away, which is geared to six to twelve
25 month olds; and lastly, a hands-on toy for older infants (twelve months on) who like to nest and stack objects, Measure Up Cups. Shake, Rattle and Roll stimulates what Piaget calls "primary circular reactions," which include systematic visual and
30 tactual exploration. With this toy, for instance, the infant touches and manipulates the five colorful, real-world objects which make up its surface: a windmill, a wheel, a duck, a boy figure, and a flower; all of which rotate or move. This toy also permits the
35 infant to self-soothe; as he shakes this toy, it "rattles" softly.

Typical of the early part of this sub-stage, the infant becomes increasingly knowledgeable about

his body; eye-hand coordination, then, is particularly
40 relevant here, and this toy generates much eye-to-hand activity as the infant moves his hand from one shape to the next. Additionally, Piaget holds that built-in reflexes such as sucking and looking are intrinsic to the earliest steps of this major stage.
45 Certainly, the variety of shapes characterizing Shake Rattle and Roll make it attractive to look at, and each of the five objects mentioned prior is small enough to fit into the infant's mouth.

Midway through the Sensorimotor Stage, the
50 infant somewhat understands that his actions can have external results—accordingly, the concept of cause-and-effect begins. Up, Up and Away demonstrates the cause-and-effect relationship: if the curious infant pushed the hot air balloon down
55 towards the floor or tabletop (whichever the suction cup happens to be attached to), then the man-in-the-balloon pops up! This reminds me of Jack-in-the-box! The infant probably notices that when the three colored balls move around inside the balloon,
60 they settle back to the bottom, once the toy stands erect and motionless.

As with the first toy discussed, sensory stimulation is relevant here, too. The three balls inside of the balloon also sound like a rattle, but louder; again,
65 auditory senses are stimulated. Also, the man's head turns round and round, and the basket at the base of the balloon is decorated with tiny, raised dots. This detail is intentional, I assume, so that the infant can experience the toy's surface texture, tactually or with
70 his mouth and tongue.

Discovery Toys recommends Measure Up Cups for ages twelve months and older. The dozen, primary-colored cups fit into one another and, if turned upside down, may be stacked one on top of the
75 other. Later in the Sensorimotor Stage, improved motor skills expand the infant's play possibilities. "Tertiary circular reactions" come into play at this time as the infant actively experiments with new ways of manipulating various-sized objects. Cogni-
80 tion-related concepts of size, position, and configuration are activated with the Measure Up Cups set. The child gains confidence in his motor abilities as he stacks the cups higher and higher, experimenting

GO ON TO THE NEXT PAGE

with the concepts of height and stability. He inde-
85 pendently learns, by trial and error, which cups—
depending on their size—fit into each other or stack
easily, one on top of another.

Measure Up Cups also entice a cognitive measure
known as "conservation," defined as the concept that
90 objects or a group of objects remains the same in fundamental ways, such as weight or number, even when
there are external changes in shape or arrangement.
Although this concept is usually achieved by children
between five and ten years of age, its investigation
95 begins, arguably, when a young child experiments
with a toy like Measure Up Cups. Specifically, the
child eventually recognizes that the number of cups
remains constant, whether or not they are spread out
over the floor, nested inside of each other, or stacked
100 in any number of piles. In other words, the set of
objects is conserved. If an adult pours water into one
cup and transfers it to another, another demonstration of conservation occurs, for a given amount of
water is not changed, regardless of the size cup it is
105 poured into.

When examining sequential stages of development, it is important to keep in mind that it is
normal for infants to acquire skills at varying times,
and to have their own developmental pace. Piaget's
110 cognitive-developmental theory is no exception; criticism questions some of this theorist's ideas, saying
that his age associations with aspects of thinking are
off, or that expertise may be more critical to cognition level than age. Some children, for example, play
115 chess at much higher thought levels than do adults
with comparable chess experience. Finally, it is as
important to question a theorist as it is to try and
apply his or her theory to real life circumstances.

11. The word "exercised" in line 2 most closely means:
(A) flexed.
(B) extenuated.
(C) implemented.
(D) put into practical effect.

12. According to the second paragraph (lines 9–18), the
typical infant cannot or is highly unlikely to do all
of the following EXCEPT:
(F) simultaneously grasp for objects while bending
and straightening his legs.
(G) grimace upon remembering something frightening he witnessed in his environment just
several minutes ago.
(H) compare, in his mind's eye, his new rattle to
his first rattle that sits on his nursery changing
table.
(J) anticipate playing with his older brothers when
they come home from school.

13. The author's main purpose in this passage is to:
(A) point out the difficulties that many adults have
in accepting the developmental limitations of
infants.
(B) discuss various and divergent perspectives on
the developmental stage spanning birth to
two years.
(C) point out how stages of infant development are
shown through how an infant interacts with
his toys.
(D) debunk the underlying assumptions of earlier
theories of infant and child development that
were widely accepted before Piaget's research.

14. Considering the context, the word "relevant" as used
in line 63 most closely means:
(F) akin.
(G) rampant.
(H) elevated.
(J) pertinent.

GO ON TO THE NEXT PAGE

15. The author's overall organization is best described as:
    (A) analyzing the developmental theories of several authorities on child psychology.
    (B) presenting examples of toys and examining how they can engage and facilitate a young child's sensory and motor development.
    (C) jumping, in a scattered fashion, from one age-appropriate skill to the next without a sense of progress or interrelationship.
    (D) sorting a human's tactual and sensory development in reverse-chronological order.

16. It can be reasonably concluded based on the information presented in the passage that which of the following also demonstrates the principle of "conservation" as mentioned in line 89?
    (F) A child can understand that by grouping blocks and rearranging them, the original number of blocks remains constant.
    (G) A child can learn a great deal by exploring objects with her mouth and hands.
    (H) A child can detect subtle differences in pattern and texture among a variety of objects.
    (J) A child can sort several marbles by their color and size.

17. The word "constant" in line 98 most closely means:
    (A) the same.
    (B) correlated.
    (C) steadfast.
    (D) dynamic.

18. It can reasonably be inferred that the author would agree that which of the following correlates best with the idea of "expertise" as referred to in line 113?
    (F) A female player's Stratego game versus that of an elder male player's
    (G) A skilled game of Stratego played by a youngster who has studied the game and practiced it versus a mature player who played the game a handful of times with little concentration
    (H) The game of Stratego played by one who holds several advanced educational degrees versus a player who is an undergraduate in college
    (J) A sixty-four-year-old's game of Stratego versus that of a sixteen-year-old

19. Which of the following play scenarios is most analogous to that delineated in lines 82–87?
    (A) As the child selects and holds up, one by one, large wooden puzzle pieces, Mom points to the place on the board where the puzzle piece belongs.
    (B) Dad helps the child to put wooden shape blocks into matching slots that line the exterior of a large, colorful cube.
    (C) With a friend, the child lines up action figures in a three-foot row, then one child knocks them down, one by one, as the other watches and laughs.
    (D) The child builds a tower, using donut-shaped rings in various colors and sizes; autonomously, he decides which rings are best suited for the bottom layers and which are best suited for the top.

20. The author's closing sentence suggests that he would most likely believe in:
    (F) believing something until you or someone else has proven it false.
    (G) scientific themes that manifest themselves over and again in contemporary writing that has been published on behavioral studies.
    (H) exploring ideas in greater depth and conducting experiments that you have independently devised.
    (J) taking an expert's advice at face value.

GO ON TO THE NEXT PAGE

Passage III

HUMANITIES: This passage on "Single Breath Meditation" is written by Dr. Rebbie Straubing, developer of The Yoga of Alignment (YOFA), and co-author of *101 Great Ways to Improve Your Life*. She is a workshop leader, Abraham Coach, and spiritual writer.

In less than a minute you can complete a single breath meditation session. Start to finish, it will take you about thirty seconds. There are as many instants of now in a minute as there are in an hour.
5 The now is infinite no matter how long you linger there. Sometimes, when we sit to meditate for twenty minutes or longer, big segments of that time slot lose their immediacy. We drift into default thinking and ride the shallow turbulence of our mental activity.
10 We miss the depth of the moment completely.

By narrowing the time of your meditation session to one breath, you send a message to your consciousness. "This is your only chance. Pay attention now or you'll miss it!" In the beginning, you may be
15 amazed at how much your mind can wander even in the space of one breath. Don't worry about that. It's natural.

How can one breath provide any kind of practice at all? For now, we want to go short and deep rather
20 than long and shallow. We want to be awake and aware for the simple matter of seconds it takes to complete one single cycle of breathing. When you think about it, it seems manageable. You may feel a surge of confidence. "This is something I might actu-
25 ally be able to do!" When you realize that each breath holds the hologram for all your breathing, you may begin to honor the power of one pure breath. When you sense that each now is nested within all "nows," you realize that an instant of pure consciousness will
30 take you further than a marathon of habit-driven practice.

In preparation for your brief session of meditation, consider this question: Who is breathing? Then release the question completely into the nonverbal
35 realm. Accept no answers that come in words. Let this question hover in the silence of your one breath. Let your one, single, on-stage, in-the-spotlight breath be completely natural. Let it move at its own pace and achieve only the depth it seeks on its own. Don't

40 force. Don't push. Don't direct it. Simply follow it. It is the only breath you will be attending to in this way so give it all your attention. There's not enough time to get bored. This is as easy as it gets.

When you are ready to begin, close your eyes.
45 Once you have completed one cycle of in and out (or out and in), open your eyes. You're done. Using the opening and closing of your eyes to punctuate your session accomplishes two things. It funnels your attention inward as your eyes close for your
50 very brief chance at sensing this unique breath which will never occur again in all of creation. It also makes distinct your session. It tells your conscious mind that you have started something and you have completed it.

55 Distortions in our thinking create physical and emotional pain. This single breath meditation is so simple and unintimidating that it does not create anxiety or inspire much resistance. It does, however, begin the unraveling of deep patterns of distortion.
60 In a soft and gentle way, it loosens the ties that hold resistant thought-forms in place. It creates little regions of space in your consciousness each time you do it. In this way it begins to undo those templates that keep replicating your challenges. It introduces
65 tiny hints of freedom into physical and emotional areas of constriction. Ultimately, this subtle sense of liberation filters down to your relationships, your health, your work and more. It brings space, light and openness. It gives you some room to be yourself.

70 These single breaths become like cookies. They taste sweet and once you have one you want another. They are small and individual and you can have one as a treat or you can sit down with the whole box and meditate for an hour.

GO ON TO THE NEXT PAGE

21. Which of the following statements best describes this passage's form and structure?
    (A) It is made up of a series of lively and exaggerated anecdotes.
    (B) It consists of a significant event in the author's life, but culminates with an insignificant conclusion.
    (C) It introduces a principle, and then elaborates on the process of putting this principle into practice.
    (D) It compares the author's perspective with that of another spiritual writer.

22. In context, "linger" (line 5) most nearly means:
    (F) become lazy.
    (G) loiter.
    (H) sit down.
    (J) remain.

23. In the first paragraph, the author suggests that:
    (A) the more time one allocates to meditation, the less meaningful and profound becomes the session.
    (B) water imagery disrupts clear thinking.
    (C) when time is limited, time is essentially lost.
    (D) meditation is an inactive state of body and mind.

24. In terms of mood, the third paragraph primarily conveys a sense of:
    (F) humor undermined by pessimism.
    (G) urgency buoyed by fanciful and pleasant daydreams.
    (H) steadily increasing zeal and enlightenment.
    (J) consistent doubt and disillusionment.

25. As it is used in line 37, the phrase "on-stage, in-the-spotlight" most nearly refers to:
    (A) an image of arrogance linked to a central premise of the author's argument.
    (B) an allusion to improvisational theater.
    (C) the author's unrealized dream of becoming an actress.
    (D) the attention and respect given to one breath.

26. As discussed in the third paragraph, which of the following provides the LEAST benefit?
    (F) a "short and deep" breath (line 19)
    (G) "a marathon of habit-driven practice" (lines 30–31)
    (H) "one pure breath" (line 27)
    (J) "an instant of pure consciousness" (line 29)

27. As used in their respective contexts, the questions, "How can one breath . . . practice at all?" (lines 18–19) and "Who is breathing?" (line 33) function as follows:
    (A) The first is used as a topic sentence, and the second is intended as a question for the reader to ponder.
    (B) The first is used sarcastically; the second, somberly.
    (C) The first is a rhetorical question posed for the purpose of persuasion; the second is intended as an ironic, interrogative statement.
    (D) The first undermines the author's underlying assumptions; the second is an unrealistic stretch of the imagination.

28. In context, the word "funnels" (line 48) most nearly means:
    (F) burrows.
    (G) restricts.
    (H) withdraws.
    (J) directs.

29. Which of the following questions is NOT answered by the information provided in this passage?
    (A) About how long does single-breath meditation take?
    (B) Are yoga practice and meditative breathing inextricably tied?
    (C) How can eye movement enhance breath meditation?
    (D) Can emotional anguish derive from warped thoughts?

30. A negative association or connotation characterizes which of the following images?
    (F) hologram (line 26)
    (G) deep patterns (line 59)
    (H) cookies (line 70)
    (J) whole box (line 73)

GO ON TO THE NEXT PAGE

Passage IV

NATURAL SCIENCE: This excerpt about storm warnings was written by Greg Goebel, an electronics engineer who writes on many science topics, and was taken from *www.vectorsite.net*.

Climatology was once a generally quiet and dull science, but now it's become politicized and quarrelsome. Hurricanes are a major case in point. Climatologists have always been interested in hurricanes
5 because of their destructive power, with the interest picking up after 1995 when, after three relatively quiet decades, the number and power of the storms began to increase. Interest shifted into high gear in 2004, an unusually severe hurricane season; the 2005
10 season was worse, being marked by the devastating Hurricane Katrina.

Although there has been a trend, it's much harder to quantify and nail down hurricanes than temperatures. There's always a temperature to measure, but
15 hurricanes are infrequent events even in the worst case, and the number of data points is unsurprisingly small. Records before 1970 are spotty. The data did suggest—from a rash of severe hurricanes in the 1940s, then the 1960s, and then in the 1990s—
20 that there was an "Atlantic Multidecadal Oscillation (AMO)."

At first, climatologists thought the nasty hurricanes of the 1990s were just part of the AMO, but in 2005 two research papers were published that upset
25 the complacent status quo. One—by Peter Webster, Judith Curry, and colleagues—claimed that the data supported the notion that the number of unusually severe hurricanes was on the increase. The other—by MIT climatologist Kerry Emmanuel—claimed that
30 the intensity of Atlantic hurricanes had doubled over the previous thirty years. Dr. Emmanuel's paper was a particular wake-up call because of his prominence in his scientific community, and also because he had long believed in the AMO.

35 Hurricanes are an indirect product of warm sea temperatures. The level of hurricane activity rose during the first half of the twentieth century as temperatures rose, dropped for a few decades as they fell again, and since has been more or less tracking
40 the rise in sea temperatures. Or so some claim; there

being dissenters. One major dissenter is an influential meteorologist, Bill Gray of Colorado State University in Fort Collins, who runs a hurricane-forecasting center and is usually visited by reporters every
45 time a big hurricane hits. Says Dr. Gray: "I'm a great believer in computer models. I am—out to ten or twelve days. But when you get to the climate scale, you get into a can of worms." However, given the nasty hurricanes that have been blowing around as
50 of late, the view that global warming has something to do with them has a receptive audience. The only major dispute is over the degree of influence, with the views varying widely. Florida, one of the most hurricane-prone of the U.S. states, is currently
55 growing rapidly, with development heavy in high-risk coastal areas. The growth is boosted by the fact that property values are lower than they would be if insurance rates reflected the actual level of risk. In the Grand Bahamas, where insurance is provided by
60 British companies not under strong local influence, there are coastal areas that insurers simply refuse to cover. People are moving out and such structures as are being built in these areas are on stilts.

The climatologists may differ on their view of the
65 facts, but they are generally consistent in their belief that current government policies are foolish. This last summer, a group of them, including Dr. Emmanuel and Phil Klotzbach, a close associate of Bill Gray, issued a statement warning of the "lemming-like
70 march to the sea" of coastal development and calling on leadership to "undertake a comprehensive evaluation of building policies and insurance, land-use and disaster-relief policies that currently serve to promote an ever-increasing vulnerability to hurricanes."

31. According to the passage, which of the following make it hard to "quantify" (line 13) hurricanes?

   I. sketchy records of past hurricanes
  II. the severe and brute power of hurricanes
 III. poor measurement technology
 IV. hurricanes are relatively sporadic occurrences

(A) I only
(B) II only
(C) III only
(D) I and IV

GO ON TO THE NEXT PAGE

32. In context, the adjective "complacent" in line 25 most nearly means:
    (F) comfortable.
    (G) relentless.
    (H) arrogant.
    (J) agreeable.

33. One overall purpose of this passage is to:
    (A) encourage readers to consider careers in climatology.
    (B) analyze the dynamic between sea and wind temperatures.
    (C) mock former investigations into the causes of hurricanes.
    (D) warn readers about building along hurricane-prone coastlines.

34. According to the passage, all of the following elements have been indicated as indirect or direct causes of hurricanes EXCEPT:
    (F) human fallibility.
    (G) global warming.
    (H) warm sea temperatures.
    (J) Atlantic Multidecadal Oscillation.

35. Meteorologist Bill Gray's statement, "out to ten or twelve days" (lines 46–47) refers to:
    (A) his average annual vacation time, indicated in days.
    (B) the average number of days, per year, that his forecasting equipment is defunct.
    (C) the reliability of his equipment to predict, within a ten to twelve day range, when a hurricane will hit.
    (D) the average number of days per year that he is interviewed by the media.

36. Which of the following best describes the way the fourth paragraph (lines 35–63) functions in terms of the passage as a whole?
    (F) It reveals the author's attitude by relating two anecdotes.
    (G) It contradicts the premises of the first three paragraphs.
    (H) It reveals the author's international interest in climatology that was hinted at earlier in the passage.
    (J) It provides two geographical examples that foreshadow concerns expressed in the final paragraph.

37. To develop this piece of writing, the author does all of the following EXCEPT:
    (A) alludes to some obscure but great literary work.
    (B) presents a chronological perspective.
    (C) refers to authorities within a specialized field.
    (D) defines scientific terms.

38. Given that *lemmings* are mouse-like rodents that periodically mass migrate to the sea, occasionally ending in their mass drowning, the statement "lemming-like march to the sea" (lines 69–70) most nearly serves to:
    (F) deride the building methods of southern land developers.
    (G) mediate a severe outlook on coastal building with a more humorous one.
    (H) provide an ominous image that serves to admonish readers about the risks of building and living by coasts susceptible to hurricane activity.
    (J) humorously compare coastal land developers to foolish, rodent-like creatures.

39. According to the passage, which of the following is the most reliable tool when it comes to accurately predicting hurricane activity?
    (A) data points (line 16)
    (B) computer models (line 46)
    (C) climate scale (line 47)
    (D) structures…built…on stilts (lines 62–63)

40. It is reasonable to infer that the author would consider all of the following potential and worthwhile solutions to temper the destructive power of hurricanes EXCEPT:
    (F) an increased ability to measure and "nail down" (line 13) hurricanes.
    (G) an international effort to work toward cooling the sea temperatures.
    (H) an increase in hurricane-conscious policies about land use, particularly land at risk to the hurricane threat.
    (J) an improved focus, on the part of the government in particular, on land and homeowner's insurance policies.

STOP

ANSWER KEY
Practice Tests

English Test

PASSAGE I: BACI

1. D	4. F	7. D	10. F	13. D
2. J	5. B	8. H	11. D	14. F
3. C	6. H	9. C	12. G	15. C

PASSAGE II: CABO SAN LUCAS

16. H	19. A	22. G	25. A	28. J
17. D	20. J	23. D	26. H	29. B
18. H	21. D	24. F	27. C	30. J

PASSAGE III: THE HERO'S JOURNEY

31. A	34. H	37. C	40. F	43. B
32. F	35. B	38. F	41. D	44. J
33. D	36. J	39. D	42. H	45. D

PASSAGE IV: MIGUEL HIDALGO

46. F	49. B	52. F	55. C	58. F
47. A	50. G	53. D	56. J	59. D
48. J	51. A	54. H	57. C	60. G

PASSAGE V: HOW TO MAKE CINNAMON-NUT SQUARES

61. D	64. J	67. B	70. F	73. D
62. F	65. B	68. J	71. D	74. J
63. D	66. G	69. B	72. G	75. A

Reading Test

PASSAGE I: FICTION

1. B	3. D	5. A	7. D	9. C
2. J	4. H	6. H	8. F	10. G

PASSAGE II: SOCIAL SCIENCE

11. C	13. C	15. B	17. A	19. D
12. F	14. J	16. F	18. G	20. H

PASSAGE III: HUMANITIES

21. C	23. A	25. D	27. A	29. B
22. J	24. H	26. G	28. J	30. G

PASSAGE IV: NATURAL SCIENCE

31. D	33. D	35. C	37. A	39. B
32. F	34. F	36. J	38. H	40. G

ANSWERS EXPLAINED

English Test

PASSAGE I: BACI

1. **(D) Choice D** is the most clear and concise.
   Choice A, *we had the occasion to meet her*, is wordy.
   Choice B, *we had ever the occasion of meeting*, is wordy as well as awkward.
   Choice C contains a vague, unclear *on this occasion*.

2. **(J) Choice J**, *January snowstorm*, is most to the point.
   The original choice F and Choice G, *snowstorm in January that had been occurring*, are both drawn out, unnecessarily wordy.
   Choice H, *snowstorm occurring during January*, is also not as concise as the original version.

3. **(C) Choice C is best**; *a town in central Italy*, expresses a concise and clear appositive that modifies Perugia.
   Choice A, *which is the name of a town found in central Italy*, is diffusely worded.
   Choice B, *central Italy*, does not give enough information to modify the city of Perugia.
   Choice D, *which is the name of a town, found in central Italy*, is a bit wordy and contains an unneeded, awkward comma.

4. **(F) The original version, F, is best**; the colon (:) is correctly used to introduce the list of objects that Baci will retrieve.
   Choice G is not the best because a hyphen is not the correct punctuation mark to use to introduce a list of items.
   Choice H is out because it shifts from the present tense that is used throughout the paragraph to the past tense: *you have thrown to her; including*. Also, the semicolon (;) is awkwardly and ineffectively placed.
   Choice J, *you go ahead and throw.*, should be eliminated because it sounds kind of slang or, at least, overly casual.

5. **(B) Choice B is correct** because it is the clearest version: *Baci is athletic and dexterous in other ways, too.*
   Choice A is redundant because it uses the expressions *as well* and *too*.
   Choice C, *Baci is athletic and dexterous, as well, in other ways* is overdone. Choose one or the other: *as well* or in *other ways*.
   Choice D is incorrect; when used in the same sentence, *as well* and *several additional ways* is overkill.

6. **(H)** Choices G and H are close contenders, but **Choice H, runs nonstop laps, is best** because the action verb *runs* is parallel to the action verb *plays*, which is used in the preceding part of the sentence.

Choice F is out because *nonstopping* is an unsound, awkward adjective—faulty diction.

Choice J is overkill: *ceaselessly and nonstop* say the same thing. Choose one or the other.

7. **(D) Choice D**, *she's somehow playing, too?*, is concisely and clearly expressed.
Choice A, the original version, contains the redundant expressions *as well* and *too.*
Choice B is also repetitive because it uses *in addition to* in conjunction with *as well.*
Comma overload makes choice C undesirable: *she's, as well, somehow playing, along with us?*

8. **(H) Choice H, *food are*, is the correct answer** because it is grammatically correct and to the point.
Choice F, the original version, is out because it uses a singular verb along with a plural, compound subject.
Choice G is also out because it uses the singular linking verb *is*. In addition, the interrupting phrase, *so enjoyable to her*, is superfluous since the food and treats are already described in the sentence as *delights.* Remember, the ACT English Test likes language that is expressed to-the-point, leaving no room for redundancy.
Choice J is incorrect because it creates a sentence fragment (incomplete sentence). Gerunds (*-ing* ending verbs) such as *being* (which is used in this choice) cannot be used as the main verb of a sentence, unless they appear in conjunction with a helping verb such as *was.*

9. **(C) In Choice C**, the semicolon (;) correctly separates the independent clauses, which are written in parallel form.
Choice A, is incorrect because beef does not constitute a *flavor combination.*
Choice B (*combination, with beef snacks being*) sounds awkward and non-standard.
Choice D (*combination, while beef combined with vegetables, regarding flavor combinations,*) is redundant and drawn out.

10. **(F) In Choice F**, NO CHANGE is needed because the list correctly follows the verb *are* without punctuation.
Choice G (*treats are;*) is out because a semicolon is not used to introduce a list.
Choice H (*treats, them being;*) is awkwardly expressed and misuses the semicolon.
Choice J (*treats would be the following:*) is too wordy.

11. **(D) The correct answer is Choice D**; the essay would lose *an additional, fitting detail that adds a touch of humor as well as a cute image.*
Choice A is out; an engaging detail would be lost.

Choice B is incorrect. The sentence is about the dog, Baci, so it cannot be regarded as an *irrelevant detail*.

Choice C is out. This detail is far from serious, and it does not *detract from the tone of the essay*.

12. **(G) The correct answer is Choice G.** This version is most succinctly put, meaning that it is tightly worded, concise, and to the point.

    Choice F, is not the best choice. It is wordy, and *mannerism* is not the correct word form.

    Choice H is a close contender, but it is not as concise as Choice G. The ACT prefers economy of written expression.

    Choice J is very awkward. Trust your ear to hear the "ouch" factor.

13. **(D) The correct answer is D.** *First,* is expressed parallel to the sentence that immediately follows.

    Choice A, is not the most fitting choice because it is not parallel to *second,* which appears in the next sentence.

    Choice B, *Firstly,* is close, but it is not as perfectly parallel as Choice D. The preferred form is *First.*

    Choice C misuses the colon (:).

14. **(F) The correct answer is F** because it is clear, succinct, and to the point.

    Choice G (Baci- *who is weighing forty-five pounds,*) is incorrect because the hyphen mark is misused and because it is wordy.

    Choice H (Baci, *with a weight of forty-five pounds;*) is incorrect because *with a weight of* is diffusely expressed (wordy).

    Choice J (Baci, *forty-five pounds of weight,*) is incorrect because it is awkward and not as concise as Choice F.

15. **(C) Choice C,** which tells how Baci plays basketball with her brothers, is in keeping with the topic sentence of the paragraph: *Baci enjoys many activities and outings.*

    Although Choice A is a detail pertaining to Baci *she sometimes sleeps in her crate at night,* it is neither about an enjoyable activity nor about an outing.

    Choice B also relates to Baci *she is a great watchdog* but this detail does not follow the lead of the topic sentence.

    Choice D is way off: telling *about how Baci gets uptight at the groomer's* would disrupt the cohesiveness (focus) of the closing paragraph.

PASSAGE II: CABO SAN LUCAS

16. **(H) The correct answer is H**, *to reach,* because the infinitive verbal form works best here.

    Choices F, *in reaching,* and G, *in reach for,* do not flow in context.

    Choice J, *as it is reaching,* is awkward as well as drawn out.

17. **(D) Choice D**, *Nestled between*, works best as a descriptive phrase.
    Choice A is out because *Among and between* is logically unsound.
    Choice B, *Among*, is out because *among* means "through the midst of" and is used when referring to more than two.
    Choice C, *Between*, is nice and concise but not enough to eloquently and descriptively introduce the town.

18. **(H) Choice H**, *miles*, makes the point of a lengthy shoreline most succinctly.
    Choice F (*miles upon miles*) and Choice B (*miles after miles*) are unnecessarily wordy.
    Choice D, *with miles*, is wrong because the preposition *with* is superfluous.

19. **(A) Choice A**, *is enthusiastic about*, is expressed both clearly and concisely.
    Choice B (*has enthusiasm with regard to*) is incorrect because it is too drawn out (wordy).
    Choice C (*being enthusiastic about*) is out because the gerund form, *being*, cannot function as the main verb of a sentence; if it is used as the main verb, a fragment usually results.
    Choice D (*is enthusiastic for*) is out because *enthusiastic for* is idiomatically unsound.

20. **(J) Choice J**, *riding*, is parallel to the gerund verb forms in its vicinity: *snorkeling* and *taking*.
    Choice F, (*a ride on*) is not parallel and, therefore, incorrect.
    Choice G (*get ready for going for a ride on*) is out because it is diffuse (wordy, drawn out).
    Choice H (*taking a ride with*) is also not parallel structure with when one considers the surrounding language and expressions.

21. **(D) The correct answer is D**, *set*. In this particular context, a *set* refers to a group of persons.
    Choice A, (*beset*), is a verb with a negative connotation that means plagued or weighed down. It is not correct.
    Choice B (*sect*) is typically used to mean a religious group. Thus, it is not correct.
    Choice C (*being so set*) is out because it is unnecessarily wordy.

22. **(G) The correct answer is G** because the paragraph would lose *an example that further supports the focus of this paragraph*. The topic sentence summarizes the paragraph's focus: *For the more <u>adventurous</u> set, Medano Beach offers somewhat <u>daring</u> or, at least, <u>faster-velocity water sports</u>*. The underlined portions show how a slippery, speedy banana-boat ride would fit right in as a supporting detail for this paragraph.

Choice F (*a piece of information that is not pertinent to this paragraph*) is incorrect because the sentence in question is pertinent (relevant).

Choice G (*information about how people use water sports as a means of working out*) is way off! Where is there mention of *working out*? Lifting that banana boat would build muscle, but the concept of water fitness is not found in the text.

Choice J (*an irrelevant, though lighthearted, digression*) is out because the sentence in question, while lighthearted (slippery banana-boat ride!), is not a *digression* (a straying away from the topic).

23. **(D)** **The correct answer is D**, *delete the underlined portion*, because Choices A, B, and C all provide descriptions that are superfluous (unnecessary).

Choices A (*and scenic*), B (*while scenic*), and C (*as they are scenic*) add unnecessary words. *Picturesque* already means scenic, aesthetically pleasing to the eye. The ACT English Test requires you to avoid redundancy.

24. **(F)** **The correct answer is F** (*dips*) because this version has subject–verb agreement.

Choice G (*is dipping*) is out because this verb phrase is not as succinct as the action verb, *dips*.

Choice H (*is seen as it dips*) is too long-winded.

Choice J (*dip*) is incorrect because this version lacks subject–verb agreement (. . . *sun dip below the horizon.*)

25. **(A)** **The correct answer is A** (*Cabo San Lucas, many of which can be found in Cabo's splendorous resorts,*) because a pair of commas is correctly used to set off this interrupting phrase. The phrase provides more information about the Cabo restaurants. Notice how the sentence still flows even when this phrase is taken out.

Choice B (*Cabo San Lucas, many being they are found in Cabo's splendorous resorts,*) is expressed in a wordy and awkward fashion (*many being they are . . .* ouch!).

Choice C (*Cabo San Lucas—many of which can be found in Cabo's splendorous resorts,*) is incorrect because the phrase is erroneously (incorrectly) set off by a comma and a dash. A comma and dash is an odd and nonstandard combination for setting off phrases.

Choice D (*Cabo San Lucas, many of which can be found in Cabo's splendorful resorts,*) is incorrect because *splendorful* is not a word. This error falls under the category of faulty diction (word choice, usage). Be careful about misused or made-up words! Read quality books and newspapers to "tune" your ear to standard diction.

26. **(H)** **The correct answer is H** because using *being found* as the main verb of the sentence creates a fragment.

Flipping back to the English passage reveals that the subject (underlined) is plural: <u>*Great sushi, sashimi, and vegetable tempura*</u> *can be found at several Asian-style or "fusion" restaurants which are located at the downtown marina.* Choices F (*can be found*), G (*are found*), and J (*are served*) are incorrect because each of these three versions works effectively as an alternative in this sentence. Choice F flows smoothly.

Featuring plural helping verbs, Choices G and J work soundly as well.

27. **(C)** **The correct answer is C** because this is a lackluster and sleepy topic sentence—*Water sports aside, there's the shopping*—and would therefore least effectively open the paragraph and express excitement about shopping as something for vacationers to enjoy.

Choice A (*You can shop 'til you drop while in Cabo.*), B (*There are abundant prospects for the born-to-shop while in Cabo.*), and D (*Shopping enthusiasts will feel like kids in a candy shop while in Cabo*) are much more effective and inspiring as topic sentences.

28. **(J)** **Choice J**, *At*, is idiomatically correct.

Choices F (*By*), G (*Out and about*), and H (*Among*) are idiomatically unsound. In other words, these expressions do not reflect the conventions of standard, written English.

29. **(B)** **The correct answer is B**, *delete the underlined portion*; the word *shopping* is extraneous (unnecessary). The ACT English Test prefers economy of language, whenever possible.

Choice A, is incorrect because the word *shopping* is superfluous.

Choice C is also wrong; *wholesale shopping* slows down the sentence with two unneeded words.

Choice D, *moderately-priced*, is too wordy.

30. **(J)** **The correct answer is J.** It is true that *this essay mainly focuses on the positive aspects of a Cabo vacation*, so the essay does NOT fulfill the goal of expressing both the advantages and drawbacks of vacationing in Cabo.

Choice F is incorrect because the essay does not detail the pros and cons of visiting Cabo.

Choice G is out because the essay does not *present a balanced exposition that encourages readers to be aware of both the benefits and drawbacks of a Cabo vacation.*

Choice H is wrong because this essay is not completely objective; in fact, it tends to *persuade rather than dissuade readers from considering* Cabo as their next *vacation destination.*

PASSAGE III: THE HERO'S JOURNEY

31. **(A)** **The best answer is A**, *Lucas's*, because this version correctly forms the possessive proper noun by adding an apostrophe and an "s."
Choice B, *Lucas'*, is out. The name is Lucas, so *'s* must be added to show ownership.
Choice C, *Lucas'es*, is an invalid possessive form.
Choice D, *Lucas*, does not have the punctuation required to show ownership.

32. **(F)** **The best answer is F** (*are*) because the subject of this sentence is the plural *steps*.
Choice G, *was*, is a singular linking verb; thus, it is incorrect.
Choice H, *have been*, is out because there is no logical reason to put this sentence into the past tense.
Choice J, *is*, is also a singular linking verb.

33. **(D)** **Choice D** (*advancements but actually*) is the most concisely put. Succinct language is always prefered on the ACT English Test.
Choice A (*advancements—but, actually*), is incorrect because the punctuation use is erroneous.
Choice B (*advancements, but actually,*) is out because there is comma overload.
In Choice C (*advancements, but, actually,*) there are unneeded commas, which slow down the flow of the sentence.

34. **(H)** **The best answer is H** (*distraught, alone, and determined to fight back*) because this version features a list of parallel adjectives. Recall that the ACT prefers language to be expressed in a balanced and parallel fashion.
Choice F (*distraught and alone, and determined on fighting back*) is out because there is one too many *ands* used. Also, determined on is an idiomatically unsound construction.
Choice G (*distraught, and alone, and determined to fight back*) is out because there are too many *ands* and too many commas! Remember, less is more; conciseness is the preference.
Choice J (*distraughtly alone, with the determination for fighting back*) lacks parallel form.

35. **(B)** **The best answer is B**; delete the underlined phrase because it is redundant. The ACT prefers economy of language, providing that the intended meaning is preserved.
Choice A, (*and changes*), Choice C (*and is changed*), and Choice D (*in changing*) are incorrect because these versions are also redundant.

36. **(J)** **Choice J**, *separation*, is most succinct.
Choice F (*being called separation*), Choice G (*called separation*), and Choice H (*the stage known as "separation"*) are all unnecessarily and ineffectively wordy.

37. **(C)** **The best answer is C** because *accommodate* does not flow or fit in this particular context. In other contexts, *accommodate* can mean to adjust or to reconcile, among other possible meanings.

Choice A (*join in the journey with*), Choice B (*accompany*), and Choice D (*travel/with*) are incorrect answers because each of these is an effective replacement for *come with*. Even though Choice A is rather wordy, it can fly!

38. **(F)** **The best answer is F** (*explains, "It*) because it is standard to introduce a quotation with a comma followed by open quotations marks.

Choice G (explains…"It), Choice H (explains: It), and Choice J (*explains; "It*) are not the best because these versions misuse punctuation marks or neglect the appropriate use of open quotes.

39. **(D)** **The best answer is D**, *doing*, because this verb is parallel to the *doing* that precedes it.

Choice A (*to do*) lacks parallelism.

Choice B (*the doing of*) also lacks parallelism and is wordy as well as awkward.

Choice C (*about to do*) does not flow at all. This version should evoke the Ouch! factor.

40. **(F)** **The best answer is F**, *ability*, is the most specific and appropriate to insert where indicated:

Discovering the supernatural aid is the next step of separation. This ability is represented by Obi-Wan, Luke's guru, and the Force.

Discovering the supernatural aid, which serves as a context clue, is best defined as an *ability*.

Choice G *symbol*, Choice H (*character*), Choice J (*feature*) do not fit the definition.

41. **(D)** **The correct answer is D**, *to manipulate*, because the infinitive form of a verb should follow a conjugated verb. In this case, the infinitive *to manipulate* should follow the conjugated *has*.

Choice A (*of manipulating*), Choice B (*in manipulating*), and Choice C (*manipulating*) are incorrect because the simple infinitive form is best here.

42. **(H)** **The correct answer is H**, *To lose a specific aspect of Luke's personal growth*. With this part excised (deleted), the reader would be unaware that Luke has learned not to trust so easily.

Choice F, *to streamline the prose by eliminating an impertinent detail*, is incorrect because this detail is not impertinent or irrelevant.

Choice G, *to deemphasize Luke's growing sense of paranoia*, is incorrect because there is no passage proof to support that Luke has become paranoid! This is a leap: do not read into the passage or add what is not there. The text simply says that he is learning not to trust everyone.

Choice J, *to improve the essay by eliminating a stereotype*, is incorrect because the underlined portion indicated does not represent a stereotype. A *stereotype* is an idea held by people about a particular thing or group of people.

43. **(B) In Choice B** (*companions; however, the two*) a semicolon is correctly used to divide the two independent clauses that make up this compound sentence.
Choice A (*companions, however, the two*) forms a comma-splice run on sentence.
Choice C (*companions, however being them two*) because it has the Ouch! factor. It is awkwardly expressed.
Choice D (*companions: However, the two of them*) is out because a colon is incorrectly used and *of them* is superfluous. Sorry to beat a dead horse, but it bears repeating: The ACT English Test prefers economy of language.

44. **(J) The best answer is J** (*next phase: initiation, in which he gains*). The colon (:) is correctly used to introduce the specific phase, and the phrase *in which* flows best. *Which*, a relative pronoun, correctly refers back to the "phase."
Choice F (*next phase: initiation, where he gains*) is incorrect because *where* should refer back to a place or location, which is not the case in this context.
Choice G (*next phase; initiation, where he gains*) is incorrect because the semicolon is ineffective. It neither divides two independent clauses nor serves as a "big comma."
Choice H (*next phase: being initiation, where he will gain*) is incorrect because *being* is unnecessary and awkward.

45. **(D) The correct answer is D** (*gain instinctive impulses and sensations*) because these details pertain to the topic sentence of the paragraph, which says, *After completing the separation state, Luke must complete the next phase: initiation, where he gains confidence in himself and learns how to rely on instinct as well as feeling*. As expressed in Choice D, to *gain instinctive impulses and sensations* is to rely on instinct as well as feeling.
Choice A (*gain distinction*) is incorrect because Luke is not concerned, at this point in time, with gaining distinction, which is merit or worth in a particular field.
Choice B (*lose self-doubt*) is way off because this paragraph is not about Luke becoming more confident and losing his insecurities or *self-doubts*.
Choice C is also way off; even though Luke is toying with an electric saber (sword), his goal is *not* to *learn about the intricacies of electricity*!

PASSAGE IV: MIGUEL HIDALGO

46. **(F)** **The best answer is Choice F.** It is clear, correct, and concise. Choices G, H, and J all have unnecessary words (*being*, *called*, and *known as*) that do not enhance or clarify meaning in any way. Remember, less is more when it comes to succinctly expressed language.

47. **(A)** **Choice A** is *not* clear and sound. The part that is most problematic is *which having proving myself* because it is awkward and sluggish (slow-moving, without saying much).
All other versions—Choices B, C, and D—are grammatically sound.
Choice B is a clear and complete sentence.
Choice C flows nicely and has parallel form.
Choice D is also effectively put.

48. **(J)** **Choice J** is the most clear and precise.
Choices F, G, and H are unnecessarily wordy, making this introductory phrase sluggish (slow moving).

49. **(B)** **The best answer is B** because it is to the point.
The remaining choices—A, C, and D—are all unnecessarily wordy. The relative pronouns *who*, *that*, and *which* are not needed to express the desired meaning. The ACT likes language as clear and concise as possible.

50. **(G)** **The best answer is G** because it is worded most clearly and concisely and uses the comma to set apart the noun *educator* with the participle phrase that modifies it. A participal phrase has qualities of both verb and adjective.
Notice how Choices F and G are nearly the same, except that Choice F lacks the comma that is necessary to set off the gerund phrase, *pushing myself to assist . . .*
Choice H creates a sentence fragment.
The underlined part of Choice J is non-idiomatic: *educator pushing myself in assisting*.

51. **(A)** **Choice A** (*public and wanted*) is clear, short, and sweet—just what the ACT looks for.
Choice B (*public, and wanted,*) suffers from comma overload!
Choice C (*public and wanted,*) is incorrect because the comma is not needed.
Choice D (*public while I was wanting*) is awkward and drawn out.

52. **(F)** **Choice F** (*a tremendously essential*) most concisely modifies *point*.
Choice G (*a tremendous while being essential*) is incorrect because it is wordy. Remember that the ACT English Test prefers language that is short and to-the-point.

Choice H (*a tremendous, essentially,*) is incorrect because the commas make this version staccato- or unconnected-sounding.

Choice J (*a tremendous as well as essential*) is wrong because it is not as succinct as Choice A.

53. **(D) The best answer is D,** *inspiring,* because it is the most succinct.
Choice A (*to inspire*) is out because the infinitive form here does not flow. Remember, infinitive forms of verbs usually follow conjugated verbs.
Choice B (*in inspiring*) is incorrect because the preposition *in* is superfluous (not needed).
Choice C (*regarding the inspiration of*) is too diffuse (spread out in a wordy fashion).

54. **(H) The best answer is H,** *respected,* because this word form makes the most sense in context: after all, Mexico should be respected after achieving its independence!
Choice F (*respectful*) because showing reverence does not make as much sense in this context as earning it (*respected*).
Choice G (*respective*) is wrong because *respective* is typically used to mean separate (Following the meeting, the colleagues returned to their *respective* offices).
Choice J (*retrospective*) is out because *retrospective* is typically used to mean a review of past performance or of one's track record.

55. **(C) The best answer is C** (*from harm.*). It is the most concise.
Choice A (*from harm's way.*) is not as concise as Choice B.
Choice B (*from being harmed in any way.*) is ineffectively wordy.
Choice D (*from the way of harm.*) is diffuse (wordy).

56. **(J) The best answer is J:** *No, because the information provides another reason why it is prudent* (wise) *for the men to retreat.* Yes, this piece of information fits as part of the topic sentence of the paragraph.
Choice F is incorrect because the information does not impair the paragraph's focus; the paragraph is about why Hidalgo has his men retreat.
Choice G is incorrect because the information does not *weaken Hidalgo's decision to turn back*; on the contrary, this additional point edifies (builds up, informs) the rationale behind the retreat.
Choice H is way off because the information does not *contain an allusion* (indirect reference) *to a former battle.* Typically, allusions refer to works of literature.

57. **(C) The best answer is C.** It is true that this sentence does not accurately *reflect the author's positive mindset.* This sentence should *not* be added.

Choice A is incorrect because the author has not maintained an attitude of cynicism. Vocabulary sharpener: cynicism has to do with thinking negatively about others, particularly in terms of their false or self-serving motives.

Choice B is incorrect because this author's attitude has not been shown as pessimistic (negative thinking).

Choice D is out because the author does not envision *global unity*, only unity within his own country.

58. **(F)** **The best answer is F** (*in*) because, of all the choices given, *I made a clear fundamental change __in__ Mexico's status* is idiomatically preferable.

Choice G is out because the preposition *with* is idiomatically incorrect in this context.

Choice H is incorrect because *regarding* is not as streamlined or smooth-flowing as the simple preposition *in*.

Choice J is also incorrect because the preposition *on* is non-idiomatic.

59. **(D)** **The best answer is D.** The singular possessive *its* is needed here to express belonging to Mexico. Review the context: *a clear fundamental change in Mexico's status and __its__ peoples' determination.*

Choice A (*it's*) is out because the contraction *it's* stands for *it is*. *It is* does not work in the context.

Choice B is incorrect because *they're* a contraction standing for *they are*; this pronoun–verb pair does not work in the context.

Choice C is incorrect because *their* is a plural-possessive pronoun and, therefore, cannot show belonging to Mexico, which is singular (*one* country).

60. **(G)** **The best answer is G** because there is a bevy (a great amount) of textual evidence to support Hidalgo's feeling of pride about *all that he has accomplished.*

Choice F is incorrect because Hidalgo indeed does reflect on his past and *revel* (*take pleasure in*) in his merits.

Choice H is incorrect because Hidalgo does not express, in this passage, a sincere wish to *have led his people differently.*

Choice J is incorrect because while a reader may interpret Hidalgo as having somewhat of a *boastful personality or arrogant leadership style*, there is not passage proof to support his losing friends over such personal shortcomings.

PASSAGE V: HOW TO MAKE CINNAMON-NUT SQUARES

61. **(D)** **The correct answer is D**, *"Aunt Louisa from Texas," as we called her,* because this choice flows best and most naturally.

While not a terrible choice, A, *"Aunt Louisa from Texas" we'd call her,* reads somewhat awkwardly and the contraction, *we'd,* is not particularly well suited for standard, written English.

Choice B, *calling her "Aunt Louisa," the one from Texas,* and Choice C, *as we were calling her "Aunt Louisa from Texas,"* both contain unnecessary words.

62. **(F)** **Choice F** is a logical closing sentence to the first paragraph. Leave it where it is.

Choice G (*Begin new paragraph with this sentence.*) is not the best choice because the beginning of the essay would become too choppy and there are no supporting details to "flesh out" this particular sentence.

Choice H (*Delete the underlined portion.*) is also not a good idea. Why eliminate a perfectly good sentence that relates to the topic and enlivens the essay with some vivid detail: *hand-written recipe, Long Island, niece Brandy, 1978.*

Choice J (*Move this sentence to the very beginning of the passage.*) is incorrect. For one thing, readers would not know who *she* is. Also, Brandy is not a key player in this essay, so we would not want her name to be mentioned in the opening sentence.

63. **(D)** **Choice D** (*1, 2, 4, 3, 5*) provides the most logical sequence of sentences for this opening paragraph. The ideas build upon each other, and the placement of ideas flows in a way that makes sense.

Choice A, NO CHANGE, does not work because in this original structure the description of Aunt Louisa's voice is too removed from the first mention of Aunt Louisa.

Choice B (*4, 3, 2, 1, 5*) and Choice H (*4, 5, 3, 2, 1*) do not work because starting off with sentence 4 (*She had a slow and soft way of talking, and she was as sweet as the powdered sugar she'd sprinkle on her nut squares.*) could lead to some confusion; for example, who is *she*? Furthermore, beginning with sentence 4 leads the reader to believe that the essay will be more of a character portrait (of Aunt Louisa) and less of a how-to about making a particular type of cookie.

64. **(J)** **The correct answer is J** (*sister-in-law, Helen,*) because the commas are needed to set off the nonessential element of the sister-in-law's name. In other words, the name *Helen* is not essential in order to understand who carried on the tradition of making the cookies. Louisa had only one sister-in-law. If she had more than one sister-in-law, then a comma should not be used. Also, the hyphens are needed to join together the three words that make up the name of this relative, *sister-in-law.*

Choice F (*sister-in-law Helen*), is incorrect because it lacks the commas.

Choice G (*sister in law called Helen,*) is out for a few reasons: it lacks hyphens, it lacks a comma, and it contains the superfluous word, *called.*

Choice H (*sister in-law, who was named Helen,*) is missing one hyphen mark and is unnecessarily wordy.

65. **(B) The correct answer is B:** cookies, *for.* This comma-conjunction pair correctly divides the two independent clauses that make up this sentence and provides the reason for doubling the decadent cookie recipe!
Choice A (*cookies for*), lacks the necessary punctuation mark: the comma!
Choice C, (*cookies—for,)*, misuses the dash, creating an awkward construction.
Finally, Choice D (*cookies; for*) does not work. If the semicolon (;) is present, there is no need for the conjunction *for* to follow; on its own, the semicolon correctly separates the two independent, yet correlated, clauses.

66. **(G) The correct answer is G**; the sentence should be kept because it *elaborates on the* <u>process</u> *(this step reflects the end of the process) of making, baking, and* <u>serving</u> *these cookies.*
Choice F is out: the sentence by no means elucidates (clearly explains) the benefits of *using a cookie sheet instead of a baking pan.* Where did that come from? Choice H is out because there is no sound rationale for moving this sentence to Paragraph 4.
Choice J is invalid. This sentence does not confuse the readers because it is about serving and slicing, not about the quantity of dough to prepare.

67. **(B) The correct answer is B**, *So,* because this transitional word is most effective regarding the logical organization of ideas.
Choice A (*Also,*) is out because this transitional word suggests that a prior recipe was given.
Choice C, *Though,* is incorrect because this connecting word is illogical in this context; the purpose of this paragraph is *not* to oppose or contradict the preceding content.
Choice D, *Lastly,* does not work because this paragraph is not the last in a sequence of steps within a process.

68. **(J) The correct answer is J**, *three heaping teaspoons of cinnamon,* because this expression is parallel to the other members of the series comma.
Choice F (*three teaspoons, heaping, of cinnamon*) is out because it not only features a comma overload, but it also lacks parallelism within the series.
Choice G (*three teaspoons of cinnamon-heaping-)* creates awkwardness because the adjective *heaping* is strangely tacked onto the end with hyphen marks.
Choice H (*threefold teaspoonsful of heaping cinnamon*) is incorrect for these reasons: *threefold* really means having three parts, <u>teaspoonsful</u> should be spelled *teaspoonfuls*, and this version creates an error in parallel form.

69. **(B) The correct answer is B**, *a sprinkle of.* This choice is parallel to the other measurements (precise or estimated) of ingredients that appear within the list.

Choice A (*sprinkle*) does not work because it lacks parallel form.

Choice C, *you should then sprinkle*, is too drawn out and lacks parallelism.

Choice D, *to sprinkle*, is also not parallel to the rest of the members in the listing of ingredients.

70. **(F) The correct answer is F** (*which is*). This answer correctly links powdered sugar to the subordinate clause that modifies it.

Choice G (*being*) is incorrect because it sounds awkward.

Choice H (*as it is*) is a bit wordy and presents the possibility for an ambiguous pronoun, *it*.

Choice J, (*for it is*) doesn't make sense. There's no reason to use the conjunction *for* because the purpose of the latter part of this sentence is not to emphasize a cause-and-effect relationship. Again, this choice presents the potential for an ambiguous *it*.

71. **(D) The correct answer is D**, *after the word Next* because *using your hands* modifies the action verb *press*. To decide on the best placement for this phrase, carefully reread around this section:

Once all of the ingredients are fully incorporated and the dough is formed, shape into two balls. Next, press the balls of dough about one-quarter inch flat onto an ungreased cookie sheet, using your hands.

Choice A (*where it is now*) is incorrect because, positioned here, the phrase seems to relate more to the *cookie sheet* than to the action of *pressing*.

Choice B (*before the word Once*) is incorrect because one might understand this to mean that the *hands* have no part in this baking process until all of the ingredients have been fully blended!

Choice C (*after the word <u>incorporated</u>*) is faulty because it's not too much of a stretch to say that the reader may conclude that *only* the hands should be used to blend the ingredients and nothing else, like a mixing spoon or electric mixer!

72. **(G) The correct answer is G**; certainly this clause should be *kept, because it aids the reader in more fully understanding the specifics of the baking process.* The type or rolling pin to use can be a significant factor. For example, some baking instructions might call for a marble rolling pin, or even one filled with ice water.

Choice F is incorrect. First, this is not much of a vivid description; second, this essay is more explanatory than descriptive in purpose.

Choice H is incorrect because the actual material and composition of the rolling pin may not necessarily be *irrelevant* (of little importance to the matter at hand; impertinent) to the baking process.

Choice J is incorrect, a bit ridiculous even. If there are bakers out there with plastic rolling pins, power to them! It is a big stretch to conclude that owners of *plastic* rolling pins might be reluctant to carry on with this cookie recipe.

73. **(D) The correct answer is D** (*preferences; you*) because the semicolon is correctly used to separate the two independent clauses that make up this compound sentence.

Choice A (*preferences, you*) is incorrect because the comma creates a comma splice, which is a type of run-on sentence.

Choice B (*preferences; You*) is out; a capital letter should not follow the semicolon when attempting to create a compound sentence.

Choice C (*preferences you*) is incorrect; this is a fused run-on sentence that lacks the necessary punctuation.

74. **(J) The correct answer is J.** It makes sense that this sentence should be moved to Paragraph 4 because this is the paragraph in which the reader is told to gather the ingredients. At this point, it is most advisable to have the baker preheat the oven.

Choice F is wrong because Paragraph 1 is primarily about the origins of this recipe.

Choice G is incorrect because Paragraph 2 is primarily about Helen and Anne baking these cookies for their families.

Choice H is out because Paragraph 3 is mostly about pragmatic things like the number of servings the recipe makes, how to cut the cookies, and that they can be made ahead of time and frozen.

75. **(A) The correct answer is A** (*5, 6, 7, 8*) The original ordering of paragraphs makes the most sense because these paragraphs delineate a logical process. In abridged (shortened) form, the steps can be roughly sketched as follows: Paragraph 5: incorporate the required ingredients and flatten dough onto cookie sheet; Paragraph 6: smooth out dough, then coat with egg whites and nuts; Paragraph 7: cook dough then dust with powdered sugar; and Paragraph 8: cut, serve, and enjoy the cookies!

Reading Test

PASSAGE I: FICTION

1. **(B) This question addresses the narrative effect of a fiction passage.**
Cross off Choice A, *affection and compassion*, as these are not emotions necessarily evoked by the fiction excerpt. Eliminate Choice C, *reverence and trepidation*; while a level of fear is palpable in the story, reverence (respect) is not. Likewise, eliminate Choice D, *envy and mistrust*, because while there's a sense of mistrust in the passage, envy (jealousy) is not prevalent. **The correct answer is Choice B**, *anticipation and suspense.*

2. **(J) This is an inference question, which requires higher order critical thinking. Carefully reread the referenced opening lines.** *"You've done well, Rainsford," the voice of the general called. "Your Burmese tiger pit has claimed one of my best dogs. Again you score. I think, Mr. Rainsford, I'll see*

what you can do against my whole pack. I'm going home for a rest now. Thank you for a most amusing evening." The question asks you to infer the air with which *General Zaroff regards Rainsford.* Choice F, *contentedness,* is incorrect because while Zaroff may be a happy chap, he is not regarding Rainsford with an air of happiness or satisfaction. Also, cross off Choice H, *contrition,* as Zaroff's words are not expressing remorse for his actions or conduct. Likewise, cross off Choice G, *contention* because contention (argumentativeness, disagreement) is too strong of an emotion in this scenario. **The best answer is Choice J**, *condescension,* given the tone of Zaroff's comments, particularly when he says, "You've done well, Rainsford" and "Thank you for a most amusing evening."

3. **(D) This question requires a combination of inferencing and paraphrasing skills.** The question asks about the meaning of the phrase in lines 8–9 *he had new things to learn about fear.* Eliminate Choice A, *Rainsford lives an insulated life,* as it is on the extreme side; there is little to no evidence that he lives an isolated or cloistered life. Likewise, Choice B, *Rainsford is a daredevil who seeks risky situations,* is rather extreme, as the text does not substantiate his being a "daredevil." Cross off Choice C, *Rainsford has difficulty dealing with his emotions,* as we don't know that Rainsford is emotionally struggling or ill-equipped with regard to his emotions. **The best answer is Choice D**, *Rainsford experiences a level of trepidation that he had not encountered until this moment,* as this is the most accurate paraphrasing of the referenced lines; trepidation means fear.

4. **(H) This question requires using context clues to deduce the meaning of an idiomatic expression**, *an animal at bay.* The question asks about the effect of the expression in characterizing Rainsford. Eliminate Choice F, *an intruder who has an aggressive stance,* as given the context of the story and circumstances, Rainsford is not poised aggressively. Choice G, *a beast at heart who feels close to animal life,* is also incorrect, as the text does not evidence Rainsford feeling bonded and intimate with animals. Cross off Choice J, *a nature-lover who communes with the spirit world,* as we also lack evidence for this description of Rainsford. **The best answer is Choice H**, *a fugitive who can no longer flee from danger,* as Rainsford is trapped and feeling like he's between a rock and a hard place, as another idiom goes.

5. **(A) This is a holistic ALL/EXCEPT question, in that the evidence can come from any part of the passage.** The question asks you to select from the options the aspect of discomfort the character does NOT experience. Eliminate Choice B, *hunger;* this answer is validated by these lines in Paragraph 3: *Ralph's nostrils flared and his mouth dribbled. He wiped his nose and mouth with the back of his hand and for the first time since the morning felt hungry.* Cross off Choice C, *physical pain,* as the opening two lines

provide evidence for this answer. Cross off Choice D, *fear*, as in addition to snippets of textual evidence appearing elsewhere in the passage, "first panic" and "terrified" are associated with Ralph in Paragraph 2. **The best answer is Choice A**, *excessive heat* as minimal evidence, if any, substantiates this choice.

6. **(H) This is a word-in-context question. Reread the entire sentence in which the word appears:** *At last Ralph* <u>wormed</u> *out of the ferns and sneaked forward to the edge of that impenetrable thicket that fronted the neck of land.* In this case, the question asks about the meaning of the action verb, *wormed* in line 65. Choice F, *wallowed*, is incorrect because wallowed means floundered and this meaning does not fit as well as the best answer. Cross off G, *wheedled*, because this means cajoled or coaxed using one's words to get what he or she wants. *Wobbled* doesn't quite fit the scene, so cross off Choice J. **The best answer is Choice H**, *wiggled*, as it flows most effectively in the context of the setting and story.

7. **(D) This question is about the rhetorical effect of a sentence.** The question asks about the type of rhetoric used in the sentence *"The breaking of the conch and the deaths of Piggy and Simon lay over the island like a vapor."* Choice A, *as hyperbole to illustrate how Ralph obsesses about his circumstances unreasonably*, is incorrect because hyperbole (exaggeration) is not evidenced by this sentence or the sentences prior and post in context. Likewise, Choice B, *as imagery to lend a poetic tone to the narrative*, is invalid as a poetic tone is inconsistent with the narrative as a whole and, thus, this purpose would lack a certain cohesiveness with the rest of the text. Eliminate Choice C, *as a comparison to illustrate Ralph's overactive, pessimistic perspective*; while a comparison is being made, the events referenced (breaking of the conch, deaths of Piggy and Simon) do not validate "an overactive" perspective or imagination regarding the events at hand. **The best answer is Choice D**, *as a simile that emphasizes Ralph's grim and foreboding mental outlook*, as the word "like" establishes the simile, and "vapor" connotes a foreboding mental outlook.

8. **(F) This is a comparative question, in that it is based on understanding the circumstances and characters depicted in both fiction passages.** The question asks you to select which characters in both passages share similar experiences. Cross off Choice G: Bill and General Zaroff are not character counterparts. Cross off Choice H, as Ivan and Piggy are not similar character types. Finally, cross off Choice J, for Simon and Ralph are not experiencing similar circumstances or challenges. **The best answer is Choice F**, as Ralph and Rainsford both endure the struggles and fears of one being pursued.

9. **(C) This is a holistice question, requiring an understanding of theme.** Although Choice A, *Nothing ventured, nothing gained.*, is a popular maxim, this saying is not implicitly or explicitly illustrated in the exploits of Ralph and Rainsford. Even though Choice B, *The early bird gets the worm.*, is a timeworn and favorite saying, there is not a predominant message about the advantages of rising or showing up early. Finally, although Choice D, *Give them an inch, and they take a mile.*, often holds true in interpersonal relationships, this dynamic is not firmly illustrated by the character interactions in these passages. **The best answer is Choice C,** *Better to be the hunter than the hunted,* as the passages definitely depict scenes of the pursuer and the pursued, and the latter is having a difficult time.

10. **(G) This question is based on both passages, so it is a comparative reading question.** The question asks what the lines from both passages *"He had to stop to get his breath"* (line 37) and *"By the time his breathing was normal again"* (lines 46–47) can reveal about the characters of Rainsford and Ralph. While Choice F, *possess superhuman stamina and fortitude*, may sound exciting, it is not validated by the passage evidence. There are no statements or suggestions to support Rainsford and Ralph neglecting their health in the pursuit of beating their opponent or being out of shape physically, so eliminate Choices H and J. **The best answer is Choice G,** *have endured physical stress and anxiety,* as both male protagonists are dealing with physical stresses (pain, hunger, fatigue) and feel a level of anxiety with regard to their strife-filled circumstances and pursuers.

PASSAGE II: SOCIAL SCIENCE

11. **(C) Reread the entire sentence in which the word in question (*exercised*) appears to get a clear sense of its meaning and usage:** *During infant play, Jean Piaget's cognitive-developmental stages are exercised, to some degree, by the use of toys with developmental play value.*
Choice A, *flexed,* does not fit the context of this sentence. This is more of a physical exercise term that relates to flexing (contracting, stretching, moving) muscles.
Choice B, *extenuated,* also does not fit. Extenuated means provided an excuse that lessened the severity of what has transpired.
Choice D is an undesirable choice because it is unnecessarily verbose (wordy): *put into practical effect.*
The best answer is C, *implemented,* because it succinctly expresses "put into effect," a meaning that fits the context.

12. **(F) ALL/EXCEPT questions require you to validate three of the four answer choices (based on what the infant *cannot* or is *unlikely* to do); the one remaining is the correct answer.**

Choice G is invalid because the paragraph tells us that the infant responds only to the *immediate present*; therefore, he could not *grimace (express disgust, fear) upon remembering something frightening he witnessed in his environment just several minutes ago.*

Choice H is invalid because the paragraph tells us that the infant has *no mental pictures or words that stand for objects and that can be manipulated mentally*; therefore, the infant would not have the faculties to *compare, in his mind's eye, his new rattle to his first rattle that sits upon his nursery changing table.*

Choice J is invalid because the paragraph says that infants respond only to the *immediate present*; therefore, the infant could not *anticipate playing with his older brothers when they come home from school.*

The correct answer is F, *simultaneously grasp for objects while bending and straightening his legs*, because the paragraph says that he responds to the world primarily in *sensory and motor* modalities (manners or modes of activity).

13. **(C) Sharp test takers know that the author's main purpose spans and "flavors" the entire piece; these test takers also know that the main purpose is often laid out in the introductory material and/or in the opening paragraph, as such:** *This passage on child development examines Jean Piaget's theory on infant developmental stages in relation to their play with toys.* Based on the preceding passage evidence, Choice A, *the difficulties that many adults have in accepting the developmental limitations of infants*, is therefore invalid.

Choice B is also unsubstantiated because the passage does not investigate *various and divergent perspectives on the developmental stage spanning birth to two years*; only Piaget's is addressed.

Choice D is also off-the-mark; in consideration of the passage as a whole, the author does not strive to *debunk (disprove, contradict) the underlying assumptions of earlier theories of infant and child development that were widely accepted prior to Piaget's research* even though many theories were in existence then.

Using process of elimination and considering what is stated in the passage, **the correct answer is C:** *how stages of infant development are shown through how an infant interacts with his toys.*

14. **(J) Reread the entire sentence in which *relevant* appears. The best choice has to make sense in context and flow in a non-awkward manner.** The sentence reads, *As with the first toy discussed, sensory stimulation is relevant here, too.*

Choice F may be tempting because *akin* means alike or similar, and *relevant* (in its most popular usage) means related or applicable. Still, the usage of *akin* is off and the sentence does not flow logically.

Choice G does not work; *rampant* means widespread or extensive, with a bent toward being "out of control." We don't want to put a negative spin on the word *relevant* in terms of how it is used in the sentence reproduced above.

Choice H does not work. *Elevated*, which means place high or superior, doesn't fit here either. **The correct answer is J**, *pertinent*, which is a nice synonym for relevant.

15. **(B) Make it a habit to keep organization in mind as you read the passages because this type of question is predictable.**
    Choice A is invalid. Even though it sounds open-minded and thorough—*analyzing the developmental theories of several authorities ...* —only one authority (Piaget) is mentioned.
    Choice C is way off—this passage is not presented in a *scattered fashion* and there is a firm line of relationship between the toys examined since they all engage the child's sensorimotor faculties.
    Choice D is unsubstantiated; even though *tactual (hands-on) and sensory development* is a centerpiece idea of the passage, *reverse-chronological order (time order)* is not happening!
    The best answer is B, *presenting examples of toys and examining how they can engage and facilitate a young child's sensory and motor development.*

16. **(F) Locate conservation and reread the entire sentence (at minimum) in which it is used:** *Measure Up Cups also entice a cognitive measure known as "conservation," defined as the concept that objects or a group of objects remains the same in fundamental ways, such as weight or number, even when there are external changes in shape or arrangement.*
    Choice G, *A child can learn a great deal by exploring objects with her mouth and hands,* is a true and reasonable statement that is supported elsewhere in the passage; however, it is not directly relevant to the concept of conservation.
    Choice H is not relevant to conservation because this principle does not focus on a child's ability to *detect subtle differences in pattern and texture among a variety of objects.*
    Choice J is off because conservation does not focus on sorting.
    The best answer is F: A child can understand that by grouping blocks and rearranging them, the original number of blocks remains constant.

17. **(A) To answer this word-in-context question, revisit the passage and reread the section in which the word appears:** *Specifically, the child eventually recognizes that the number of cups remains <u>constant</u>, whether or not they are spread out over the floor, nested inside of each other, or stacked in any number of piles.*
    Choice B does not fit because *correlated* means related to. This choice does not flow.
    Choice C does not fit either because *steadfast* means unwavering, faithful, typically in the manner in which one supports a cause, holds a belief, or shows dedication.
    Choice D, *dynamic*, is incorrect because *dynamic* means "changing, inconstant."

The correct answer is A, *the same*, because the number of cups remains the same whether they are spread out, nestled, or stacked.

18. **(G) Be a page flipper! Return to the passage and read broadly around this line to determine which of the four cases, as described in the answer choices, most closely correlates (compares) to the one described in the passage.** To be prudent, reread and concentrate on this portion of the passage: *. . . it is important to keep in mind that it is normal for infants to acquire skills at varying times, and to have their own developmental pace. Piaget's cognitive-developmental theory is no exception; criticism questions some of this theorist's ideas, saying that his age associations with aspects of thinking are off, or that* expertise *may be more critical to cognition level than age. Some children, for example, play chess at much higher thought levels than do adults with comparable chess experience.*

Choice F is out because nothing in the excerpt above suggests that the player's gender has to do with his expertise (knowledge and proficiency).

Choice H is incorrect because nothing in the passage states or suggests that *one who holds several advanced educational degrees* might be a more adept (skillful) player than an undergrad.

Choice J (*A sixty-four-year old's game of Stratego versus that of a sixteen-year-old.*) is incorrect because, according to Piaget, proficiency is not based fundamentally and solely on age.

Choice G is the best answer. The passage suggests that Piaget thinks that skill level has less to do with age and more to do with *cognition level* (which you can think of as a level of intellectual activity, such as logic and reasoning). Therefore, a game of Stratego played by a younger person who has studied and practiced the game versus an older player who played with little concentration would be most comparable to the scenario delineated in the excerpt above. Skill level is not necessarily a function of age.

19. **(D) To select the most analogous (similar) situation, reread the lines that are referenced, paying close attention to the details (which are underlined in the excerpt that follows) that characterize this particular scenario:**

The child *gains confidence in his* motor abilities *as he stacks the cups higher and higher,* experimenting *with the concepts of height and stability. He* independently learns, *by* trial and error, *which cups—depending on their size—fit into each other or stack easily, one on top of another.*

Choice A does not work because, in this circumstance, Mom is assisting the child with the task at hand as she *points to the place on the board where the puzzle piece belongs.*

Choice B is also invalid because the child is not working independently as *Dad helps the child to put wooden shape blocks into matching slots that line the exterior of a large, colorful cube.*

Choice C is not most analogous either because the child is not playing alone: *With a friend, the child lines up action figures in a three-foot row, then one child knocks them down, one by one, as the other watches and laughs.*

The correct answer is D: *The child builds a tower, using donut-shaped rings in various colors and sizes; autonomously, he decides which rings are best suited for the bottom layers and which are best suited for the top*—because the child is playing by himself and experimenting while engaging in the trial-and-error method.

20. **(H) Focus carefully on the last sentence of the passage, trying to get inside the author's head to determine some aspect of his belief system:** *Finally, it is as important to question a theorist as it is to try and apply his or her theory to real life circumstances.* This author apparently believes in actively finding the truth oneself: *question a theorist, apply his theory to real life circumstances.*

Choice F, *believing something until you or someone else has proven it false*, is invalid because it promotes the idea of blindly believing without first inquiring and testing.

Choice G, *scientific themes that manifest* (show) *themselves over and again in contemporary writing that has been published on behavioral studies*, also promotes a blind acceptance of that which is popular and published. Given what he says in that final line, our author would not go for this.

Choice J is way off the mark, for this author would never advocate *taking an expert's advice at face value.*

The correct answer is H: *exploring ideas in greater depth and conducting experiments that you have independently devised*; it promotes an active and autonomous search for the truth of things.

PASSAGE III: HUMANITIES

21. **(C) Consider the passage as a whole—skim if you need to—to get a sense of its form and structure.** Choice A is off because it does not contain a bevy (a great deal) of *lively and exaggerated anecdotes* (personal stories, often humorous, that have been stretched for rhetorical effect).

Choice B may sound riveting, but *a significant event in the author's life* is hard to pinpoint in this passage and the concluding remarks are far from *insignificant.*

Choice D is way off the mark, particularly because reference to another spiritual writer is mentioned. Stick with what's actually in the passage.

Choice C is correct: *It introduces a principle (single breath meditation), and then elaborates on the process of putting this principle into practice.*

22. **(J) Return to the passage and reread, at minimum, the sentence in which this word appears to get the gist of this word's contextual**

meaning: *There are as many instants of now in a minute as there are in an hour. The now is infinite no matter how long you <u>linger</u> there.*

Choice F is incorrect; even though the notion of lingering around may have connotations of laziness, *become lazy* does not fit in this sentence.

Choice G is way off because *loiter* has a negative association that implies an idle or even "up-to-no-good" use of time.

Choice H, *sit down*, is too literal to fit into this abstract presentation of ideas. **The correct answer is J**, *remain*, which fits and flows seamlessly.

23. **(A) To nail this question, peruse the first paragraph again (reproduced below). Consider which statement the author is suggesting "between the lines."**

In less than a minute you can complete a single breath meditation session. Start to finish, it will take you about thirty seconds. There are as many instants of now in a minute as there are in an hour. The now is infinite no matter how long you linger there. Sometimes, when we sit to meditate for twenty minutes or longer, big segments of that time slot lose their immediacy. We drift into default thinking and ride the shallow turbulence of our mental activity. We miss the depth of the moment completely.

Even though several words that one might associate with water, such as *drift, shallow, turbulence,* and *depth*, are used in the latter half of the paragraph, Choice B, *water imagery disrupts clear thinking*, is still invalid because this idea is neither explicitly stated nor implied.

Choice C (*when time is limited, time is essentially lost*), a bit of a brainteaser, is also unsubstantiated. What is this choice saying, anyway?

Even though sentence 4 says *when we sit to meditate . . .* , the paragraph is not suggesting that *meditation is an inactive state of body and mind*, so Choice D is out. As suggested by the last three lines of the paragraph, **Choice A**, *The more time one allocates to meditation, the less meaningful and profound becomes the session,* **is the best answer.**

24. **(H) Savvy test takers don't rely on their memories alone. Revisit the third paragraph (reproduced below), intent upon determining its mood:** *How can one breath provide any kind of practice at all? For now, we want to go short and deep rather than long and shallow. We want to be awake and aware for the simple matter of seconds it takes to complete one single cycle of breathing. When you think about it, it seems manageable. You may feel a surge of confidence. "This is something I might actually be able to do!" When you realize that each breath holds the hologram for all your breathing, you may begin to honor the power of one pure breath. When you sense that each now is nested within all nows, you realize that an instant of pure consciousness will take you further than a marathon of habit-driven practice.*

Choice F is invalid. Where is the *humor*? The *pessimism*? Although a sense of *urgency* may be detected, *fanciful daydreams* are a stretch!

Cross off Choice G.

Even a cursory review of the paragraph on the previous page reveals that answer Choice J, *consistent doubt and disillusionment*, is way off the mark. **The correct answer is H**, *steadily increasing zeal* (*enthusiasm*) *and enlightenment* (*awareness*); this is a feel-good paragraph that crescendos—ends on a high note.

25. **(D) Revisit the lines in which this phrase appears:**

    . . . consider this question: Who is breathing? Then release the question completely into the nonverbal realm. Accept no answers that come in words. Let this question hover in the silence of your one breath. Let your one, single, <u>on-stage, in-the-spotlight</u> breath be completely natural. Let it move at its own pace and achieve only the depth it seeks on its own. Don't force. Don't push. Don't direct it. Simply follow it. It is the only breath you will be attending to in this way so give it all your attention.

    As you consider the above context, Choice A (*an image of arrogance linked to a central premise of the author's argument*) seems off-the-mark; there is no passage evidence to support an emotion as negative as arrogance.

    Choice B (*an allusion to improvisational theater*), while it sounds creative and lofty, does not have textual support either; where is the reference to a theater?

    Choice C (*the author's unrealized dream of becoming an actress*) might be tempting because the excerpt above can be interpreted as dramatic but, still, this choice involves reading into the passage or adding something that really isn't there.

    Process of elimination and the words of the passage point to **D as the correct answer**; *the attention and respect given to one breath* is supported in many ways: how the breath is given silence, how it is given freedom to move at its own pace, and how the reader is asked to "Simply follow it."

26. **(G) Peruse the third paragraph (reproduced in answer explanation 24) with a specific quest: Which of the quoted expressions provides the LEAST benefit?**

    In the paragraph, *a "short and deep" breath* (Choice F) as well as "*one pure breath*" (Choice H) are shown to have significant benefits and rewards for the one who meditates. **The correct answer is G:** "*a marathon of habit-driven practice*" contrasted with "*an instant of pure consciousness*" (Choice J); the sentence is written to suggest that the former holds less value.

27. **(A) Be a page flipper! Return to the passage, find the two questions, and consider their respective (separate, particular) function and purpose.**

    Choice B is incorrect because there is no evidence to support the idea that the first question is posed *sarcastically*. Where are the references to mocking, satirizing, or poking fun? There aren't any. It is also unreasonable to conclude that the second question is expressed *somberly*. What is gloomy or sad about asking readers to consider a lofty or "high minded" question? Cross off Choice B.

Choice C is also incorrect. While it is fairly reasonable to decide that *the first is a rhetorical question posed for the purpose of persuasion*, it is far less reasonable to say that the second question—while, without a doubt, an interrogative sentence—is *ironic*. Irony pertains to written or verbal expression that is purposely intended as opposite to that which one actually means. Choice D is incorrect because the first question does not have the power or intent to *undermine* (weaken, contradict) *the author's underlying assumptions*. A quick review of the third paragraph reveals that one breath has power and, in fact, is something to be honored. Choice D is also incorrect because the second question is not necessarily *an unrealistic stretch of the imagination*. Again, context reveals that this question is simply one to be pondered.

The correct answer is A. Revisit the third paragraph to understand that it is true that *the first* [question] *is used as a topic sentence* for the third paragraph; after all, the contents of the third paragraph answers this question. It is also true that *the second* [question] *is intended as a question for the reader to ponder*. Notice that the question *Who is breathing?* is preceded by *In preparation for your brief session of meditation, consider this question:*. The context reveals that this is a question to be pondered or considered.

28. **(J) Reread the sentence in which this verb appears. Plug in each answer choice to see which one makes the most sense in context:** *It funnels your attention inward as your eyes close for your very brief chance at sensing this unique breath which will never occur again in all of creation.* A close reread helps you to understand that *It* stands for the process described in the preceding sentence: *Using the opening and closing of your eyes to punctuate your session accomplishes two things.*
    Choice F, *burrows,* doesn't work because *burrows* means digs a tunnel.
    Choice G, *restricts,* is not a good fit because this word means limits.
    Choice H, *withdraws,* is also incorrect because this word is more often used to mean pulls away from social interaction.
    The correct answer is J, *directs,* because this word suggests the direction of movement inward of the breath as well as one's focus as he or she practices this type of meditation.

29. **(B) Find evidence for three of the four answer choices listed. The one that lacks proof is the correct answer.**
    In the opening lines, Choice A is answered. A *single breath meditation* takes *less than a minute*.
    Choice C, *eye movement,* is addressed in the fifth paragraph.
    Choice D, *Can emotional anguish derive from warped thoughts?*, is addressed in the second to last paragraph.

And Choice B, *Are yoga practice and meditative breathing inextricably* (cannot be freed from) *tied?* is never definitively answered by the information provided in the passage, so **B is the best answer**.

30. **(G) This question is time-consuming because you need to skim around all four referenced images to get a sense of their treatment or portrayal. Are they negative, positive, or neutral?** A negative association surrounds "deep patterns" because this phrase is modified by the prepositional phrase *of distortion* that follows. Distortion, in this sense, is negative and something that the author wishes to "unravel." **The correct answer is G.**
Choice F is incorrect because *hologram for your breathing* is something to *honor,* so it has a positive association.
Choice H is incorrect because *cookies* are described as *sweet,* again positive.
Choice J is out because *whole box* (in the last sentence) is something to savor and enjoy.

PASSAGE IV: NATURAL SCIENCE

31. **(D) Use your memory and skim around the passage to find evidence for the items listed. Using process of elimination, check off the ones that are supported by the text.** Roman Numeral I is supported by line 17, *Records before 1970 are spotty,* and Roman numeral IV is supported by lines 15–17, *hurricanes are infrequent events even in the worst case, and the number of data points is unsurprisingly small.* **Therefore, process of elimination reveals that the best answer is D.**

32. **(F) Savvy test takers take no shortcuts. Diligently return to the text, and carefully review the sentence in which the word appears:** *At first, climatologists thought the nasty hurricanes of the 1990s were just part of the AMO, but in 2005 two research papers were published that upset the complacent status quo.* The context reveals that new information in the form of *research papers* upset the ways things were, *status quo.* So, that which was accepted and *comfortable* was altered based on the new finding. *Relentless* means persistent, and *arrogant* means conceited; neither of these terms works.

33. **(D) Consider the passage as a whole.** In the closing paragraph, the author mentions climatologists who put forth a "warning of the 'lemming-like march to the sea' of coastal development and call on leadership to 'undertake a comprehensive evaluation of building policies and insurance, land-use and disaster-relief policies that currently serve to promote an ever-increasing vulnerability to hurricanes.' " This is most closely the author's indirect attempt to *warn readers about building along hurricane-prone coastlines.* The remaining choices are not firmly supported by the text.

34. **(F) Use your memory and skim the passage as well to pinpoint the specific causes of hurricanes that the author expressed.** The following evidence supports answer choices G, H, and J, respectively: "the view that *global warming* has something to do with them [hurricanes] has a receptive audience" (lines 50–51), "Hurricanes are an indirect product of *warm sea temperatures*" (lines 35–36), and "climatologists thought . . . hurricanes . . . were part of the AMO." (lines 22–23) **Choice F is the correct answer**, for *human fallibility* (the human ability to fail, to make errors) is not cited anywhere as a cause of hurricanes.

35. **(C) Read up, down, and around the referenced portion of the passage, lines 46–47, and consider *ten or twelve days* in a generous context.**
There is no mention of Gray's vacation habits or his equipment breaking down, so Choices A and B are out.
Choice D is out, too, since we don't get much detail about his interviewing stints. The quote, "out to ten or twelve days" refers to the reliability of his equipment to predict, within this indicated time range, when a hurricane will hit.

36. **(J) Reread the fourth paragraph, considering its primary role in the reading selection as a whole.**
Choice F is out since two anecdotes (personal, often humorous, autobiographical accounts) cannot be found.
The fourth paragraph does not belie the first three paragraphs, so Choice G is out.
No clear international interest is stressed on the part of the author; Choice H is also out.
Choice J is the correct answer. The fourth paragraph provides the geographical examples of Florida and the Grand Bahamas to foreshadow concerns expressed in the final paragraph.

37. **(A) Since this is an ALL/EXCEPT question, you need to skim the passage to find evidence to support three of the four answer choices. The answer choice without substantiation is the correct answer.** The author presents a chronological perspective in the first paragraph, so Choice B has support.
In line 29, he mentions MIT climatologist Emmanuel, so Choice C has support.
The author defines AMO in lines 20–21, so Choice D also has support.
Choice A is the correct answer since there are no references (allusions) to literary works.

38. **(H) Consider the ominous imagery behind this statement and get a sense of its purpose in the reading selection.**
This statement and its ominous (gloomy) image (*mass death by drowning*) serve as a warning to readers, so **the correct answer is Choice H**.

Choice F is out since *building methods* are not being mocked.

Choice G is out since the author is serious about this topic and does not wish to temper or *mediate* his outlook on coastal building. The lemmings and developers are not being compared.

Choice J is out.

39. **(B) Once again, skim the reading selection for passage evidence. Do not rely on your memory alone.**

The passage says that *the number of <u>data points</u> is unsurprisingly small. Records before 1970 are spotty . . .* , so cross off Choice A.

The correct answer is B because lines 45–48 clearly state that *computer models* are more reliable predictors than *climate scales*.

The text says, "I'm a great believer in computer models. But when you get to the climate scale, you get into a can of worms." Cross off Choice C.

Choice D is also out since these coastal structures have nothing deliberately to do with hurricane forecasting.

40. **(G) Notice the key word *except* that appears at the end of this question.**

The author would consider Choices F, H, and J (see final paragraph) as worthwhile efforts to temper the destructive power of hurricanes.

Choice F is supported by what the author discusses in the second paragraph, and how he wished we had better methods of measurement.

Choice G is the best choice since the author never speaks of *an international effort* or a global solution.

DIAGNOSTIC CHARTS
ACT English Test

45 MINUTES—75 QUESTIONS

<u>Note</u>: For the purpose of this self-assessment test, there is flexibility among these subdivision categories: writing strategy, organization, author's style. English is an art, not a science, so some questions overlap to a degree. On the ACT, you will have to answer 40 questions pertaining to usage and mechanics and 35 questions pertaining to rhetorical skills.

Skills	Questions	Possible Score	Your Score
Usage/Mechanics			
Punctuation	4, 10, 14, 31, 33, 38, 51, 64, 65, 73	10	
Grammar and Usage	6, 8, 16, 17, 19, 24, 26, 28, 32, 39, 41, 59	12	
Sentence Structure	3, 5, 9, 13, 20, 34, 36, 43, 44, 46, 49, 50, 53, 58, 61, 68, 69, 70	18	
Rhetorical Skills			
Writing Strategy	11, 15, 22, 30, 37, 40, 42, 45, 47, 56, 60, 72	12	
Organization	27, 48, 55, 57, 62, 63, 66, 67, 71, 74, 75	11	
Author's Style	1, 2, 7, 12, 18, 21, 23, 25, 29, 35, 52, 54	12	

Total: 75

Percent correct: _____

ACT Reading Test

40 MINUTES—35 QUESTIONS

Passage Type	Referring	Reasoning	Possible Score	Your Score
Prose Fiction	1, 2, 4, 7	3, 5, 6, 8, 9, 10	10	
Social Science	11, 13, 17	12, 14, 15, 16, 18, 19, 20	10	
Humanities	21, 22, 25	23, 24, 26, 27, 28, 29, 30	10	
Natural Science	32, 33, 37, 40	31, 34, 35, 36, 38, 39	10	

Total: 40

Percent correct: _____

Score Conversion Table*

English Raw Score	Reading Raw Score	Scaled Score
70–75	34–40	31–36
61–69	27–33	25–30
46–60	20–26	19–24
31–45	12–19	13–18
14–30	4–11	7–12
0–13	0–3	1–6

*Note: This chart is designed to give you a general approximation of the number of questions you need to get right to fall into a general score range on the actual test. It is *not* designed to give you an exact score or to predict your actual ACT score. The variance in difficulty levels and testing conditions can affect your score range.

PRACTICE TESTS

Index